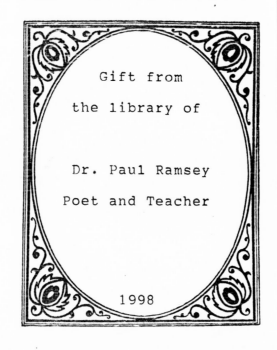

CLASSICAL GENRES AND ENGLISH POETRY

CLASSICAL GENRES and ENGLISH POETRY

WILLIAM H. RACE

CROOM HELM
London • New York • Sydney

135657

© 1988 William H. Race
Croom Helm Ltd, Provident House,
Burrell Row, Beckenham, Kent BR3 1AT
Croom Helm Australia, 44-50 Waterloo Road,
North Ryde, 2113, New South Wales

Published in the USA by
Croom Helm
in association with Methuen, Inc.
29 West 35th Street
New York, NY 10001

British Library Cataloguing in Publication Data

Race, William H.
    Classical genres and English poetry.
    1. English poetry—Classical influence
    2. Classical poetry—History and criticism
    I. Title
    821'.009   PR508.C68
    ISBN 0–7099–4272–9

Library of Congress Cataloging-in-Publication Data

ISBN 0–7099–4272–9

Printed and bound in Great Britain by Mackays of Chatham Ltd, Kent

Contents

For
N. Gregson Davis

teacher and friend

Preface

E.R. Curtius called rhetorical topics 'the cellars — and foundations! — of European literature'. While the present study is far less ambitious than his monumental *European literature and the Latin Middle Ages* and contains little material from the medieval period, it also deals with some of the building-blocks of poetry: topics, themes, formal structures, rhetorical arguments, and genres that were developed in Graeco-Roman culture and continued to exert an influence through the Renaissance to the twentieth century.

Although I include occasional examples from French poetry, the bulk of examples are in Greek, Latin and English, and, for the sake of brevity, most of them are from lyric poetry. Since the work is intended for diverse readers who may be unfamiliar with some of the languages, authors and periods covered, I have provided my own prose translations that follow as closely as possible the lineation of the original, and have tried to offer aid, where appropriate, in the form of background and bibliography.

Each chapter proceeds inductively — that is, the generalisations are drawn from the poetry itself. For that reason, I provide extensive quotations and make constant reference to them. My aim throughout is to be as faithful to the texts as possible and to elucidate specific passages by comparing them with others of the same kind. I have limited myself in the discussions, however, to particular points, and as a result, the analyses are never intended to be exhaustive. In addition, since it is impossible to cover more than a small sample of poems, I have provided an annotated list of 'Additional Examples' at the end of the book for those who wish to pursue the inquiry further.

I intend this work to be helpful to students of Classics, English, and Comparative Literature. As a graduate student at Stanford I was fortunate to have taken Professor N. Gregson Davis's course on the classical tradition, which presented many of the poems covered here. I have always found that course of great value to me, and I have taught a similiar one for several years at Vanderbilt University, adding and changing here and there and profiting from students' suggestions. Professor Davis has generously allowed me to use materials covered in his course. He is, of course, in no way responsible for the directions in which I have taken them, but I hope that he will be pleased and accept the book's heartfelt dedication.

Finally, I would like to thank my friend, Professor Andrew M. Miller; my colleagues, Donald Davie, Laurence Lerner, and Harold L. Weatherby for their generous help and criticism; my student, Mr Anthony Lombardy; and especially Mr G. Robert Rust for his encouragement, suggestions and painstaking assistance.

Acknowledgements

W. H. Auden, 'Law Like Love', 'Musée des Beaux Arts' and 'In Memory of W. B. Yeats', reprinted from *Collected Poems* by W. H. Auden by permission of Faber and Faber Ltd. Copyright 1940 and renewed 1968 by W. H. Auden. Reprinted from W. H. Auden: *Collected Poems* edited by Edward Mendelson, by permission of Random House, Inc.

J. V. Cunningham, 'For My Contemporaries' from *The Collected Poems and Epigrams of J. V. Cunningham*, Swallow Press, 1971. Reprinted with the permission of Ohio University Press, Athens.

John Hollander, 'Refusing to Tell Tales', from *Powers of Thirteen*. Copyright (c) 1983 John Hollander. Reprinted with the permission of Atheneum Publishers.

A. E. Housman, 'Loveliest of Trees, the Cherry Now', copyright 1939, 1940, (c) 1965 by Holt, Rinehart and Winston, Inc. Copyright (c) 1967, 1968 by Robert E. Symons. Reprinted from *The Collected Poems of A. E. Housman*, by permission of Henry Holt and Company, Inc.

John Crowe Ransom, 'Blue Girls', reprinted from *Selected Poems*, by permission of Laurence Pollinger Ltd. on behalf of Methuen Ltd. Copyright 1927 by Alfred A. Knopf, Inc. and renewed 1955 by John Crowe Ransom. Reprinted from *Selected Poems, Third Edition, Revised and Enlarged* by John Crowe Ransom, by permission of Alfred A. Knopf, Inc.

Adrienne Rich, 'Versailles: Petit Trianon', reprinted by permission of the author, from *The Diamond Cutters and Other Poems* (N.Y.: Harper and Brothers, 1955) by Adrienne Rich.

Dylan Thomas, 'Do Not Go Gentle Into That Good Night' reprinted from *The Poems of Dylan Thomas*, copyright 1952 by Dylan Thomas, by permission of New Directions Publishing Corporation and by permission of the Trustees for the Copyright of Dylan Thomas and J. M. Dent & Sons Ltd.

William Carlos Williams, 'Landscape With the Fall of Icarus', reprinted from *Pictures from Brueghel*, copyright (c) 1960 by William Carlos Williams, by permission of New Directions Publishing Corporation.

Yvor Winters, 'A Prayer For My Son', reprinted from *The Collected Poems of Yvor Winters, With an Introduction by Donald Davie*, by permission of Carcanet Press Ltd. and from Yvor Winters, *Collected Poems*, copyright 1943, by permission of New Directions Publishing Corporation.

W. B. Yeats, 'A Coat', reprinted with permission of Macmillan Publishing Company from *Collected Poems* by W. B. Yeats, copyright 1916 by Macmillan Publishing Company, renewed 1944 by Bertha Georgie Yeats and by permission of A. P. Watt Ltd. on behalf of Michael B. Yeats and Macmillan London Ltd.; 'An Irish Airman Foresees His Death', reprinted with permission of Macmillan Publishing Company from *Collected Poems* by W. B. Yeats, copyright 1919 by Macmillan Publishing company, renewed 1947 by Bertha Georgie Yeats and by permission of A. P. Watt Ltd. on behalf of Michael B. Yeats and Macmillan London Ltd.; and 'A Prayer For My Son', reprinted with permission of Macmillan Publishing Company from *Collected Poems* by W. B. Yeats, copyright 1928 by Macmillan Publishing Company, renewed 1956 by Georgie Yeats and by permission of A. P. Watt Ltd. on behalf of Michael B. Yeats and Macmillan London Ltd.

An adapted version of the translation and discussion of Pindar's *Pythian* 1 is reprinted by permission of Twayne Publishers, a division of G. K. Hall & Co., Boston, from *Pindar*, by William H. Race, copyright 1986.

Introduction

Let us imagine a reader encountering Shelley's 'Ode to the West Wind' for the first time. Its subject (the West Wind as a symbol both of death and of poetic inspiration), its mood of conflicting emotions ('Sweet though in sadness'), its images of the wandering boy ('The comrade of thy wanderings over Heaven') and of the Aeolian harp ('Make me thy lyre'), and its identification with nature ('Be thou me') clearly mark it as a product of the Romantic period — and the list of such particulars could be continued at great length. At the same time, however, the poem contains another set of significant particulars which will escape the reader unless he recognises that its *form* is very traditional. The title 'Ode' is too vague to be of much help in classifying its form, since by Shelley's time the word loosely referred to any ambitious lyric poem, but in the course of the poem Shelley indicates its genre by the words 'with thee in prayer'. When one realises the simple fact that the poem is a prayer (or more precisely, a Classical hymn), then a number of its formal and stylistic features begin to take on additional significance: for example, the apostrophes ('O Thou'), relative clauses ('from whose unseen presence') and imperatives ('O hear!') are characteristic of hymnal style. Shelley, who was familiar with Graeco-Roman poetry, is putting an ancient form to new use.

Once the genre of the poem has been identified, the studious reader will naturally go on to ask a number of questions: how are hymns in general constructed?; what rhetorical strategies are used to persuade the god?; what topics regularly occur in hymns?; what are the literary functions of hymns?; what kind of style is deemed appropriate?; what are the major examples and how are they similar? In pursuing the answers to questions such as these, the reader discovers that there is a long tradition of poetic hymns to which Shelley's ode belongs. The reader is then in a position to ask more specific questions about Shelley's poem: which features has Shelley chosen from the tradition?; how typical is the form of his poem?; in what ways does his hymn differ?; how has he adapted generic form to fit his particular concerns?; what does a detailed comparison with another example (say the opening hymn of Lucretius' *De Rerum Natura* or a hymnal proemium from *Paradise Lost*) reveal about the intentions of each poet and about the predominant concerns of his period?

These are, I believe, basic questions, which it is essential to answer if one is to discover what is traditional and what is new in a poem. The answers which are found lay the foundations for assessing the poem's merits and achievements; they are a first step towards the goal of criticism. Yet in spite of the importance of these preliminary questions, the student of poetry faces an impasse from the very start. To my knowledge, for instance, there is no work that can provide even the most basic information about the rhetoric, form and style of literary hymns, particularly of those in Greek and Latin which served as the models for later poetry. Useful information is scattered in large works by classical scholars such as E. Norden, R. G. M. Nisbet and M. Hubbard, and G. Williams, but remains in the domain of specialists. Even Curtius' massive *European literature and the Latin Middle Ages* offers no help; nor does Francis Cairns's otherwise very detailed study of ancient generic topics, *Generic composition in Greek and Latin poetry*. Surprising as it may seem, this fundamental issue of generic form has received very little attention. The student simply does not have access to the essential information about the hymnal genre that would permit the comparison of Shelley's poem with others of the same kind from Homer to the present, and thereby facilitate a more precise appreciation of Shelley's intention and achievement.

To take another example on a smaller scale, classicists have come to realise in recent years that the priamel is one of the most important formal elements in Graeco-Roman poetry, but its existence in subsequent poetry has not even been recognised. It is the purpose of this book to begin to fill some of the gaps in generic criticism that exist between English poetry and its Classical past. The task is obviously beyond the scope of one book (or even a series of books), but a beginning must be made, even if the topics are few and can only be illustrated by selecting a few examples from many. Below I set out the chapter titles and some of the questions that underlie the selections and discussions of the poems.

1. 'Modifying the Poetic Tradition: The *Recusatio*': when a poet wishes to change the tradition and defend his new poetic, what form does his poem often take?

2. 'Introducing a Subject: The Priamel': what is the rhetorical

device often used to introduce and highlight a subject in a poem, and what are its forms and functions?

3. 'Poetry and the Visual Arts: The *Ekphrasis*': how do descriptions of artworks in poems capture the prevailing concerns of historical periods and concurrently reveal literary principles?

4. 'The Rhetoric of Lament and Consolation': what are the rhetorical strategies for expressing grief and offering consolation, and what topics and styles have been deemed appropriate?

5. 'The Argument of *Carpe-diem* Poems': what topics and logical arguments have regularly occurred in this intensely developed subgenre of consolation?

6. 'Forms of Persuasion in Hymns': what are the intention, form and style of literary hymns and prayers, and how do they function in larger works?

7. 'Praise and Counsel: Eulogy': what are the standard topics of praise, and how do poets keep their praise from being mere flattery?

The concept of genre and generic

It is apparent from the table of contents that I am using the words 'genre' and 'generic' in a sense which is sufficiently inclusive to embrace both broad types such as hymns and specialised forms such as priamels. The concept of genre is notoriously elusive: it can indicate formal characteristics (sonnet, epigram), occasions (*epithalamium, epinikion*), content (*carpe-diem*, amatory elegy), or mode (pastoral, vituperation). Like the Persian chain it can measure miles (epic, drama, lyric), or it can be calibrated to measure inches (*blason*, simile, *adynaton*). Indeed, genres can theoretically be subdivided to the point at which they all but vanish into the particular poem under consideration, in accord with a Crocean nominalism (*quot poemata, tot genera*). In practice, however, one chooses generic classifications broad enough to include a number of poems or passages, but not so broad as to lose their capacity for describing similarities. In the terms formulated by A. Rosmarin (*The power of genre*), one must strike a balance between a generic term's *extensiveness*, its ability to subsume surprisingly many poems; and its *intensiveness*, its ability to unfold a given poem in surprising detail.

This adjustment of generic categories to describe passages within larger works is theoretically and practically necessary because a given poem or work is often compounded of various generic elements which it shares with other works, some of which often belong to different formal genres. This phenomenon, which has received considerable attention in biblical form criticism, applies equally to the Western poetic tradition, in which large genres such as epic, drama, and lyric contain many smaller generic units. There is evidence to show that the Homeric epics were largely composed of 'typical scenes' such as arming, eating, debating in council and fighting, that were woven into the plot and subtly varied according to need. Likewise, types of speeches (e.g. prayers, laments, exhortations, praise, blame, persuasion, orders, messages) could be adjusted to the occasional demands of the plot. For that reason, the *Iliad* and *Odyssey* became the literary Bible of the Greeks, providing paradigms for all forms of poetry (and prose) that followed. As late as the third century AD, when Menander Rhetor was providing rules for hymns and farewell speeches, it was only natural for him to cite as models Chryses' prayer in the *Iliad* and Odysseus' parting words to Alcinous in the *Odyssey*. In a similar fashion, drama and lyric poetry consist of many smaller generic types, most of which they borrowed from epic. Indeed, five of the seven topics treated in this study (priamel, *ekphrasis*, lament and consolation, *carpe diem*, and hymns) have clear models in Homer that were subsequently adapted to drama and lyric poetry, where they were put to new use and combined with other generic forms. This creative adaptation of models constitutes a large part of the literary tradition, and is one that has received considerable attention from scholars of Renaissance English poetry.

Genre is also related to typical occasions and the rhetoric associated with them. If there is one main subject of poetry, it is (as Yvor Winters maintained) human experience, and the generic types that portray this experience are rooted in occasions that occur in real life, not just in a Greek *polis* or Roman villa, but universally. People in all societies argue, lament, describe, praise, blame, console and (usually) compose hymns. For that reason, the occasional aspect of genre inevitably links it with rhetoric, in a mother–daughter relationship, as R. Colie (*The resources of kind*) terms it. It was not by accident that Romantic and post-Romantic theorists felt compelled to banish both the parent (genre) and her child (rhetoric) from what they considered to be 'true' poetry. Generic types remain, however, in spite of theories — even, as we shall see, among Romantics — and it was the genius of the Greeks, beginning with Homer, to capture the essential forms and topics of these types in their poetry. They were successful to such an extent that the Romans largely despaired of excelling them. By their own admission they invented only one formal genre — satire; and even in that case, Horace knew well that although Lucilius was indeed the first to compose separate poems in hexameter verse which could be called 'satires', 'satiric' poetry itself really stemmed from Greek iambic poetry and Attic old comedy. The Romans' originality did not consist of inventing new genres, but in redirecting existing ones. Catullus, Lucretius, Vergil, Horace and Ovid, as we shall see, gave new life to generic forms by exploiting latent possibilities. They were great poets precisely because they built on existing forms. As Wellek and Warren (*Theory of literature*) note, 'By and large, great writers are rarely inventors of genres . . . [they] enter into other men's labours'.

Genres and literary history

As Fowler (*Kinds of literature*) has most recently reminded us, generic categories are not fixed entities, but are subject to constant 'historical mutability'. All new examples subtly alter the overall concept of a genre, not only those which extend its dimensions by realising latent potentialities or by combining it with other generic forms, but even those which reduce it to banality by slavishly repeating its elements. Genres and generic forms therefore have a history: they flourish and wane, and some all but disappear, only to reappear in a new context. In addition, and conversely, changes in generic form are also indicative of larger historical changes: for example, Classical hymns were eclipsed in the early Middle Ages by a new generic type occasioned by the influence of Hebrew psalms (themselves a mine of generic types) and the demands of Christian liturgy and doctrine. These changes in the generic form of hymns reflect profound changes in theology and worship, a subject that deserves much more study than it has received; and when the Christian–Humanist tradition began to decline during the eighteenth century, Classical hymns reappeared with entirely new content in the works of Gray, Wordsworth and Shelley. For a variety of reasons, mainly political and philosophical, eulogy (particularly public praise of statesmen) has been moribund for almost three centuries. This does not mean that eulogy itself is extinct; it still exists, but is carefully qualified and safely ensconced in other generic types such as the funeral elegy, one of the few ancient forms which retains enough of its occasional validity to permit an appeal to shared values and the straightforward use of rhetorical *commonplaces*. A society's values are implicit in the genres it uses and develops. A society that has nothing to praise, or which cannot offer hope in the face of suffering and death, is one that cannot compose eulogistic or consolatory poetry without irony. Such seems to be the case today, whereas *ekphraseis* are flourishing.

Because of this important interrelationship between genre and literary history, I discuss the examples in each chapter in roughly chronological order — not, however, in order to provide a thorough history of the genre, nor to trace direct influence from one poet to another, but rather to maintain a sense of literary history. Genres are embodied in particular poems from particular periods, and the only way of appreciating the interaction between a tradition and individual poets is to examine how they adapt common generic forms to express their own ideas and the concerns of their age.

For the purpose of locating poems within larger *literary* traditions, I have divided the poetry into three large classes: Classical, Hellenistic and Romantic. 'Classical' refers to the period and literature from Homer through Aristotle (that is, from approximately 750 BC to 323 BC), and to the prevailing attitude towards experience that was formed by the life of the *polis*. 'Hellenistic' refers to that period and literature from the death of Alexander until the Roman domination (that is, from approximately 323 BC to 146 BC), when the poet became separated from active political life. The distinction between Classical and Hellenistic is essential for understanding not only Greek poetry, but also Roman (and subsequently Renaissance) poetry, which inherited both traditions, and maintained a tension between them, often without realising that it did so. Simply labelling all Graeco-Roman poetry as Classical creates hopeless confusion.

'Romantic' refers to that body of poetry from Wordsworth to the present which makes 'feeling', particularly the speaker's own emotion, the primary subject of poetic imitation.

These brief sketches are not intended to be definitions of these three complex traditions, nor do I mean to suggest that these three are the only major traditions (indeed, the medieval developments are largely omitted in this work since my purpose is to show lines of continuity between Graeco-Roman and English poetry), but they are, I think, of crucial importance for understanding how generic form persisted, although it was adapted to radically different poetic programmes.

Generic criticism and conscious imitation

A word is in order about the limits of the book's methodology. I consider generic criticism to be a necessary starting-point for the understanding of poetic texts. If we do not know what *kind* of poem we are reading, or what elements it shares with others of the same type, then we shall be able only to view the poem as an isolated entity in a poetic oeuvre. We shall ultimately be unable to ascertain what is original and important in it, for there will be no tradition consisting of comparable examples within which to measure its particular qualities. Generic criticism is just a starting-point, however: it does not replace or even displace other types of analysis and criticism. Thus, for example, only the researches of literary history and biography can ascertain whether a poet is consciously or unconsciously using a genre. Generic criticism can show what is traditional in Shelley's ode; but only the biographer and historian can determine what precise models Shelley actually used. Both methods have their own, complementary functions.

In many cases, conscious *imitatio* is obvious. Catullus wrote a mock elegy on his mistress' sparrow and Ovid did him one better with one on Corinna's parrot, both of whom were followed by Statius. Milton had command of the entire tradition of pastoral lament when he composed his 'Lycidas', and Auden consciously drew on that same tradition in his 'In Memory of W.B. Yeats'. However, there are cases where direct influence is questionable: for example, as we shall see, the wording of Wordsworth's rejection of eighteenth-century poetry in his *Preface to lyrical ballads* (1800) is strikingly similar to that used by the Silver Latin poets. Was he aware of it? He certainly read the Latin poets at Hawkshead and at Cambridge. Or was it that, finding himself in a situation of attacking an outmoded poetic tradition, he unconsciously used the same terms that poets in a similar situation had used centuries before in a genre known as the *recusatio*? As T.S. Eliot points out in 'The music of poetry', 'Every revolution in poetry is apt to be, and sometimes announces itself as, a return to common speech. That is the revolution which Wordsworth announced in his prefaces.' Do the generic affinities alone account for the similarities?

The priamel provides a particularly interesting case, for only within recent years has it been recognised as a form. Thus, none of the authors treated in Chapter 2 knew that he was composing such a thing; and yet the form is recognisable in so many examples that the poets must have been at least partially aware of what they were doing. Here the literary historian is at a loss. Did Baudelaire, steeped as he was in Latin poetry, borrow the form unconsciously from Horace?; and what about Dylan Thomas, who had very little traditional training? The fact is that the form is so basic to speech and rhetoric that one can naturally use a priamel without being conscious of it — like Molière's M. Jourdain, who used prose without knowing it. Nor is the priamel the only anachronistic term in literary criticism: for example, dramatic irony is a strictly modern term, but there is abundant evidence to show that the Greek playwrights were consciously using the technique, even though they lacked a precise name for it. Generic criticism cannot answer the question as to how consciously Dylan Thomas was adapting the tradition of lament and consolation (he certainly did not know that he was composing a priamel) when he wrote 'Do Not Go Gentle Into That Good Night' — that is an issue for literary biographers to decide.

Generic criticism creates a context within which to analyse a poem, but it does not claim to provide a final analysis. Indeed, its value lies in establishing a background against which the particular merits and innovations of individual poems can be seen. One can show *that* an author uses a priamel and *what* elements it has in common with the tradition, but the next step — a step that takes one beyond the strict confines of generic criticism — is to understand *why* the poet chose that form in this instance, and *how* effectively it is used. For this reason, the reader may sense from time to time that the analysis in the following chapters stops just short of questions of evaluation. That is done on purpose. Like every reader of poetry, I have my own tastes and preferences, and I am convinced that some of the examples I provide are better poetry than others, but that is not a question that generic criticism can adequately treat, and I have refrained on the whole from offering my own judgements.

There is a great deal of spadework in the book, some very detailed examinations of poems with many cross-references, and occasionally lists and tables are necessary to sum up the material. I hope that the reader will persevere. The following chapters are certainly not the last word on the subject — they are, in fact, only a necessary beginning.

1

Modifying the Poetic Tradition: The *Recusatio*

What is commonly referred to as Classical poetry, as if it were a simple entity, is in reality a complex phenomenon consisting of various poetic programmes, often in conflict with each other. Although the Homeric epics set an early standard for excellence in poetic composition and remained the dominant model throughout antiquity, other types of poetry successfully competed for recognition and gained a permanent place in the tradition. In fact, those poems in which poets announced and defended their programmes became conventional in their own right, so that the Graeco-Roman tradition actually possessed a means for its own renewal and change, which was subsequently adopted by Renaissance and later poets. In this chapter we shall chart some of the major trends of Graeco-Roman poetry by examining a subgenre of poetic apology called the *recusatio* ('refusal'), which Graeco-Roman poets developed to express and defend their poetic aims. Although fragmentary, a poem of Sappho (*fr.* 16) provides a good starting point.

> ο]ἰ μὲν ἰππήων στρότον οἰ δὲ πέσδων
> οἰ δὲ νάων φαῖσ᾽ ἐπ[ὶ] γᾶν μέλαι[ν]αν
> ἔ]μμεναι κάλλιστον, ἔγω δὲ κῆν᾽ ὄτ-
> τω τις ἔραται·
>
> 5 πά]γχυ δ᾽ εὔμαρες σύνετον πόησαι
> π]άντι τ[ο]ῦτ᾽, ἀ γὰρ πόλυ περσκέθοισα
> κάλλος [ἀνθ]ρώπων Ἐλένα [τὸ]ν ἄνδρα
> τὸν [πανάρ]ιστον
>
> καλλ[ίποι]σ᾽ ἔβα ᾽ς Τροῖαν πλέοι[σα
> 10 κωὖδ[ὲ πα]ῖδος οὐδὲ φίλων το[κ]ήων

1

πά[μπαν] ἐμνάσθη, ἀλλὰ παράγαγ' αὖταν
  ]σαν

  ]αμπτον γὰρ [
  ] . . . κούφως τ[   ]οηο[.]ν
15 . .]με νῦν 'Ανακτορί[ας ὀ]νέμναι-
σ' οὐ] παρεοίσας·

τᾶ]ς κε βολλοίμαν ἔρατόν τε βᾶμα
κἀμάρυχμα λάμπρον ἴδην προσώπω
ἤ τὰ Λύδων ἄρματα κἀν ὄπλοισι
20 πεσδομ]άχεντας.

Some say an array of cavalry, others of infantry,
and others of ships, is the most beautiful thing
on the black earth, but I say it is whatever
a person loves.

 5 It is perfectly easy to make this understood
by everyone: for Helen, who by far surpassed
mankind in beauty, abandoned her
most noble husband

and went sailing off to Troy with no consideration
10 whatever for her child or dear parents,
but [love?] led her astray . . .

  .   .   .   .

15 [This?] has now reminded me of Anactoria
who is not here;

I would rather see her lovely walk
and the bright sparkle of her face
than those Lydians' chariots and armed
20 footsoldiers.

When reduced to its simplest terms, the argument of the poem is
most unusual: people disagree on what is most beautiful: some
think it is military arrays; but I think it is what one loves (as the
example of Helen proves), and I would rather see Anactoria than
Lydian armies. One might have expected a contrast between

other charming women and Anactoria: a choice between an army and a girl makes little sense, until one realises that the poem has a literary dimension. Sappho is not only talking about her girlfriend but also about her poetry: she is, in effect, rejecting the grand martial themes of epic poetry (specifically Homer's *Iliad*, as the reference to Helen suggests) in favour of the theme of individual love in lyric poetry. The reduction in scope from 'impersonal' epic poetry narrated in the third person to the small compass of 'personal' lyric poetry expressed in the first person is hyperbolically characterised by Sappho's preference for the mere sight of her beloved's features over all those Lydian arms — and the power and wealth that they represent. This is an early expression of a poetic form that later became so frequent and so explicit that classical scholars have given it a technical name: *recusatio*, a literary 'refusal'.[1]

Recusationes provide one of the most important means for redirecting a poetic tradition, for they allow the poet to make a place for his poetry by 'rejecting' certain elements of the past and substituting new ones. Often the poet dramatises his choice of theme or manner of treating it: he may claim to have been asked to compose something else, or he may even claim to have tried to do so; he may pretend to be responding to the criticism of others; often a god appears to rebuke the poet or give his approval. *Recusationes* tend to employ the methods of forensic rhetoric. On the one hand, they are always apologetic (in the Greek sense of the word), for they 'defend' the poet's choice of subject matter or style. On the other hand, they also undermine the merits of his opponents' position. For that reason, the literary polemic in *recusationes* tends to create exaggerated dichotomies which allow the poet to deflate the views of unnamed 'others' and assert his own preference. 'I would rather see her lovely walk . . . than those Lydians' chariots', concludes Sappho in triumphant defiance.

As one would expect, *recusationes* tend to proliferate in periods of great change in literary tastes, and this is especially true of the Hellenistic period (c. 323–146 BC), when there was a widespread shift of favour away from epic, tragedy and the more Classical varieties of lyric poetry such as Pindar's, to shorter, more personal forms of expression. In the hands of Hellenistic poets, especially Callimachus, the *recusatio* became a vehicle for literary manifestos. At the end of his 'Hymn to Apollo', Phthonos (Envy) suddenly appears, whispering criticisms of the poet in Apollo's ear (105–13):

3

105 ὁ Φθόνος 'Απόλλωνος ἐπ' οὔατα λάθριος εἶπεν
    'οὐκ ἄγαμαι τὸν ἀοιδὸν ὃς οὐδ' ὅσα πόντος ἀείδει.'
    τὸν Φθόνον ὡπόλλων ποδί τ' ἤλασεν ὧδέ τ' ἔειπεν·
    ''Ασσυρίου ποταμοῖο μέγας ῥόος, ἀλλὰ τὰ πολλὰ
    λύματα γῆς καὶ πολλὸν ἐφ' ὕδατι συρφετὸν ἕλκει.
110 Δηοῖ δ' οὐκ ἀπὸ παντὸς ὕδωρ φορέουσι Μέλισσαι,
    ἀλλ' ἥτις καθαρή τε καὶ ἀχράαντος ἀνέρπει
    πίδακος ἐξ ἱερῆς ὀλίγη λιβὰς ἄκρον ἄωτον.'
        χαῖρε ἄναξ· ὁ δὲ Μῶμος, ἵν' ὁ Φθόνος, ἔνθα
    νέοιτο.

105 Envy spoke secretly into Apollo's ear,
    'I do not like the poet who does not even sing as much as
    the sea.'
    Apollo drove away Envy with his foot and spoke thus:
    'Great is the flow of the Euphrates River, but it carries
    all that
    filthy dirt and much refuse on its water.
110 But Demeter's Melissae do not bring her water from
    every source,
    but a small drop that trickles up pure and undefiled
    from a holy spring, a thing of highest quality.'
        Farewell, Lord. May Criticism go where Envy went.

The exact meaning of Envy's complaint is a subject of debate,[2]
but it is clear that he is objecting to the present hymn primarily
on the grounds of its deficient quantity, for not being 'as much as
the sea' (106). As if he were an adviser, Envy whispers his
disapproval into Apollo's ear. If we compare the 'Homeric' *Hymn
to Apollo* of 546 lines (written in the archaic period sometime
before 600 BC) with Callimachus' hymn of one-fifth that length,
we see that Envy's criticism may have some point. But Apollo is
not impressed with mere size, and the water imagery which he
employs to compare the old and new poetic traditions will be
echoed frequently by later authors: the Euphrates is big (μέγας,
108), but carries all that refuse along with it. Instead, he
approves the small (ὀλίγη, 112) drop brought by Demeter's
Melissae ('Bees') that is pure (καθαρή, 111) and untainted
(ἀχράαντος, 111). These adjectives convey the gist of Callimachus' poetics and of Hellenistic taste in general: a preference
for the small and refined (of which the bee is a fitting symbol) to
the vast and inclusive. In this dramatised *recusatio*, Apollo, as the

god of poetry, makes a place for the new poetry of Callimachus
by expelling Envy (and his companion Criticism), who represent
the previous literary tradition at its most conservative.

However, the most important manifesto of the new poetic only
came to light in this century on a papyrus[3] containing verses
which served as a prologue to Callimachus' *Aetia*, a collection of
elegiac poems on diverse, often mythological subjects. In spite of
the fragmentary state of the text, the passage has proved to be
crucial for understanding Hellenistic and Roman poetics. I have
omitted some lines that would require explanations.

> Οἶδ' ὅτ]ι μοι Τελχῖνες ἐπιτρύζουσιν ἀοιδῇ,
>   νήιδες οἳ Μούσης οὐκ ἐγένοντο φίλοι,
> εἵνεκεν οὐχ ἓν ἄεισμα διηνεκὲς ἢ βασιλ[η
>   .....]ας ἐν πολλαῖς ἤνυσα χιλιάσιν
> 5 ἢ.....]ους ἥρωας, ἔπος δ' ἐπὶ τυτθὸν ἐλ[ίσσω
>   παῖς ἅτε, τῶν δ' ἐτέων ἡ δεκὰς οὐκ ὀλίγη.
> ....] καὶ Τελχῖσιν ἐγὼ τόδε·
>
> . . . .
>
> 17 "ἔλλετε Βασκανίης ὀλοὸν γένος· αὖθι δὲ τέχνῃ
>   κρίνετε,] μὴ σχοίνῳ Περσίδι τὴν σοφίην·
>   μηδ' ἀπ' ἐμεῦ διφᾶτε μέγα ψοφέουσαν ἀοιδήν
> 20 τίκτεσθαι· βροντᾶν οὐκ ἐμόν, ἀλλὰ Διός."
>   καὶ γὰρ ὅτε πρώτιστον ἐμοῖς ἐπὶ δέλτον ἔθηκα
>   γούνασιν, Ἀπόλλων εἶπεν ὅ μοι Λύκιος·
>   "........] ἀοιδέ, τὸ μὲν θύος ὅττι πάχιστον
>   θρέψαι, τὴ]ν Μοῦσαν δ' ὠγαθὲ λεπταλέην·
> 25 πρὸς δέ σε] καὶ τόδ' ἄνωγα, τὰ μὴ πατέουσιν ἅμαξαι
>   τὰ στείβειν, ἑτέρων δ' ἴχνια μὴ καθ' ὁμά
>   δίφρον ἐλ]ᾶν μηδ' οἶμον ἀνὰ πλατύν, ἀλλὰ κελεύθους
>   ἀτρίπτο]υς, εἰ καὶ στεινοτέρην ἐλάσεις.
>   τεττίγω]ν ἐνὶ τοῖς γὰρ ἀείδομεν οἳ λιγὺν ἦχον
> 30   θ]όρυβον δ' οὐκ ἐφίλησαν ὄνων."
>   θηρὶ μὲν οὐατόεντι πανείκελον ὀγκήσαιτο
>   ἄλλος, ἐγ]ὼ δ' εἴην, οὑλαχύς, ὁ πτερόεις . . .

I know that the Telchines[4] grumble about my poetry,
   (for they are ignorant of the Muse and no friend of
      hers),
   because I have not composed one continuous poem

5

of many thousand lines about kings
5 or heroes, but instead spin out a short tale
   like a child, although the decades of my years are not
     few.
   . . . and I say this to the Telchines:

   .   .   .   .

17 'Off with you, baneful brood of Envy. From now on
   judge poetic skill by means of art, not with a Persian
   chain.
   Do not expect me to produce a song with lots of noise;
20   Zeus is the one to thunder, not I.'
   For when I first put tablets on my knees,
     Lycian Apollo said to me:
   '. . . poet, raise the fattest animal you can to sacrifice,
   but, my friend, keep your Muse slender.
25 Furthermore, I urge you to walk the path where no
   wagons
     come and go; do not drive your chariot on the
     common tracks
   of others nor on the wide road, but on ways
     untravelled, although your course will be narrower.
   For we sing among those who [appreciate] the high
   chirp
30   of crickets and detest the noise of donkeys.'
   Others can bray just like the long-eared beast;
     let me be that little, winged one . . .

Instead of one continuous poem dealing with kings and heroes
(one thinks of the Homeric epics and their imitators), the poet
prefers a short tale or poem, which should not be measured by its
length (the 'Persian chain', a humorous exaggeration, measures
miles), but by its art. The effects should not be grandiose (like
Zeus' thunder), but quiet and diminished. In this poetic
programme Callimachus proposes sweeping changes, for he not
only rejects the subject matter of epic, but also its form and style.
At the end of his *Hymn to Apollo*, the god in person had sanctioned
his new way of writing hymns: here again Apollo makes a
dramatic appearance to present Callimachus' new poetic. The
injunctions he puts into Apollo's mouth (to keep his Muse
slender, to take the narrow, unworn path, and to imitate the

sound of the crickets, not of asses) show that Callimachus intends his new poetry to treat small topics in highly artful and unusual ways, a programme that is borne out in what survives of the *Aetia*, a series of relatively short, highly artful and original poems not in epic metre (dactylic hexameter) but in elegiac couplets. For him the earlier tradition has become a common highway; he will try a new path. The spirit (as well as the terminology) of this manifesto will exert a permanent influence on subsequent poetry, particularly upon the Augustan poets, who were consciously reshaping the Greek poetic tradition to the Roman language and tastes.[5] One of the clearest examples is the imitation by Vergil at the beginning of his sixth *Eclogue*:

> Prima Syracosio dignata est ludere versu
> nostra nec erubuit silvas habitare Thalia.
> cum canerem reges et proelia, Cynthius aurem
> vellit et admonuit: 'pastorem, Tityre, pinguis
> 5 pascere oportet ovis, deductum dicere carmen.'
> nunc ego (namque super tibi erunt, qui dicere laudes,
> Vare, tuas cupiant et tristia condere bella)
> agrestem tenui meditabor harundine Musam.

> At first my Muse Thalia saw fit to play in Theocritean
>   verses
> and was not ashamed to dwell in the woods.
> But when I sang of kings and battles, Cynthian Apollo
> pulled my ear and warned: 'Tityrus, a shepherd should
>   feed
> 5 his sheep to be fat, but sing a fine-spun song.'
> So now — since you will have many poets eager to recite
> your praises, Varus, and to compose sad wars —
> I shall meditate my rustic Muse on a thin reed.

This *recusatio* appropriately occurs in Vergil's *Eclogues*, his lightest poetry, modelled on the *Idylls* of Theocritus, who was a contemporary of Callimachus and shared his Hellenistic poetics.[6] Here in his sixth *Eclogue* Vergil 'refuses' to sing of Varus' military exploits on the grounds that plenty of others will be eager to do so and invokes the authority of Apollo, as Callimachus had done. The words 'play' (*ludere*, 1), 'woods' (*silvas*, 2), 'fine-spun' (*deductum*, 5), 'rustic' (*agrestem*, 8), and 'thin' (*tenui*, 8) are all semi-technical terms that characterise Vergil's pastoral poetry as a minor genre, in contrast with the grand genres dealing with 'kings and battles' (*reges et proelia*, 3), 'praises' (*laudes*, 6), and 'sad wars' (*tristia bella*, 7). Although Vergil (following Callimachus) unflatteringly compares the grand genres to 'fat' (*pinguis*, 4) sheep, he manages to turn his programmatic verses into an indirect compliment to the achievements of Varus by pretending that they are beyond his power to celebrate, a manoeuvre that his contemporary Horace uses to great effect. A good example is Horace, *Odes* 1.6, written for Marcus Agrippa, the general responsible for the most important military victories of Augustus (called Caesar by Horace).

> Scriberis Vario fortis et hostium
> victor Maeonii carminis alite,
> quam rem cumque ferox navibus aut equis
>   miles te duce gesserit.
>
> 5 nos, Agrippa, neque haec dicere nec gravem
> Pelidae stomachum cedere nescii
> nec cursus duplicis per mare Vlixei
>   nec saevam Pelopis domum
>
> conamur, tenues grandia, dum pudor
> 10 imbellisque lyrae Musa potens vetat
> laudes egregii Caesaris et tuas
>   culpa deterere ingeni.
>
> quis Martem tunica tectum adamantina
> digne scripserit aut pulvere Troico
> 15 nigrum Merionen aut ope Palladis
>   Tydiden superis parem?
>
> nos convivia, nos proelia virginum
> sectis in iuvenes unguibus acrium
> cantamus, vacui, sive quid urimur,
> 20   non praeter solitum leves.

> You will be celebrated by Varius (who soars to
> Homeric song) as he writes of your bravery and victories
> over enemies and all the exploits of the daring sailors
>   and soldiers under your command.

5 I, Agrippa, do not attempt to sing those deeds,
   nor the tragic bile of stubborn Achilles,
   nor the journeys on the sea of tricky Odysseus,
      nor the savage house of Pelops,[7]

   for I am too frail for grand themes, since modesty
10 and the Muse who possesses the lyre of peace forbid
   me to detract from glorious Caesar's fame and yours
      through defect of talent.

   Who could adequately write of Mars in his armour
   of adamant? or of Meriones blackened with dust at Troy?
15 or of Diomedes, who with Athene's aid
      was a match for the gods?

   I sing of parties, I sing of battles waged by fierce
   girls with sharpened nails against boys,
   and whether I am fancy-free or deeply in love, I maintain
20   my customary levity.

The future tense of the opening verb *scriberis* ('You will be celebrated') is one of the marks of a *recusatio*. Vergil used it at *Eclogue* 6.6: 'you will have many poets eager to recite your praises.' The future tense is a polite way of leaving open the possibility for 'others' to do what the poet refuses to do himself.[8] Here, instead of anonymous 'others', Horace suggests his friend Varius as a worthy candidate to sing the martial exploits of Agrippa, since he writes in the high epic style.

The prominent *nos Agrippa* ('I, Agrippa') at the beginning of the second stanza brings together the poet and his subject, but turns on Horace's inability to write about such deeds as those of Agrippa or about the prominent heroes of Homer's epics. This is, of course, an urbane compliment to Agrippa: it suggests that his deeds are of the same stature as those of epic heroes; but at the same time, by undercutting the grand-style portrayals with such expressions as 'tragic bile' (6) and 'tricky Odysseus' (7), he both demonstrates his own lack of ability to handle such themes and suggests that epic portrayals are no longer appropriate to contemporary achievements. In line 9 occur two programmatic adjectives: *tenues grandia* ('too *frail* for *grand* themes'). The same adjective, *tenuis*, was used by Vergil at *Eclogue* 6.8 to describe his

9

'thin' poetry. By juxtaposing its opposite *grandia* ('grand' themes), Horace drives home their incongruity.

Horace pretends that the Muse and his own modesty both prevent him from composing inadequate poetry that might detract from Agrippa's and Augustus' glory; both of these motivations, external and internal, belong to the tradition of the *recusatio*. Apollo had deterred Callimachus and Vergil from writing about war; here the Muse of lyric poetry — specifically, of Horatian lyric poetry — stops Horace from doing the same. Implicit in the word *pudor* (9) is the topos of 'affected modesty', a rhetorical strategy to disarm critics which Horace often employs in his *recusationes*.[9]

The answer to the rhetorical question in the penultimate stanza ('Who could adequately write of' the deeds of epic heroes?) is, of course, only Homer (and perhaps Varius), but not Horace, since the emphatic 'I' (*nos*, 17) finally brings us to the positive programme of the poet, who does indeed sing of 'battles' (*proelia*, 17), but they are lovers' battles,[10] that take place in the context of symposia (*convivia*, 17).[11] The very last word of the poem, *leves*, 'light', commonly refers to the less serious genres (e.g. love lyric) as opposed to the heavier ones (e.g. epic and tragedy). It is obvious that Horace has it both ways in this poem; he slyly gets in his praise while claiming that he is incapable of writing it.[12]

Horace's contemporary Propertius also wrote *recusationes* in the tradition of Callimachus.[13] The most famous is the third elegy in the Third Book, of which I quote the first 24 lines.

> Visus eram molli recubans Heliconis in umbra,
>   Bellerophontei qua fluit umor equi,
> reges, Alba, tuos et regum facta tuorum,
>   tantum operis, nervis hiscere posse meis;
> 5 parvaque tam magnis admoram fontibus ora,
>   unde pater sitiens Ennius ante bibit;
> et cecinit Curios fratres et Horatia pila,
>   regiaque Aemilia vecta tropaea rate,
> victricesque moras Fabii pugnamque sinistram
> 10   Cannensem et versos ad pia vota deos,
> Hannibalemque Lares Romana sede fugantes,
>   anseris et tutum voce fuisse Iovem:
> cum me Castalia speculans ex arbore Phoebus
>   sic ait aurata nixus ad antra lyra:

15 'Quid tibi cum tali, demens, est flumine? quis te
    carminis heroi tangere iussit opus?
non hinc ulla tibi speranda est fama, Properti:
    mollia sunt parvis prata terenda rotis;
ut tuus in scamno iactetur saepe libellus,
20   quem legat exspectans sola puella virum.
cur tua praescripto sevecta est pagina gyro?
    non est ingenii cumba gravanda tui.
alter remus aquas alter tibi radat harenas,
    tutus eris: medio maxima turba mari est.'

I dreamed that I was lying in the soft shade of Helicon
    where flows the fountain of Pegasus, Bellerophon's
    horse.
I thought, Alba, that your kings and their deeds — a
    great
    undertaking — were within my power to mouth.
5 Already had I brought my small lips to those great
    fountains
    where Father Ennius had once quenched his thirst
and sung of the Curian brothers, the spears of the Horatii,
    the royal spoils carried on the ship of Aemilius Paulus,
the delays of Fabius that brought victory, the fateful fight
10   at Cannae, the gods won over by pious prayers,
Hannibal chased by the Lares from their Roman home,
    and the goose's cackling that saved Jupiter.
But from his Castalian grove, Phoebus Apollo saw me
    and, leaning on his golden lyre near a cave, said:
15 'Madman, what are you doing with a river like that? Who
    ordered you to undertake the task of heroic song?
You cannot hope for any fame in that way, Propertius;
    you must roll your small wheels over soft meadows,
so your little book may be tossed again and again on a stool
20   by a lonely girl who reads it as she waits for her lover.
Why has your writing turned from its prescribed course?
    The rowboat of your talent cannot bear heavy cargo.
If you scrape the water with one oar and the shore with the
    other,
    you will be safe: the middle of the sea is heavy going.'

The poem is an example of a dream-vision, a narrative setting
that had a long history in Graeco-Roman poetry and continued to

be popular in medieval (and even Renaissance) poetry.[14] The mention of Helicon clearly indicates that the speaker's experience concerns poetic inspiration.[15] The prominent *reges*, 'kings', in line 3 indicates that his themes are those appropriate to the grand style, and in lines 7–12 he provides a sample by recounting heroic episodes of the sort Ennius, the early Roman poet, treated in his *Annales*. As in Callimachus' *Aetia* and Vergil's *Eclogue* 6, Apollo suddenly appears and warns him not to essay such grand subjects.[16] Apollo's prescriptions are clearly in the tradition of Callimachean poetics. The 'river' (*flumen*) in line 15 and the following reference to the sea (*mari*) in line 24 indicate by their large size the epic themes.[17] In contrast, the poet must travel over 'soft' (*mollia*, 18) terrain, with 'little' (*parvis*, 18) wheels; or, with another metaphor, his 'rowboat' (*cumba*, 22) cannot bear 'heavy' (*gravanda*, 22) cargo. Instead, his format is to be a *little* book (*libellus*, 19) and his audience a love-sick girl, who (we may infer) will have no time or inclination to read lengthy, epic accounts since she is anxiously awaiting her lover.

From the examples so far, we can set out a table of vocabulary frequently encountered in *recusationes* stemming from Callimachus. The list is far from complete, but it gives a good indication of the terms used in this highly developed subgenre (those in the first column are always used pejoratively).[18]

The 'heavy' genres:	The 'light' genres:
epic, tragedy, history, Pindaric lyric	personal lyric, love elegy, satire

grand (*grandia*)	small (*parva*)
heavy (*gravem, gravanda*)	light (*leves*)
fat (πάχιστον, *pinguis*)	thin (λεπταλέην, *deductum, tenui*)
wide (πλατύν)	narrow (στεινοτέρην)
common (ὁμά)	unique (ἀτρίπτους)
hard (*adamantina*)	soft (*mollia*)
combats (*proelia, pugnam*)	parties (*convivia*)
battles (*bella*)	lovers' quarrels (*proelia virginum*)
war (*Martem*)	peace (*imbellis*)
loud (ψοφέουσαν, θόρυβον)	quiet (λιγὺν ἦχον)
large (μέγα, *magnis*)	small (ἐλαχής, *parva*)

long (σχοίνῳ Περσίδι)   short (τυτθόν)
vast (μέγας)   minute (ὀλίγη)

Although there are many other *recusationes* in Augustan poets,[19] probably the most important is *Odes* 4.2 of Horace. Since it sums up so well Horace's relationship to the Classical and Hellenistic traditions and has been so influential in European poetry from the Renaissance on, it is worthwhile quoting all of it.[20]

Pindarum quisquis studet aemulari,
Iule, ceratis ope Daedalea
nititur pinnis vitreo daturus
    nomina ponto.

5 monte decurrens velut amnis, imbres
quem super notas aluere ripas,
fervet immensusque ruit profundo
    Pindarus ore,

laurea donandus Apollinari,
10 seu per audaces nova dithyrambos
verba devolvit numerisque fertur
    lege solutis,

seu deos regesque canit, deorum
sanguinem, per quos cecidere iusta
15 morte Centauri, cecidit tremendae
    flamma Chimaerae,

sive quos Elea domum reducit
palma caelestes pugilemve equumve
dicit et centum potiore signis
20   munere donat,

flebili sponsae iuvenemve raptum
plorat et vires animumque moresque
aureos educit in astra nigroque
    invidet Orco.

25 multa Dircaeum levat aura cycnum,
tendit, Antoni, quotiens in altos

nubium tractus. ego apis Matinae
   more modoque

   grata carpentis thyma per laborem
30 plurimum circa nemus uvidique
   Tiburis ripas operosa parvus
     carmina fingo.

   concines maiore poeta plectro
   Caesarem, quandoque trahet feroces
35 per sacrum clivum merita decorus
     fronde Sygambros;

   quo nihil maius meliusve terris
   fata donavere bonique divi,
   nec dabunt, quamvis redeant in aurum
40   tempora priscum.

   concines laetosque dies et urbis
   publicum ludum super impetrato
   fortis Augusti reditu forumque
     litibus orbum.

45 tum meae, siquid loquar audiendum,
   vocis accedet bona pars, et 'O sol
   pulcher, o laudande!' canam recepto
     Caesare felix.

   tuque dum procedis, 'io Triumphe!'
50 non semel dicemus, 'io Triumphe!'
   civitas omnis dabimusque divis
     tura benignis.

   te decem tauri totidemque vaccae,
   me tener solvet vitulus, relicta
55 matre qui largis iuvenescit herbis
     in mea vota,

   fronte curvatos imitatus ignis
   tertium lunae referentis ortum,
   qua notam duxit, niveus videri,
60   cetera fulvus.

14

Whoever strives to rival Pindar,
Jullus, relies on wings waxed by
Daedalus' craft and will give a
    transparent sea its name.

 5 Like a river rushing down a mountain
which rains have swollen above its normal banks,
the deep-voiced Pindar seethes and floods
    far and wide,

sure to win Apollo's laurels
10 when he tumbles new words through his
daring dithyrambs, carried along by
    rhythms without restraint;

or when he celebrates gods and kings,
and the heroes who justly slew the
15 Centaurs and quenched the flame
    of the dread Chimaera;

or when he exalts Olympic victors returning home
with the palm for boxing or horse-racing
and presents them with a gift surpassing
20   a hundred statues;

or when he laments the youth snatched
from his sobbing wife and lauds his strength,
intelligence and golden character to the stars
    and cheats black Hades of them.

25 A great breeze lifts up the Swan of Dirce,
Antonius, whenever he soars high
among the clouds; but I, just like
    a bee from Mt Matinus,

that gathers pleasing thyme with greatest
30 effort about the woods and banks of lush
Tibur, painstakingly compose songs
    in my small way.

You will celebrate Caesar in grander style,
as he leads the fierce Sygambri

35 up the Sacred Way, his deserving brow
     wreathed with garlands,

     and declare that no greater or better gift
     has been bestowed by fate and the kind gods
     on the earth, nor will ever be, even though
40   the Golden Age return.

     You will celebrate the holidays and the public
     games on the event of brave Augustus'
     return and the forum that is
        free from litigation.

45 Then, if my best voice can add anything
     worth hearing, I shall sing, 'O beautiful
     day, o give him praises', in my joy
        at Caesar's return.

     And as you step forward, all of us citizens
50 will repeat, 'Hail to the Victor, Hail to the
     Victor', and offer incense
        to the generous gods.

     You can offer ten bulls and as many cows;
     I shall offer a tender calf, that has just
55 left its mother, and is maturing in the pasture
        to fulfil my vows;

     its brow resembles the curved light
     of the new moon at its third rising;
     it bears a snowy-white mark,
60   but the rest is brown.

The theme is very similar to that of *Odes* 1.6, where the deeds of
Agrippa require the exalted poetic gifts of a Varius. Here the occasion is the return of Augustus from a victorious campaign against
the Sygambri, a German tribe that was threatening Gaul. As in the
earlier poem, Horace actually praises the event while declining to
celebrate it. In the course of this ode, however, he contrasts his own
poetic achievement in lyric poetry with that of Pindar, and provides
later ages with an influential distinction between the 'greater'
Pindaric ode and the 'lesser' Horatian one.[21]

The poem begins with the assertion that Pindar's lofty achievement is impossible to equal, and that anyone who tries to imitate him will, like Icarus, plunge into the sea (the Icarian Sea was named for him). In support of this claim, Horace describes the genres and style of Pindar's lyric poetry — specifically, his dithyrambs, hymns, athletic victory odes and dirges — and compares him with a swollen river rushing down from the heights without restraint. The much more supple metres that Pindar used in his lyrics, meant to be sung by a choir, allowed him considerably more latitude than Horace, whose odes are in the simpler metres primarily intended for solo performance. Moreover, Pindar's bold metaphorical language and sudden shifts from one subject to another gave him the appearance of unrestrained impetuosity, as in his 'daring' (*audaces*, 10)[22] dithyrambs. The five stanzas which describe Pindar's achievement (5–24) consist of one sentence, a *tour de force* that in fact imitates the very Pindaric style in which Horace refuses to write.[23]

The two flying creatures that Horace takes as emblematic of the two kinds of poetic achievement each represent a side of the diagram on pp.12–13. On the one hand, a 'great' (*multa*, 25) breeze uplifts the Swan of Dirce (a spring near Thebes, Pindar's home), who soars in the clouds. The image of flight returns us to the opening comparison with Icarus and once again characterises Pindar's grand style as lofty. On the other hand, Horace compares himself with a bee from Mt Matinus (in the region where Horace was born), a small (*parvus*, 31) creature who flies close to the ground, and whose songs are painstakingly fashioned (*operosa*, 31). In other words, Horace confines himself to smaller themes, but composes his odes with greater care.[24]

Horace then leaves it up to one Antonius to sing of the achievements of Augustus 'in grander style' (*maiore plectro*, 33) with a tactful future tense, 'You will celebrate' (*concines*, 41), such as we saw at Vergil, *Eclogue* 6.6 and at *Odes* 1.6.1. Once again, he puts into another's mouth the praise that he himself refuses to utter — and the praise (37–40) is high indeed! By simply joining the rest of the citizens in shouting 'Io triumphe!' as Augustus returns, Horace portrays his modest, personal devotion to the emperor — and indirectly portrays the universal joy at Augustus' triumph.[25]

The last two stanzas employ yet another image to contrast the two types of poetry. Antonius will sacrifice 20 head of cattle; the poet will offer 'a tender calf', but it is special because it is his very own; he thus describes it in loving detail. It stands for his own modest but painstaking achievement and undercuts the grand gestures attributed to Antonius. The poem is at once a fine tribute to Augustus, who is declared worthy of celebration in the grand Pindaric manner, and an affirmation of Horace's Hellenistic poetics.

Although there are many excellent *recusationes* in the elegiac love poetry of Tibullus, Propertius, and Ovid (see 'Additional Examples'), we shall conclude this brief survey of Latin poets with examples from two other genres: satire and epigram. Whereas the Augustan poets, Vergil, Horace and Propertius, declined to write in the grand style because they preferred smaller, more personal lyric and elegiac genres, satiric poets of the succeeding 'Silver Age' offered a new reason for rejecting grand-style poetry: it was not true to life. A growing realism, particularly prominent in satire, is evident in the prose (e.g. Petronius) and poetry of the Neronian and Flavian authors and finds its place in their literary manifestos. An influential example is the epigram that prefaces the *Satires* of Persius (of which I quote the first seven lines):

> Nec fonte labra prolui caballino
> nec in bicipiti somniasse Parnaso
> memini, ut repente sic poeta prodirem.
> Heliconidasque pallidamque Pirenen
> 5 illis remitto, quorum imagines lambunt
> hederae sequaces: ipse semipaganus
> ad sacra vatum carmen adfero nostrum.

> I never washed my lips in the horse's fountain;
> nor do I remember dreaming on the twin peaks
> of Parnassus, so that I suddenly came forth a poet.
> The Heliconian Muses and pale Pirene
> 5 I leave to those whose busts are licked
> by clinging ivy; as for me, it is as a half-member
> that I bring my poetry to the rites of the bards.

In the first three lines Persius dissociates himself from those poets such as Hesiod and Ennius who claimed to experience a sudden call to the bardic profession. In the following lines he leaves traditional invocations to the Muses — and the grandiose poetry such appeals betoken — to those who fancy themselves fully established poets laureate. To such awesome poetic rites, he is a mere semi-initiate. The satiric tone that underlies the words *sacra vatum* (7), which suggest a pretentious 'bardic' religion, and *semipaganus*, which characterises his own status as an outsider of sorts, is more mordant than that in the *recusationes* of Horace and Propertius. They admitted the inherent superiority of the grander genres; Persius simply deflates them.

Persius' programme is portrayed in even greater detail in the *recusatio* that opens his Fifth Satire, where the poet's mentor, a Stoic philosopher named Cornutus, deters him from writing grand-style poetry.

> Vatibus hic mos est, centum sibi poscere voces,
> centum ora et linguas optare in carmina centum,
> fabula seu maesto ponatur hianda tragoedo,
> volnera seu Parthi ducentis ab inguine ferrum.
> 5   'Quorsum haec? aut quantas robusti carminis offas
> ingeris, ut par sit centeno guttere niti?
> grande locuturi nebulas Helicone legunto,
> si quibus aut Procnes aut si quibus olla Thyestae
> fervebit saepe insulso cenanda Glyconi.
> 10 tu neque anhelanti, coquitur dum massa camino,
> folle premis ventos, nec clauso murmure raucus
> nescio quid tecum grave cornicaris inepte,
> nec scloppo tumidas intendis rumpere buccas.
> verba togae sequeris iunctura callidus acri,
> 15 ore teres modico, pallentis radere mores
> doctus et ingenuo culpam defigere ludo.
> hinc trahe quae dicis mensasque relinque Mycenis
> cum capite et pedibus plebeiaque prandia noris.'

> Bards customarily demand a hundred voices and call for
> a hundred mouths and a hundred tongues to recite their
>   poems,
> whether putting on a play to be mouthed by a miserable
>   tragedian,
> or a Parthian pulling a lance from his wounded groin.
> 5   'What is all this about? How many globs of solid poetry
> are you cramming down, so that you need a hundred-fold
>   throat?
> Let the grand-style poets gather clouds on Helicon,
> if they plan to boil the pots of Procne and Thyestes,
> the bread and butter of insipid Glycon.
> 10 But you are not one to squeeze air from a puffing bellows

while the furnace smelts ore, nor do you hoarsely mutter
some grave matter to yourself to caw out ineptly,
nor do you strain your swollen cheeks until they burst with
a pop.
No, you seek everyday words, your skill is in pointed
combinations,
15 your diction is rounded and reserved, and your *forte* is
scraping sickly morals and pinning down faults with frank
wit.
Let this be the source of your poetry; leave Mycenae to her
feasts of head and feet and get to know ordinary peoples'
dinners.'

In *Odes* 4.2, Horace had used pairs of animals (swan, bee; bulls, calf) to contrast his style and subject matter with Pindar's; here the dominant metaphor is food. The lengthy epics and tragedies that form the staple for bards (*vatibus*, 1) are compared with 'globs of solid poetry' (5), and their themes are also conceived in terms of food: Persius alludes to two popular tragic incidents in which sons were served for dinner to their unsuspecting fathers — subjects which, Cornutus cynically remarks, provide the actor Glyco with his own meals. The metaphor continues to the end of the passage, when Persius' proper subject is compared with dinners of ordinary people (*plebeia prandia*, 18),[26] that is, themes of everyday life. Whereas the grandiose style of tragedy and martial epic is characterised by such adjectives as 'hundred' (1, 2, 6), 'miserable' (3), 'solid' (5), 'grand-style' (7), 'grave' (12), and 'swollen' (13), his own language consists of 'everyday words' (*verba togae*, 14), and his style is 'rounded' (*teres*, 15), 'moderate' (*modico*, 15), and, most characteristically, adept at creating a 'pointed combination' (*iunctura acri*, 14).[27] A final indication of Persius' realism is the introduction of his contemporary, Cornutus, in the role of adviser instead of Apollo, who had been the conventional spokesman for the poet in the *recusationes* by Callimachus, Vergil, Horace and Propertius. The stoic sage has replaced the gods of lyric poetry.

Martial's realism is even more pronounced in the following defence of his epigrams (10.4):

Qui legis Oedipoden caligantemque Thyesten,
  Colchidas et Scyllas, quid nisi monstra legis?
quid tibi raptus Hylas, quid Parthenopaeus et Attis,
  quid tibi dormitor proderit Endymion?

5 exutusve puer pinnis labentibus? aut qui
   odit amatrices Hermaphroditus aquas?
quid te vana iuvant miserae ludibria chartae?
   hoc lege, quod possit dicere vita 'Meum est.'
non hic Centauros, non Gorgonas Harpyiasque
10   invenies: hominem pagina nostra sapit.
sed non vis, Mamurra, tuos cognoscere mores
   nec te scire: legas Aetia Callimachi.

If you read about Oedipus and Thyestes' deed that
   darkened the sun,
and about Medeas and Scyllas, you are just reading
   about monsters.
What good will you get from Hylas' rape? from
   Parthenopaeus?
   from Attis? or from the sleeping Endymion?
5 what from the boy who lost his gliding wings? or from
   Hermaphroditus who hates the waters that love him?
Why do you enjoy the empty shams of a wretched scroll?
   Read this, about which Life can say, 'It is mine.'
Here you will not find Centaurs nor Gorgons
10   nor Harpies: man is the subject of my page.
But, Mamurra, since you do not wish to recognise your
   character
   nor to know yourself, you can read Callimachus' *Aetia*.

This epigram brings us full circle. We began with the very
influential *recusatio* at the beginning of Callimachus' *Aetia*. Now
Martial rejects that very work because it contains the fictional
story-telling that for Martial has become 'empty shams' (*vana
ludibria*, 7), whereas his satirical epigrams deal with real people
and speak the language of Life. Lines 9 and 10 single out the real
subject of Martial's epigrams: 'man' (*hominem*, 10).[28]

In these Greek and Latin examples, we have seen poets
rejecting previous poetic traditions that they considered outmoded with regard to subject matter (e.g. kings and battles,
mythology, panegyrics), genre (e.g. epic and tragedy), and
language (e.g. grand style, seen as inflated, bombastic). The
recusatio thus provides an effective means for correcting a tradition
a poet feels has become excessive or misdirected in its practice.

Recusationes ceased to be written in the later centuries of the
Roman empire and during the Latin phase of the Middle Ages,

but with the rise of vernacular poetry they again made an appearance. In English poetry, brief examples can be found in Chaucer, where characters contrast their 'pleyn' style with the high style full of rhetorical 'colours' and figures,[29] but *recusationes* become especially frequent in the Renaissance, as poets reacted against the excesses of the courtly and Petrarchan conventions. An early example in English is Sir Thomas Wyatt, whom D.L. Peterson describes in these terms:[30]

> Wyatt appears to have been constitutionally at odds with the values and mores of court society. If we are to judge from the tone of his poetry he found the empty rhetoric of courtly verse and the mock subservience of the courtly lover about equally offensive. His opposition to both is expressed in the plain style stripped of its didactic excesses and employed with a flexibility it had never before achieved.

One example is his lyric poem 'Blame Not My Lute', where he refuses to flatter his mistress in grandiose terms (in the Petrarchan convention) and describes his songs as 'somewhat plain' (12). Even more explicit is his rejection of the eloquent courtly poetry of his time in 'Mine Own John Poins', 56–60:

> None of these points would ever frame in me.
> My wit is naught. I cannot learn the way.
> And much the less of things that greater be,
> That asken help of colours of device
> 60   To join the mean with each extremity:
> With the nearest virtue to cloak alway the vice . . .

This disclaimer fittingly occurs in one of Wyatt's epistolary satires (a traditionally plain-style genre), where the poet's intention is to speak honestly and straightforwardly to a friend about the moral corruption in the court: to that end he follows the example of Horace and Persius of eschewing flattering rhetoric.

It was in the sonnet, however, that the *recusatio* found a particularly congenial setting. Its brevity, its minor status and the demand for novel treatment of conventional subjects all contributed to the popularity of the *recusatio* in collections of sonnets. We can begin with an example from Du Bellay's *Regrets*, Sonnet 4, in which he declares his modest intention to write simply and plainly:

Je ne veulx feuilleter lex exemplaires Grecs,
Je ne veulx retracer les beaux traicts d'un Horace,
Et moins veulx-je imiter d'un Petrarque la grace,
Ou la voix d'un Ronsard, pour chanter mes Regrets.

5 Ceulx qui sont de Phoebus vrais poëtes sacrez
Aimeront leurs vers d'une plus grand' audace:
Moy, qui suis agité d'une fureur plus basse,
Je n'entre si avant en si profonds secretz.

Je me contenteray de simplement escrire
10 Ce que la passion seulement me fait dire,
Sans rechercher ailleurs plus graves argumens.

Aussi n'ay-je entrepris d'imiter en ce livre
Ceulx qui par leurs escripts se vantent de revivre
Et se tirer tous vifz dehors des monumens.

I do not wish to thumb through Greek models,
I do not wish to retrace Horace's fine strokes,
Even less do I wish to imitate Petrarch's grace,
Or Ronsard's voice, in singing my 'Regrets'.

5 Those who are truly Apollo's sacred poets
Will prefer their verse of greater daring:
As for me, who am stirred by a lesser inspiration,
I am not so far advanced in such deep secrets.

I will be content to write simply
10 What my feelings alone make me say,
Without going off in search of weightier arguments.

Therefore, I have not undertaken to imitate in this book
Those who by their writings boast of coming back to life
And of rising alive out of their tombs.

This is one of many such Renaissance sonnets that claim to eschew learned affectation and grand effects in favour of a more straightforward account of experience. The adjectives used to characterise the grand style ('plus grand' audace', 6; 'profonds', 8; and 'graves', 11) and his own less pretentious style ('plus basse', 7; 'simplement', 9) are familiar from the tradition, but the announcement that he will simply write just what his feelings ('la passion', 10) dictate is striking. Taken out of context, this statement appears to anticipate nineteenth- and twentieth-century Romanticism, but his actual practice is far from a Romantic indulgence of the feelings, for as a member of the Pléiade, Du Bellay was very learned and still very much a part of the Graeco-Roman poetic and rhetorical tradition. He is drawing attention, though, to the fact that this collection of sonnets breaks new ground, that it is not indebted to the Greek models, to Horatian refinement, to Petrarchan charm, or (closer to home) to Ronsard's eloquence; and as its title, '(mes) Regrets', indicates, its primary subject is the poet's bitter personal experiences. In generic terms, as Colie has pointed out, Du Bellay's programme consists of mixing the *mel* ('honey') characteristic of the sonnet with the *fel* ('gall') of the epigram.[31]

Several of the opening sonnets of Sidney's *Astrophil and Stella* are witty variations that express a similar claim to break away from convention by presenting actual experience. In Sonnet 1, after the poet's vain attempts to find in other writings aids to expression and invention, the Muse tells him, 'Look in thy heart and write!'[32] In Sonnet 3, 'Let dainty wits cry on the sisters nine', he rejects the extravagant ploys of other love poets in praising their beloved, and claims that he merely copies what Nature writes in Stella's face.[33] However, probably the best-known of Sidney's *recusationes* is Sonnet 74:

> I never drank of Aganippe well,
> Nor ever did in shade of Tempe sit,
> And Muses scorn with vulgar brains to dwell;
> Poor layman I, for sacred rites unfit.
> 5 Some do I hear of poets' fury tell,
> But God wot, wot not what they mean by it;
> And this I swear by blackest brook of hell,
> I am no pick-purse of another's wit.
> How falls it then that with so smooth an ease
> 10 My thoughts I speak; and what I speak doth flow
> In verse, and that my verse best wits doth please?
> Guess we the cause. What, is it thus? Fie, no.
> Or so? Much less. How then? Sure thus it is:
> My lips are sweet, inspired with Stella's kiss.

Although Sidney claims no dependence on earlier poets, the very form which he uses is traditional, and many of the ideas as well as much of the vocabulary comes directly from Persius' prefatory epigram (see p. 18). Even the order of the first four verses closely follows its model: Persius never washed his lips in the 'horse's fountain' (i.e. Hippocrene), Sidney never drank from the well of Aganippe; Persius did not dream on Parnassus, Sidney did not sit in Tempe (a valley in Thessaly celebrated for its beauty); Persius leaves the Muses to other poets, Sidney is too 'vulgar' for them; Persius comes as a 'half-pagan' to the poetic rites, Sidney is a 'layman' unfit for them.[34] Throughout the first two quatrains, Sidney echoes Persius' disassociation from grand-style poetry with its claim to semi-religious inspiration that possesses the poet ('poets' fury', 5). In the third quatrain, however, when he turns to the merits of his own programme, he departs from Persius' plain-style realism, for in describing his verse as smooth (9), flowing (10), pleasing (11) and sweet (14), Sidney is drawing on rhetorical vocabulary which describes the middle (or florid) style.[35] This sweetness, he wittily concludes, is inspired by his subject matter itself, withheld until the very end of the poem, 'Stella's kiss'.

George Herbert, who conscientiously set out to redirect English poetry to treat spiritual subjects, wrote a pair of *recusationes* called 'Jordan I' and 'Jordan II', in which he adapts the subgenre to his religious poetry. I give the second:

> When first my lines of heavenly joys made mention,
>   Such was their luster, they did so excel,
> That I sought out quaint words, and trim invention;
>   My thoughts began to burnish, sprout, and swell,
> 5 Curling with metaphors a plain intention,
>   Decking the sense, as if it were to sell.
>
> Thousands of notions in my brain did run,
>   Offering their service, if I were not sped:
> I often blotted out what I had begun;
> 10   This was not quick enough, and that was dead.
> Nothing could seem too rich to clothe the sun,
>   Much less those joys which trample on his head.
>
> As flames do work and wind when they ascend,
>   So did I weave myself into the sense;
> 15 But while I bustled, I might hear a friend

> Whisper, 'How wide is all this long pretense!
> There is in love a sweetness ready penned:
> Copy out only that, and save expense.'

The dramatic framework of the poem is familiar. Just as Apollo (in the case of Callimachus, Vergil, Horace and Propertius) and Cornutus (in the case of Persius) suddenly appeared to deter the poet from writing in the grand style, here it is 'a friend' (God?), who suggests the proper course for Herbert to follow.[36] The first 14 lines that describe his attempt to portray the joys of heaven are a compendium of the stylistic embellishments commonly used in the Petrarchan tradition to describe one's beloved. And just as Sidney in *Astrophil and Stella* 3 claims to eschew all the poetic devices commonly used by love poets and merely to copy what Nature writes in Stella's face, so Herbert claims, with considerably more seriousness than Sidney, that he need only copy the sweetness written in love to depict the joy of heaven.[37]

Perhaps because poetic *recusationes* had themselves become conventional, the early Romantics avoided them, but when Wordsworth sought to redirect a poetic tradition which he also felt to be excessively artificial, the terms he chose to set forth his Romantic programme in '*Preface* to the Second Edition of *Lyrical ballads* (1800)' are surprisingly close to those of the Silver Latin poets. In opposition to the 'gaudiness and inane phraseology'[38] of contemporary writers which they inherited from eighteenth-century notions of poetic diction, he set out to compose in a simpler style: 'The principal object, then, proposed in these Poems was to choose incidents and situations from common life, and to relate or describe them, throughout, as far as was possible in a selection of language really used by men . . .' Like Persius and Martial, he is weary of far-fetched themes and grandiose diction; he also desires to return to 'situations from common life' (cf. Persius' *plebeia prandia*, 5.18), to 'language really used' (cf. Persius' *verba togae*, 5.14), and to the subject of Martial's epigrams: 'men' (cf. *hominem*, 10.4.10). Up to this point, at least, he remains within the Graeco-Roman system of poetic theory. In the continuation of the sentence, however, he announces his revolutionary Romantic objectives:

> and, at the same time, to throw over them a certain colouring of imagination, whereby ordinary things should be presented to the mind in an unusual aspect; and, further,

and above all, to make these incidents and situations interesting by tracing in them, truly though not ostentatiously, the primary laws of our nature: chiefly, as far as regards the manner in which we associate ideas in a state of excitement. Humble and rustic life was generally chosen, because, in that condition, the essential passions of the heart find a better soil in which they can attain their maturity.

Whereas Persius and Martial adopted a plainer language for the purpose of better portraying character (*mores*) in the satirical vein of Roman realism, Wordsworth, who is principally concerned with emotions, wishes to show how people think 'in a state of excitement', and therefore turns to rustics in order to portray more effectively 'the essential passions of the heart'. Wordsworth is refusing much the same artificiality as did the Silver Latin poets: it is his positive programme that is truly revolutionary.

Recusationes reappear in the twentieth century. A brief example is W.B. Yeats's 'A Coat', the penultimate poem in *Responsibilities* (1914), in which Yeats announces his intention to change his earlier, decorative poetry to a more straightforward kind. In his rejection of 'old mythologies', he echoes Persius and Martial:

> I made my song a coat
> Covered with embroideries
> Out of old mythologies
> From heel to throat;
> 5 But the fools caught it,
> Wore it in the world's eyes
> As though they'd wrought it.
> Song, let them take it,
> For there's more enterprise
> 10 in walking naked.

The elaborate decorations ('embroideries') are the Gaelic legends that had fascinated Yeats. Since the stylistic garment that these legends once embroidered has suffered poor imitation and now seems faddish, Yeats proposes to strip it off to reveal the plain song underneath. This affected nakedness and plain style (which the poem itself exhibits) is but one pole of a constant tension in Yeats's poetry, and the word 'enterprise' (9) suggests that the poet is less interested in a style that is truer (as in the case of

Persius and Martial), than in one which is bolder (OED, s.v. 'enterprise'). With this poem, as W.H. O'Donnell points out, 'he left the nineteenth century behind him and adopted instead a boldly direct, modern manner.'[39]

We shall conclude with two very different examples of recent *recusationes*, both by authors very aware of the traditions in which they are writing. The first, 'For My Contemporaries' by J.V. Cunningham, who was very familiar with Latin poetry, is clearly in the vein of Persius and Martial.

> How time reverses
> The proud in heart!
> I now make verses
> Who aimed at art.
>
> 5 But I sleep well.
> Ambitious boys
> Whose big lines swell
> With spiritual noise,
>
> Despise me not,
> 10 And be not queasy
> To praise somewhat:
> Verse is not easy.
>
> But rage who will.
> Time that procured me
> 15 Good sense and skill
> Of madness cured me.

The poem serves as a manifesto for Cunningham's own short, unpretentious, often satiric poems and epigrams, in which he opposes the excesses of certain post-Romantic poets, who aim at grand effects in 'big lines' (7). Although by disavowing 'art' Cunningham seems to diverge from the Callimachean–Horatian tradition, in which the copiousness and natural genius (φύσις, *ingenium*) of the grand-style writers is normally countered by the greater art (τέχνη, *ars*) of the smaller-scale poet, he is actually using the word 'verses' (3) to carry the value that *ars* has in the Callimachean programme. Since the writers of contemporary poetry have appropriated the concept of 'art' (and 'the artist') to their own pretentious programmes, where it becomes almost synonymous with inspired genius, Cunningham resorts to 'verses' (3, 12), incidentally scoring a hit at the modern propensity for irregular or free verse as a sign of *furor poeticus* ('spiritual noise', 8; 'rage', 13; 'madness', 16), which he opposes with his 'good sense and skill' (15). The epigram proposes a radical redirection of modern poetry from 'bardic' effusions to verses based on reason.

In contrast, the sonnet that opens John Hollander's collection, *Powers of thirteen*, is a *recusatio* closer in spirit to those of the Renaissance sonneteers, particularly Sidney:

> This is neither the time nor the place for singing of
> Great persons, wide places, noble things — high times, in
> short;
> Of knights and of days' errands to the supermarket;
> Of spectres, appearances and disappearances;
> 5 Of quests for the nature of the quest, let alone for
> Where or when the quest would start. You are the wrong
> person
> To ask me for a circus of incident, to play
> Old out-of-tunes on a puffing new calliope,
> Or to be the unamused client of history.
> 10 But tell me of the world your word has kept between us;
> I do what I am told, and tell what is done to me,
> Making but one promise safely hedged in the Poets'
> Paradox: *I shall say 'what was never said before.'*

The formal structure of the poem and its wittiness have much in common with Sidney's sonnets such as 'I never drank of Aganippe well'. The structure is simple: the word 'But' (10) signals the break between the catalogue of rejected subjects and the positive programme, much as Sidney's sonnets break between the octave and sestet. Sidney's playful indulgence of puns and paradoxes is more than matched by Hollander (e.g. in lines 2 and 3).[40] In fact, the message is so 'hedged' (12) in pun and 'Paradox' (13) that it is not quite clear what the poet's real claim is. The title of the poem, 'Refusing to Tell Tales', suggests that the poem follows the tradition of *recusationes* which espouse truthfulness, but the secondary meaning of 'tale' — namely, a story which relies on a succession of incidents — may rather be intended, since the poet refuses to provide 'a circus of incident' (7) — that is, an extended narrative. Line 10 announces what will be the true subject of the sonnet sequence: 'the world your word has kept between us' — that is, the relationship between the speaker and the anonymous addressee. The closing claim to say 'what was never said before' mockingly reuses the conventional promise of originality.[41] This ironic, sophisticated poem, which plays with the tradition of the *recusatio* much as Sidney did — but almost to the extent of becoming a parody — makes explicit the irony that poets have a fully traditional means of subverting tradition.

Notes

1. The rejection of martial themes (i.e. epic) for erotic themes (i.e. love lyric), implicit in the Sapphic example, becomes explicit in the later imitation of *Anacreontea* 26 (West):

> You sing of the Seven against Thebes,
> he sings of Phrygian battle cries,
> but I sing of the attacks on me.
> No horseman defeated me,
> 5   no footsoldier, no ships,
> but a new and different army did it,
> striking me with glances from eyes.

This light poem is one of several *recusationes* written by anonymous authors in the Hellenistic and later periods in imitation of Anacreon, the sixth-century poet, and collected in the *Anacreontea* (cf. also 2, 4 and 23 West). The first three verses reject tragic and epic themes (the Phrygian battle cries refer to the Trojan War) in favour of personal love themes, while verses 4–6 reproduce not only the form of Sappho's opening stanza, but even the same order of horsemen, footsoldiers and ships. For a good assessment of the poems in the *Anacreontea*, see G. Braden, *The Classics and Renaissance poetry: three case studies* (Yale University Press, New Haven, 1978), pp. 196–216.

2. In the latest commentary on the hymn, F. Williams, *Callimachus hymn to Apollo* (Oxford University Press, Oxford, 1978), pp. 87–9, argues that the Ocean refers to Homeric epic and the Euphrates to inferior Homeric imitators.

3. *P. Oxy.* 2079 in A.S. Hunt (ed.), Oxyrhynchus Papyri, Vol. XVII (Oxford University Press, Oxford, 1927).

4. These legendary wizards stand for old-fashioned critics of Callimachus' new poetic and are similar to Envy and Criticism in the passage quoted above from his 'Hymn to Apollo'.

5. For a thorough examination of Callimachus' influence on Roman poets, see W. Wimmel, *Kallimachos in Rom. Die Nachfolge seines apologetischen Dichtens in der Augusteerzeit. Hermes Einzelschriften*, vol. 16 (F. Steiner, Wiesbaden, 1960). For a brief treatment of Callimachus' influence on Catullus and Vergil, see W. Clausen, 'Callimachus and Latin poetry', *Greek, Roman, and Byzantine Studies*, vol. 5 (1964), pp. 181–96. For a

discussion of Callimachus' influence on the 'new poets', see R.O.A.M. Lyne, 'The Neoteric poets', *Classical Quarterly*, vol. 28 (1978), pp. 167–87.

6. Cf. Theocritus, *Id.* 7.45–50, where Lycidas attacks poets who attempt to achieve Homeric grandeur, and instead offers a little song (μελύδριον, 51) in the pastoral tradition, which he has taken pains to compose (ἐξεπόνασα, 51), and which he hopes will please (ἀρέσκει, 50) his listener. This preference for a small, carefully wrought song whose purpose is to please will recur in Horace's *recusationes* (see p. 17 with Note 24).

7. The 'savage house of Pelops' refers to the cycle of tragic stories dealing with Atreus, Thyestes and Agamemnon. The grotesque account of Atreus inviting his brother Thyestes to a banquet where he served him his own children became a standard topic in *recusationes* (cf. Persius, *Satires* 5.8 and Martial, *Epigrams* 10.4.1, pp. 19 and 20). Furthermore, Varius was famous for his tragedy *Thyestes*.

8. The next poem in Horace's collection, *Odes* 1.7, is also a *recusatio* that begins with a future tense: 'Others shall praise famous Rhodes or Mytilene' (*Laudabunt alii claram Rhodon aut Mytilenen*). It continues with a list of Greek cities that are rejected for the poet's own preference: Roman Tibur.

9. Cf. Horace, *Satires* 2.1–19, *Epistles* 2.1.145–270 (note *pudor*, 259); see R.G.M. Nisbet and M. Hubbard, *A commentary on Horace: Odes Book I* (Oxford University Press, Oxford, 1970), p. 87 and below, Note 22 and 34.

10. In the poem from the *Anacreontea* quoted above in Note 1, epic battles are also replaced by amatory battles. For a delightful poem that plays on all the similarities between soldiers and lovers, cf. Ovid, *Amores* 1.9: *militat omnis amans* ('every lover is a soldier').

11. Note the emphatic juxtaposition of 'I' and his chosen themes in line 17: *nos convivia, nos proelia*, which corrects the earlier *nos Agrippa* (5).

12. The manoeuvre is similar to that of *praeteritio* ('bypassing') in oratory, where the speaker declares that he will not mention the fact that his opponent did *x*, *y* and *z*, but by saying it he actually does mention them.

13. The first poem of the third book begins with a *recusatio* addressed to the spirit of Callimachus (*Callimachi manes*, 'Shade of Callimachus'). See 'Additional Examples'.

14. The general theme of a dramatic encounter with deities of poetry who initiate the poet into his calling first appears at Hesiod, *Theogony* 22–34. Callimachus refers to Hesiod's calling in a dream at the beginning of the *Aetia*, but too little remains to know how he treated it. Ennius began his *Annales* with a dream in which Homer appeared to him, but since only fragments of Ennius' dream are extant, we cannot determine how much Propertius may have parodied it in this poem. The *recusatio* that opens Ovid's third book of *Amores* presents a variation: it takes place in an ancient, out-of-the-way grove, where Dames Tragedy and Elegy vie for the poet's allegiance. For a detailed account of the poetic calling in antiquity, see A. Kambylis, *Die Dichterweihe und ihre Symbolik* (Winter, Heidelberg, 1965).

15. Mt Helicon, the highest mountain in Boeotia, was the locus for Hesiod's commission from the Muses (cf. *Theogony* 22–34). The nearby

spring of Hippocrene was supposedly formed when Pegasus' foot struck the rock.

16. Horace uses this topic in his first collection of verse at *Satires* 1.10.31–5, where Quirinus (the deified Romulus who exemplifies the Roman tradition) appeared to him in a dream and forbade his writing in Greek. In the last ode of his collection (4.15), Horace gives the *topos* of Apollo's warning a final twist (1–4): 'When I wished to sing of battles / and conquered cities, Apollo struck his lyre / and warned me not to spread my small sails / upon the Tyrrhenian sea.' This *recusatio* (in which the sea once again represents grand-style poetry) neatly serves as an excuse for praising the benefits of the *Pax Augusta* in the remainder of the poem.

17. This elaborate use of water imagery derives directly from the epilogue to Callimachus' 'Hymn to Apollo', and is resumed at the end of Propertius' poem, where the great fountains (*magnis fontibus*, 5) that slaked Ennius' thirst are contrasted with the fountain (*fonte*, 51) that had inspired Philetas, Propertius' Hellenistic model, and whose water the Muse of poetry sprinkles on Propertius' lips.

18. Often these dichotomies are specified by concrete illustrations such as sea–pool, river–stream, ship–rowboat, highway–path, ass–cricket, mountain–house, and swan–bee.

19. Augustan poets considered *recusationes* so important that they often placed them at the head of their books. Thus, Tibullus begins his *Elegies* with a brief one (1.1.1–6), while more elaborate ones open the second and third books of Propertius' *Elegies* and all three books of Ovid's *Amores*.

20. In the terms developed by A. Fowler, *Kinds of literature: an introduction to the theory of genres and modes* (Harvard, Cambridge, MA, 1982), p. 275, Horace's poem achieves the status of being 'definitive', of summing up the generic tradition, as, for example, does Marvell's 'To His Coy Mistress' in the *carpe-diem* subgenre and Milton's 'Lycidas' in pastoral elegy.

21. For a brief discussion of this ode and its influence on Pindaric criticism, see W.H. Race, *Pindar* (G.K. Hall, Boston, 1986), pp. 122–8.

22. Pindar's boldness contrasts with Horace's modesty (*pudor*, 1.6.9) and Propertius' caution (*tutus*, 3.3.24). The 'new words' (10–11) in Pindar's dithyrambs are made possible by the facility in Greek for inventing new and impressive compounds. Latin is much more limited in this respect.

23. At 3.3.7–12 Propertius also indulges the grand style in his list of heroic highlights from Roman history and legend.

24. This is in line with Callimachus' desire to be judged by the canons of *art*, not length or grandeur. The Horatian combination of smallness (*parvus*, 31), pleasure (*grata*, 29), and laborious craftsmanship (*per laborem*, 29; *operosa*, 31) is reminiscent of the same three qualities at Theocritus *Id.* 7.50–51 (see above Note 6). His image of the bee recalls the Melissae in Callimachus' 'Prologue' to the *Aetia*.

25. Cf. the similar effect of the closing verse of Herbert's *recusatio*, 'Jordan I': 'Who plainly say, *My God, My King*'.

26. For an analysis of the imagery in Persius' satires, see J.C.

Bramble, *Persius and the programmatic satire: a study in form and imagery* (Cambridge University Press, Cambridge, 1974). For a good overview of Persius' poetic programme, see M.P.O. Morford, *Persius* (G.K. Hall, Boston, 1984), pp. 25–38 and 54–8. For a survey of *recusationes* in which food is a metaphor for style, see W.H. Race, '*Odes* 1.20: an Horatian *Recusatio*', *California Studies in Classical Antiquity*, vol. 11 (1978), pp. 179–96.

27. For a detailed account of the *iunctura acris* in Persius (of which the phrase itself is a good example), see R.A. Harvey, *A commentary on Persius* (Brill, Leiden, 1981), pp. 130–1. For an excellent discussion of Persius' style, see Morford, *Persius*, pp. 73–96.

28. This couplet, which emphasises Martial's true subject, is in the form of a priamel (see p. 54, Note 7). The word *mores* (11) here and at Persius, *Satires* 5.15 indicates the satiric intention of these two authors to ridicule vices of character.

29. Cf. the Franklin's disingenuous apology for his 'rude speche' in his prologue (12–14): 'Thyng that I speke, it moot be bare and pleyn. / I sleep nevere on the Mount of Pernaso, / Ne lerned Marcus Tullius Scithero,' which contains a learned allusion to Persius' epigram. Also, in the *Clerk's Prologue* Harry Bailley, afraid that the Clerk will speak over his listeners' heads, requests (15–20):

15 Telle us some murie thyng of aventures.
     Youre termes, youre colours, and youre figures,
     Keepe hem in stoor til so be that ye endite
     Heigh style, as whan that men to kynges write.
     Speketh so pleyn at this tyme, we yow preye,
20 That we may understonde what ye seye.

30. D.L. Peterson, *The English lyric from Wyatt to Donne* (Princeton University Press, Princeton, 1967), p. 87. Peterson's treatment of Wyatt in light of the plain and eloquent styles in the Renaissance is very helpful. For a detailed account of the Classical styles and their influence in the Renaissance, see W. Trimpi, *Ben Jonson's poems: a study in the plain style* (Stanford University Press, Stanford, 1962), pp. 1–114.

31. R.L. Colie, *The resources of kind: genre-theory in the Renaissance*, B.K. Lewalski (ed.), (University of California Press, Berkeley, 1973), pp. 68–9. In a similar fashion, Juvenal justified his satiric genre by claiming that indignation created his verse (*facit indignatio versum, Satires* 1.79). Du Bellay lists the four languages and literatures most influential in his day and by choosing the verbs *feuilleter* (1), *retracer* (2), and *imiter* (3), he intimates that they are already well worn. For the topic of the hackneyed tradition (*omnia iam vulgata*), cf. below Note 41.

32. For a brief account of the terms 'invention' and 'imitation' in rhetorical handbooks and an explanation of the Muse's instruction ('The most quoted and least understood line of all Sidney's poetry'), see W.A. Ringler, Jr., *The poems of Sir Philip Sidney* (Oxford University Press, Oxford, 1962), pp. 458–9.

33. Sonnets 6 and 15 are also *recusationes*. Shakespeare treats similar themes in Sonnets 103, 21, and 82.

34. Sidney's 'vulgar' (3) and 'layman' (4) together convey the two

main ideas in the Latin *paganus*, which indicates both a rustic and an uninitiate, while his 'sacred rites' (4) is a literal translation of Persius' *sacra* (7). Sidney's pose as a 'poor layman' is an example of the topic of 'affected modesty', which is often a part of *recusationes*; see Curtius, *European literature*, pp. 83–5. We have seen it in Horace's 'modesty' (*pudor*) at *Odes* 1.6.9, in his 'small way' (*parvus*) at 4.2.31 and in Propertius' 'little wheels' (*parvis . . . rotis*) at *Elegies* 3.3.18. Later examples include Anne Bradstreet's 'The Prologue' to *The Tenth Muse* and Emily Dickinson's 'I'm Nobody! Who Are You?' and 'This Is My Letter to the World'.

35. For ancient descriptions of the three styles of oratory (and by extension of poetry), cf. Cicero, *Orator* 75–99 and Quintilian, *Inst. Or.* 12.10.58–68. For an account of their development, see G.L. Hendrickson, 'The origin and meaning of the ancient characters of style', *American Journal of Philology*, vol. 26 (1905), pp. 249–90, and for a brief overview of ancient stylistics, see D.A. Russell, 'Theories of style', in *Criticism in antiquity* (University of California Press, Berkeley, 1981), pp. 129–47. For a thorough examination of the plain style and its relationship to the grand and middle styles, see Trimpi, *Ben Jonson's poems*, pp. 1–114.

36. For an analysis of the 'Jordan' poems as part of larger issues of style in Herbert, see F. Manley, 'Toward a definition of plain style in the poetry of George Herbert' in M. Mack and G. deForest Lord (eds), *Poetic traditions of the English Renaissance* (Yale University Press, New Haven, 1982), pp. 203–17. For the 'Jordan' poems as expressive of Protestant poetics, see B.K. Lewalski, *Protestant poetics and the seventeenth-century religious lyric* (Princeton University Press, Princeton, 1979), pp. 3–4, 228–9, and 314–15; on p. 298 she discusses the role of the 'friend' and other interlocutors in Herbert's poems.

37. C.A. Patrides, *The English poems of George Herbert* (Dent, London, 1974), pp. 210–11, suggests that Herbert is parodying *Astrophil and Stella*, Sonnet 1 in 'Jordan II', but Sonnet 3 is a much closer model, for it too contains a list of poetic excesses, metaphors of expensiveness ('enrich', 7; 'cost too dear', 11), and the injunction to 'copy' that which is near at hand.

38. W. Wordsworth, '*Preface* to the second edition of *Lyrical ballads*, 1800', W.J. Bate (ed.), *Criticism: the major texts* (Harcourt, Brace, Jovanovich, New York, 1970), p. 336.

39. W.H. O'Donnell, *The poetry of W.B. Yeats: an introduction* (Ungar, New York, 1986), p. 14. For a brief analysis of the poem as part of Yeats's attempt to establish his poetic style, see R. Ellmann, 'Making a style' in *Yeats: the man and the masks* (Norton, New York, 1979), pp. 138–56.

40. Hollander's propensity for puns is evident even in the title of the collection (*Powers of thirteen*), for it contains 169 (= 13^2) sonnets of 13 lines with 13 syllables per line.

41. For the topos, frequently found in introductory *recusationes*, see Curtius, *European literature*, pp. 85–6.

2

Introducing a Subject: The Priamel

In the previous chapter we examined a subgenre of poetic apology. In this chapter we shall examine an independent poetic and rhetorical form, which can be found in every major genre of poetry in all periods. Although it is one of the most useful poetic devices, it has become the object of scholarly study for only the past 60 years. It is called a 'priamel' (pronounced pree-á-mel), and the name is a German form of the Latin *praeambulum* ('prelude', 'introduction'). Although it was originally used to describe a minor subgenre of German poetry of the fifteenth century, the term is now used by classical scholars to refer to a particular form that is very common in Greek and Latin literature.[1] As the name suggests, it is very frequently found in introductory passages, for its function is to lead up to or introduce a subject.

Many priamels already occur in Homer's *Iliad* and *Odyssey* (see 'Additional Examples'), but probably the best-known example is the opening stanza of *fr.* 16 by Sappho, which we briefly reviewed as an example of a *recusatio*:

> Some say an array of cavalry, others of infantry,
> and others of ships, is the most beautiful thing
> on the black earth, but I say it is whatever
> a person loves.

There are five elements to note in this priamel:

(I) a *general context*: 'the most beautiful thing on the black earth';
(II) an indication of *quantity* or *diversity* within the context: 'some say . . . others';

(III) a *pivotal word* that dismisses the previous examples and points to the one to come: 'but';

(IV) a *subject of ultimate interest*: 'whatever a person loves'; and

(V) an *evaluative term*: 'most beautiful'.

With the exception of the last, which may simply be implicit, these elements are present in every priamel and constitute its form. The first two elements are the 'foil', providing the background of possible choices. Within the general context the poet is free to enumerate as many examples as he wishes — sometimes a lengthy catalogue results — or he can simply summarise the possibilities with words such as 'many', 'each' or 'all'.[2] The last two elements constitute the 'climax'. They provide the subject of ultimate interest and emphasise it. The third element effects the transition from the 'foil' to the 'climax'.[3] Within this framework, a poet can achieve many subtle effects: for example, Sappho withholds the crucial term 'loves' (ἔραται, 4) until the very end of the stanza, thereby giving it added emphasis. In addition, she has carefully chosen all the items of the foil ('cavalry', 'infantry' and 'ships') from one category, war, so that although she explicitly endorses only 'whatever a person loves', her choice of foil terms suggests that she also excludes military (and perhaps all public) concerns.[4]

Sometimes the foil can be so extensive that it becomes a work of art in its own right, as in the introductory poem to Horace's *Odes*:

> Maecenas atavis edite regibus,
> o et praesidium et dulce decus meum,
> sunt quos curriculo pulverem Olympicum
> collegisse iuvat metaque fervidis
> 5 evitata rotis palmaque nobilis
> terrarum dominos evehit ad deos;
> hunc, si mobilium turba Quiritium
> certat tergeminis tollere honoribus;
> illum, si proprio condidit horreo,
> 10 quicquid de Libycis verritur areis.
> gaudentem patrios findere sarculo
> agros Attalicis condicionibus
> numquam demoveas, ut trabe Cypria
> Myrtoum pavidus nauta secet mare.
> 15 luctantem Icariis fluctibus Africum
> mercator metuens otium et oppidi

laudat rura sui; mox reficit rates
quassas, indocilis pauperiem pati.
est qui nec veteris pocula Massici
20 nec partem solido demere de die
spernit, nunc viridi membra sub arbuto
stratus, nunc ad aquae lene caput sacrae.
multos castra iuvant et lituo tubae
permixtus sonitus bellaque matribus
25 detestata. manet sub Iove frigido
venator tenerae coniugis immemor,
seu visa est catulis cerva fidelibus,
seu rupit teretes Marsus aper plagas.
me doctarum hederae praemia frontium
30 dis miscent superis, me gelidum nemus
nympharumque leves cum Satyris chori
secernunt populo, si neque tibias
Euterpe cohibet nec Polyhymnia
Lesboum refugit tendere barbiton.
35 quodsi me lyricis vatibus inseris,
sublimi feriam sidera vertice.

Maecenas, sprung from royal ancestors,
O my guardian and sweet claim to fame,
there are some who enjoy gathering Olympic
dust on their chariots as they avoid the turning-post
5 with their glowing wheels, to win the palm of glory
that raises them as earthly champions to the gods;
another rejoices if the mob of fickle citizens
strives to elevate him to triple honours;
another is glad if he stores in his own barn
10 all the grain winnowed in Libyan granaries;
not even by promising the wealth of an Attalus
could you persuade the man who enjoys hoeing
his ancestral fields to become a sailor
and risk sailing the Myrtoan sea in a Cyprian ship.
15 The merchant, in fear of the Southwester
when it batters the Aegean waves, praises
the tranquility of his hometown fields, but soon,
he repairs his damaged ships, unable to endure poverty.
Another man is not loath to take a cup
20 of vintage Massic nor to steal time from a busy day,
now resting his limbs beneath a green plane tree,

now his head by the gentle source of a sacred spring.
Many enjoy army life, the sound of the trumpet
and bugle, and the wars that mothers
25 hate. Beneath a freezing sky remains the hunter,
forgetful of his tender wife,
whether his trusty dogs have spotted a deer
or a Marsian boar has torn his pliant nets.
As for me, the ivy that rewards learned brows
30 links me with the gods on high; the cool grove
and the light-hearted choruses of nymphs and Satyrs
distinguish me from the crowd, provided Euterpe
does not withhold the flute nor Polyhymnia
refuse to tune the Lesbian lyre.
35 But if you include me among the lyric bards,
my exalted head shall strike the stars.

The two verses at the beginning and the two at the end constitute a dedication of the collection to Horace's patron, Maecenas, with whose approval Horace hopes to become one of the famous lyric poets. The middle of the poem (lines 3–34) is a long priamel that lists the activities of various types of people (athletes, politicians, farmers, sailors, merchants, hedonists, soldiers and hunters). These are contrasted with the prominent *me* (29), which signals the climactic term: Horace's choice of lyric poetry as his occupation. As Sappho had contrasted the opinions of others with her own choice of what is most beautiful, so Horace gives as background the choices of 'others' (*sunt quos*, 3, 'some there are'; *hunc*, 7, 'one man'; *illum*, 9, 'another') until he arrives at his particular choice: of all the range of human preoccupations, Horace has chosen that of poet.

It is important to note that in describing each occupation in the foil, Horace suggests, by a word or phrase, some flaw or limitation. Thus, for example, the politician is elected by the 'fickle citizens', the merchant cannot 'endure poverty', the soldier engages in wars 'that mothers hate', and the hunter forgets about his 'tender wife'.[5] In this way the poem's rhetoric and form work together to distinguish the poet 'from the crowd' (*populo*, 32) of others listed in the foil.

In the opening of the second book of his *De rerum natura* (*On the nature of things*), Lucretius uses a priamel to emphasise the joys of Epicurean philosophy, which advocated a simple life of pleasure lived in accordance with enlightened withdrawal from ambitious competition:

> Suave, mari magno turbantibus aequora ventis,
> e terra magnum alterius spectare laborem;
> non quia vexari quemquamst iucunda voluptas,
> sed quibus ipse malis careas quia cernere suave est.
> 5 suave etiam belli certamina magna tueri
> per campos instructa tua sine parte pericli.
> sed nil dulcius est, bene quam munita tenere
> edita doctrina sapientum templa serena,
> despicere unde queas alios passimque videre
> 10 errare atque viam palantis quaerere vitae,
> certare ingenio, contendere nobilitate,
> noctes atque dies niti praestante labore
> ad summas emergere opes rerumque potiri.

> Sweet it is, when winds churn the water on the vast sea,
> to watch from land the mighty toil of someone else,
> not because another's troubles are cause for pleasant joy,
> but because it is sweet to see what ills you do not have.
> 5 It is sweet as well to behold great armies in battle
> arrayed across the plain — and yet be free from danger.
> But nothing is more pleasant than to occupy the unassail-
>   able,
> peaceful sanctuaries built upon the teaching of the wise;
> from there you can look down upon others and see them
>   wander
> 10 here and there, straying in search of the path of life,
> as they compete with their talents and vie for nobility,
> struggling night and day with constant effort
> to rise to heights of wealth and dominate events.

The first word, *suave*, 'sweet', provides the general context (things pleasant) and also hints at the key principle of Epicurean ethics, 'pleasure'. The two examples in the foil, watching a ship founder and armies contending, both depict the avoidance of pain and danger, one of the goals of Epicurean ethics. The climactic example, introduced by 'but' (*sed*, 7) and the evaluative element 'nothing is more pleasant' (7), also involves withdrawal from strife but shifts the argument to a metaphorical plane by depicting the Epicurean philosopher high in his sanctuary (*templa*, 8) of wise doctrine, looking down on errant mankind, who vie endlessly with one another for wealth and power.[6]

In these examples from Sappho, Horace and Lucretius, the priamel was used to introduce a poem or book of poetry, but priamels are also an effective means for emphasising one particular item in a longer poem. In the sixth book of Vergil's *Aeneid*, for example, the hero Aeneas goes to the underworld to see his father. At the end of his speech of exhortation to his son, Anchises uses a priamel to highlight the future mission of Rome (6.847–53):

> excudent alii spirantia mollius aera,
> (credo equidem), vivos ducent de marmore voltus;
> orabunt causas melius, caelique meatus
> 850 describent radio et surgentia sidera dicent:
> tu regere imperio populos, Romane, memento
> (hae tibi erunt artes) pacique imponere morem,
> parcere subiectis et debellare superbos.

> Others will cast more supple bronzes that breathe life
> and, I am sure, will turn marble into living features,
> will plead more eloquently, chart the movements
> 850 of the sky and predict the risings of the stars:
> you, Roman, remember to rule the nations with your empire
> (this will be your art), to enforce the rule of peace,
> to spare the humbled and to battle down the haughty.

The achievements of 'others' are, of course, some of the arts in which the Greeks excelled: sculpture, oratory and astronomy. These are contrasted with the special Roman skill: to rule the nations and to provide peace through law and temperate use of force. The climax is signalled by the second-person address with the prominent *tu* (851), 'you',[7] and the proper name *Romane*, 'Roman'. In this brief but impressive passage, Vergil sets side by side the characteristic achievements of Greece and Rome, and reminds his contemporaries ('remember', 851) to live up to their tradition.[8]

The priamel is also appropriate for epigrams; a light example opens the collection of Martial on the Roman games (*De spectaculis liber* 1):

Barbara pyramidum sileat miracula Memphis,
    Assyrius iactet nec Babylona labor;
nec Triviae templo molles laudentur Iones,
    dissimulet Delon cornibus ara frequens;
5 aere nec vacuo pendentia Mausolea
    laudibus inmodicis Cares in astra ferant.
omnis Caesareo cedit labor Amphitheatro;
    unum pro cunctis fama loquetur opus.

Let foreign Memphis keep silent about the wonder of its
    pyramids,
    nor let Assyria boast of the labour that went into
      Babylon;
let not the soft Ionians be praised for the Temple of
    Artemis,
    nor let the altar of many horns distinguish Delos;
5 let not the Mausoleum that hangs on empty air be extolled
    to the stars in the boundless praises of the Carians.
All labour yields place to Caesar's Colosseum;
    Fame shall tell of this one work in place of all the others.

The context consists of *miracula* ('wonders') — specifically, the architectural wonders of the ancient world. The first three couplets list five: the pyramids at Memphis, the city of Babylon (famed for its great walls and its hanging gardens in the time of Nebuchadnezzar), the temple of Artemis at Ephesus in Ionia, the altar at Delos constructed of animal horns and the Mausoleum at Halicarnassus in Caria. As in the case of Horace, who undercut many of his examples with a pejorative word or phrase, so Martial also undermines his examples with such words as *barbara* (1), 'foreign'; *iactet* (2), 'boast'; *molles* (3), 'soft'; *vacuo* (5), 'empty'; and *inmodicis* (6), 'boundless,' (i.e. 'immoderate'). The last couplet provides the climactic term: Caesar's Colosseum. The first word *omnis* (7), 'all', sums up the previous examples, all of which 'yield place' (*cedit*)[9] to the greatest wonder. The phrase *unum pro cunctis* (8), 'one work in place of all', neatly expresses the force of this priamel, which singles out the Colosseum as the summation of all other wondrous structures. It also illustrates the ability of the priamel to amplify its subject.[10]

Although there are hundreds of other examples of priamels in Greek and Latin literature,[11] as well as in medieval poetry,[12] we shall single out some Renaissance and modern examples. A good starting-place is Shakespeare's Sonnet 91:[13]

> Some glory in their birth, some in their skill,
> Some in their wealth, some in their body's force,
> Some in their garments, though newfangled ill,
> Some in their hawks and hounds, some in their horse;
> 5 And every humor hath his adjunct pleasure,
> Wherein it finds a joy above the rest.
> But these particulars are not my measure;
> All these I better in one general best.
> Thy love is better than high birth to me,
> 10 Richer than wealth, prouder than garments' cost,
> Of more delight than hawks or horses be;
> And having thee, of all men's pride I boast:
>   Wretched in this alone, that thou mayst take
>   All this away and me most wretched make.

The form of the priamel is clear from the words 'some . . . some . . . but'. The context established in verses 1–4 concerns the various things that people 'glory in'. Verses 5 and 6 widen the sphere with a summarisation: 'And every humor hath his adjunct pleasure / Wherein it finds a joy above the rest.' These verses constitute summary foil. 'Every' sums up all the dispositions of men, the words 'pleasure' and 'joy' give the context, and 'above' supplies the evaluative motif. The foil has surveyed the various areas in which men take pride or pleasure, and we await one to be singled out by the poet 'above the rest'. Verses 7 and 8, right in the middle of the sonnet, provide the pivotal transition:

> But these particulars are not my measure;
> All these I better in one general best.

The word 'but' indicates the turning-point, while 'these particulars' sum up the preceding particular examples to be dismissed *en masse*: 'all these'[14] will be surpassed by the poet's 'one best' choice. Note also the introduction of the first person 'my' and 'I', a phenomenon we saw in Sappho and Horace. At this point, Shakespeare has provided four of the five elements of the priamel. We still await the most important: the subject of ultimate interest. The poet has purposely withheld it in order to build up suspense, so that he can state it emphatically. It comes, appropriately, at the beginning of the third quatrain, a common location for introducing a new subject: 'Thy love is better . . .' At last, we have the real subject of the sonnet, for which the preceding eight verses were foil.

It is always important to see what factors unify the terms of the foil, for they illuminate through contrast the climactic term. As we noted, Sappho implicitly contrasts war with love. All the items that Shakespeare mentions in the first quatrain are physical and material: on this level of enumeration, there would be no end to the various objects in which people could take pride. Instead, the poet's choice raises the discussion to a new level ('All these I better in one general best', 8): his lover's love, which is more inclusive, more fundamental than mere trappings of worldly success like birth, wealth, clothing and fine animals associated with the aristocracy.

Once the priamel has selected the subject, the poet is free to expatiate on it and amplify its importance. Indeed, the amplification itself is one of the signs of having arrived at the true subject. The third quatrain justifies the poet's choice by amplifying the merits of his love: 'better . . . richer . . . prouder . . . of more delight . . . all men's pride'. The closing couplet, as it often does in a Shakespearean sonnet, takes the argument in a surprising direction. In this instance, it continues to amplify the power of 'thy love', but in a mode which the rhetoricians call *ex contrario*, 'from the opposite case'. If having his lover's love makes the poet the happiest of all men, then its absence would (presumably) make him the most miserable. Such is the logic of the last couplet, but it also serves the ethical purpose of reminding the poet (and his beloved) that their happiness is precarious, and they had best enjoy it while they can.

Each of the poets examined so far has carefully adapted the priamel to the formal structure of his poem. Sappho reduced her priamel to one stanza and saved the crucial word until the last, while the turning-point between the foil and climax occurred in the middle of the verse. In the poems by Horace and Vergil, which did not employ a stanzaic form, the climactic term was emphatically introduced at the beginning of the line with a change of person (Horace, *me*; Vergil, *tu*). Martial, on the other hand, adapted the priamel to his elegiac couplets, in which the first three couplets contained the foil and the last one introduced the climactic term. The interaction between the priamel and the form of the poem often produces subtle effects of emphasis: for

43

example, when the subject of ultimate interest is introduced at the beginning of a line or stanza, the most important words tend to cluster at the beginning and to receive considerable emphasis. In the example from Horace, the word that follows *me*, *doctarum* (29), 'learned', points to the special characteristic that separates the poet's occupation from all the others that precede it. In the example from Vergil, the word that follows the *tu*, *regere* (851), 'to rule', emphatically introduces the particular forte of the Romans. Likewise, in Martial's epigram, the prominent *Caesareo* pays a clear tribute to the emperor. In the Shakespearean sonnet, 'Thy love' (8), contains the heart of the poem; it also provides the major tension; since it is 'thy' love, it is dependent upon another and can be taken away.

The 15th sonnet of Spenser's *Amoretti* also adapts the priamel nicely to the sonnet form.

> Ye tradefull merchants, that with weary toyle
> Do seeke most pretious things to make your gain,
> And both the Indias of their treasures spoile,
> What needeth you to seeke so farre in vaine?
> 5 For loe my love doth in her selfe containe
> All this world's riches that may farre be found.
> If saphyres, loe her eyes be saphyres plaine;
> If rubies, loe her lips be rubies sound;
> If pearls, her teeth be pearls both pure and round;
> 10 If yvorie, her forhead yvory weene;
> If gold, her locks are finest gold on ground;
> If silver, her faire hands are silver sheene.
> But that which fairest is, but few behold:
> Her mind, adornd with vertues manifold.

This sonnet actually contains two priamels, the second a gloss on the first. The first, in verses 1–6, concerns what are 'most pretious things' (2) to seek. The motif of the 'search' or 'journey' is often a feature of a priamel. Here the 'others' are merchants who travel the world over ('both the Indias', 3). Against this wide background, verse 5 provides the climax: 'For loe my love'. 'For' is the pivotal word, 'loe' ('right here') contrasts with the distant ('farre', 4) travels of the merchants, while 'my' signals the forthcoming climactic term by switching to the first person. In the manner of Martial's *unum pro cunctis* (see p. 41), the subject of real interest, 'my love', is said to sum up 'all' (6) treasures. Verses

44

7–12 elaborate on the word 'all', and illustrate how it is that his beloved contains the world's riches. All these examples (drawn from the conventions of the *blason*, Renaissance descriptions of the beloved's anatomy) are united by the fact that they describe the beloved's physical appearance. The concluding couplet turns this list into foil for the 'fairest' (13) quality of the lady (which is, paradoxically, invisible): her mind and virtues. Both of these priamels serve to focus attention on one item out of a wider context. Those far travels yield to one lady, while the lady's many physical beauties yield to the quality of her mind and character. In both of them (as in the Shakespearean sonnet) there is an implicit contrast between the material realm and the realm of the spirit.

One of the best-known Romantic poems to use the priamel is Keats's 'On First Looking into Chapman's Homer':

> Much have I traveled in the realms of gold,
>   And many goodly states and kingdoms seen;
>   Round many western islands have I been
> Which bards in fealty to Apollo hold.
> 5 Oft of one wide expanse had I been told
>   That deep-browed Homer ruled as his demesne;
>   Yet did I never breathe its pure serene
> Till I heard Chapman speak out loud and bold:
> Then felt I like some watcher of the skies
> 10   When a new planet swims into his ken;
> Or like stout Cortez when with eagle eyes
>   He stared at the Pacific — and all his men
> Looked at each other with a wild surmise —
>   Silent, upon a peak in Darien.

The motif of the journey also serves as the occasion for this priamel. The words 'much' (1) and 'many' (2, 3) sketch the wide scope of the poet's travels. At verse 4 we learn that these journeys are metaphorical and actually describe his wide reading of poetic works. And although the poet could not actually travel to the demesne of Homer — Keats could not read Greek — yet he could get its spirit from reading George Chapman's vigorous Renaissance translations of the *Iliad* and *Odyssey*. Out of all those (poetic) travels, Homer and his translator Chapman emerge as the centre of focus. The word 'till' signals the climactic term,

Chapman, which the sentence beginning with 'then' goes on to amplify.

Keats, however, is not ultimately interested in Chapman, but rather in his own reaction to the event. Having singled out his subject in the octave, Keats then devotes the sestet to a description not of the characteristics of Homer's poetry nor of Chapman's virtues as a translator, but of *what it felt like* when he 'discovered' Homer through Chapman. Indeed, the colon after verse 8 and the emphatic 'then' at the beginning of the sestet show that the priamel has merely singled out the occasion for the poet's feelings, which rise at the end of the poem to an emotional height: 'with a wild surmise — / Silent, upon a peak in Darien'.[15]

Wordsworth uses a priamel to introduce the principal character in his narrative poem 'The Brothers':

> 'These Tourists, heaven preserve us! needs must live
> A profitable life: some glance along,
> Rapid and gay, as if the earth were air,
> And they were butterflies to wheel about
> 5 Long as the summer lasted: some, as wise,
> Perched on the forehead of a jutting crag,
> Pencil in hand and book upon the knee,
> Will look and scribble, scribble on and look,
> Until a man might travel twelve stout miles,
> 10 Or reap an acre of his neighbour's corn.
> But, for that moping Son of Idleness,
> Why can he tarry *yonder*? — In our churchyard
> Is neither epitaph nor monument,
> Tombstone nor name — only the turf we tread
> 15 And a few natural graves.'
>
>   To Jane, his wife,
> Thus spake the homely Priest of Ennerdale.

As the priest sits with his wife, he remarks upon the different tourists that he sees before him. The words 'some (2) . . . some (5)' sketch the different kinds, all of whom share a kind of joy and delight in the natural surroundings. At verse 11, however, one individual is singled out ('But, for that . . .', 11).[16] He differs from the others, in that he is 'moping' and — unlike the rest, who are enjoying the natural beauty — he is inspecting the graves in the churchyard. As one would expect from such an introduction, he will play the major role in the rest of the poem; the happy tourists are foil for this morose native son.

The French Romantic poet Charles Baudelaire also used priamels to good effect. In the introductory poem 'Au Lecteur' ('To the Reader') to his collection *Les fleurs du mal* (*The flowers of evil*), he enumerates all of the evils that are rampant in the world, and at the end of the poem he uses a priamel to single out the worst vice of all (29–40):

Mais parmi les chacals, les panthères, les lices,
30 Les singes, les scorpions, les vautours, les serpents,
Les monstres glapissants, hurlants, grognants, rampants,
Dans la ménagerie infâme de nos vices,

Il en est un plus laid, plus méchant, plus immonde!
Quoiqu'il ne pousse ni grands gestes ni grands cris,
35 Il ferait volontiers de la terre un débris
Et dans un bâillement avalerait le monde;

C'est l'Ennui! — l'oeil chargé d'un pleur involontaire,
Il rêve d'échafauds en fumant son houka.
Tu le connais, lecteur, ce monstre délicat,
40 — Hypocrite lecteur, — mon semblable, — mon frère!

But among the jackals, panthers, bitches,
30 monkeys, scorpions, vultures, snakes,
and monsters that yap, and howl, and grunt, and crawl
in the foul menagerie of our vices,

there is one even uglier and nastier and filthier!
Although it makes no grand gestures or great cries,
35 it would gladly lay the land in ruins
and swallow the world in one yawn;

it is Ennui! — with a spontaneous tear in his eye,
he dreams of gallows as he smokes his pipe.
You know him, reader, that fastidious monster,
40 hypocritical reader, — my fellow-man, — my brother!

Just as priamels can be used to praise something above all else, here Baudelaire uses one to denounce an evil. The list of vices, all characterised metaphorically as animals in a menagerie, are outdone by the one which represented for Baudelaire the most insidious, and which preoccupied him in many poems, ennui ('boredom'). After two stanzas of preparation, he withholds the name itself until the beginning of the last stanza, where it receives added emphasis.

Baudelaire also uses a priamel at the beginning of his longest (and perhaps greatest) poem, 'Le Voyage', when he enumerates different kinds of voyagers (9–24):

Les uns, joyeux de fuir une patrie infâme;
10 D'autres, l'horreur de leurs berceaux, et quelques-uns,
Astrologues noyés dans les yeux d'une femme,
La Circé tyrannique aux dangereux parfums.

Pour n'être pas changés en bêtes, ils s'enivrent
D'espace et de lumière et de cieux embrasés;
15 La glace qui les mord, les soleils qui les cuivrent,
Effacent lentement la marque des baisers.

Mais les vrais voyageurs sont ceux-là seuls qui partent
Pour partir; coeurs légers, semblables aux ballons,
De leur fatalité jamais ils ne s'écartent,
20 Et, sans savoir pourquoi, disent toujours: Allons!

Ceux-là dont les désirs ont la forme des nues,
Et qui rêvent, ainsi qu'un conscrit le canon,
De vastes voluptés, changeantes, inconnues,
Et dont l'esprit humain n'a jamais su le nom!

Some are glad to flee their vile homeland;
10 others, the horror of their infancy; and some,
astrologers drowned in the eyes of a woman,
the tyrannical Circe with dangerous perfumes.

To avoid being changed into beasts they inebriate
themselves
on space and light and blazing skies;
15 the ice that stings and the suns that tan them
gradually erase the branded kisses.

But the true travellers are only those who depart
for the sake of going; with hearts as light as balloons,

they never diverge from their destiny,
20 and without knowing why always say: 'Onward!'

travellers whose desires are shaped like the clouds,
and who dream, like the recruit of the cannon,
of vast pleasures that constantly change, undiscovered ones
which the human mind has never been able to name.

The travellers in the foil are all united by the fact that they are
fleeing from something; 'But the true travellers' (17) are those
who journey 'for the sake of going' in search of yet undiscovered
pleasures. The rhetorical elaboration and heightening of this last
group shows that it constitutes the real subject of the poem.
These explorers, we discover in the course of the work, are driven
by *ennui* to the point of the last frontier of experience: death
itself.[17]

W.B. Yeats's celebrated poem, 'An Irish Airman Foresees his
Death', owes much of its effect to a priamel:

I know that I shall meet my fate
Somewhere among the clouds above;
Those that I fight I do not hate,
Those that I guard I do not love;
5 My country is Kiltartan Cross,
My countrymen Kiltartan's poor,
No likely end could bring them loss
Or leave them happier than before.
Nor law, nor duty bade me fight,
10 Nor public men, nor cheering crowds,
A lonely impulse of delight
Drove to this tumult in the clouds;
I balanced all, brought all to mind,
The years to come seemed waste of breath,
15 A waste of breath the years behind
In balance with this life, this death.

The priamel that follows the declaration of the speaker (Major
Robert Gregory), that he expects to die in combat (1–2), rejects
possible reasons for his choice: he does not go out of nationalistic
hatred or love (3–4); he does not fight for utilitarian reasons (5–
8); he is not obeying law or duty, or responding to public
outbursts of patriotic enthusiasm (9–10). At line 11 comes the

real reason: 'A lonely impulse of delight / Drove to this tumult in the clouds'.[18] As in Sappho's poem, where an unremarked similarity linked the members of the foil — they all pertained to war — here also a whole range of experience is rejected as a motive for action: the foil terms all justify going to war on the basis of one's responsibility to others. Instead, the speaker goes because of a 'lonely' impulse, one that is his alone; and in order to make his point more effectively, Yeats has purposely ended the foil with 'Nor public men, nor cheering crowds' (10) to sharpen the contrast between the enthusiasm of the masses and the unique experience of the solitary speaker. Fittingly for a poet steeped in the Romantic tradition, it is a whimsical 'impulse of delight' (a descendant, in minor key, of Wordsworth's 'spontaneous overflow of powerful feelings') that directs his hero's actions. The last four lines explain this paradoxical situation: his life 'seemed waste of breath' (14).[19]

A priamel can often be reformulated as the search for the answer to a question: for example, the priamel in Sappho's poem searches for the answer to 'What is the most beautiful thing on the black earth?', while Lucretius implicitly poses the question, 'What is the most pleasant thing?' Shakespeare's sonnet answers the question, 'What do I take the greatest pride in?' and Yeats's poem asks, 'What impels one to go and die in foreign combat?' We shall conclude this survey with a poem by W.H. Auden, consisting of an extended priamel that surveys answers to the question, 'What is Law?'

> Law, say the gardeners, is the sun,
> Law is the one
> All gardeners obey
> To-morrow, yesterday, to-day.
>
> 5 Law is the wisdom of the old
> The impotent grandfathers shrilly scold;
> The grandchildren put out a treble tongue,
> Law is the senses of the young.
>
> Law, says the priest with a priestly look,
> 10 Expounding to an unpriestly people,
> Law is the words in my priestly book,
> Law is my pulpit and my steeple.

Law, says the judge as he looks down his nose,
Speaking clearly and most severely,
15 Law is as I've told you before,
Law is as you know I suppose,
Law is but let me explain it once more,
Law is The Law.

Yet law-abiding scholars write:
20 Law is neither wrong nor right,
Law is only crimes
Punished by places and by times,
Law is the clothes men wear
Anytime, anywhere,
25 Law is Good-morning and Good-night.

Others say, Law is our Fate;
Others say, Law is our State;
Others say, others say
Law is no more
30 Law has gone away.

And always the loud angry crowd
Very angry and very loud
Law is We,
And always the soft idiot softly Me.

35 If we, dear, know we know no more
Than they about the law,
If I no more than you
Know what we should and should not do
Except that all agree
40 Gladly or miserably
That the law is
And that all know this,
If therefore thinking it absurd
To identify Law with some other word,
45 Unlike so many men
I cannot say Law is again,
No more than they can we suppress
The universal wish to guess
Or slip out of our own position
50 Into an unconcerned condition.

Although I can at least confine
Your vanity and mine
To stating timidly
A timid similarity,
55 We shall boast anyway:
Like love I say.

Like love we don't know where or why
Like love we can't compel or fly
Like love we often weep
60 Like love we seldom keep.

The foil in the first 34 lines contains a list of possible answers. Like that in Sappho, *fr.* 16, it surveys the opinions of 'others', and like that in Horace, *Odes* 1.1, it often undercuts them with a telling detail (e.g. 'as he looks down his nose', 13). Although these opinions differ radically from one another, they are united by the fact that they all simply identify Law with something else, and in several cases a self-serving motive underlies the identification. All in one way or another seek to reduce the scope of law or, in one extreme case, to eliminate it altogether. Indeed, the last two examples of the foil present extreme instances of law becoming the 'we' of an angry crowd or the 'me' of an idiot. Because it contrasts with 'crowd', the word 'idiot' may preserve some force of its Greek original: a private individual. Here again, the last items of foil serve to intensify the contrast with the climactic term. Law is not to be equated with the anger of a crowd, nor with the quietude (cf. 'soft', 34) of the lone individual. As we shall see, it must exist in a context of love between people.

The turning-point comes in the long stanza that begins at 35, marked by the change of syntax and person: 'If we, dear'. In the following lines Auden introduces an innovation into the structure of a priamel that is, to my knowledge, unprecedented. Instead of forcefully introducing the climactic term, he delays with a long hesitatory passage that lays the basis for his eventual opinion. These lines attest to the speaker's character as a reasonable, indeed modest man, for unlike those who boldly claimed to know what Law was, the poet hesitates to commit himself, until he (speaking also for his addressee) finally offers a 'timid similarity' (54): 'Like love I say' (56). As is often the case in priamels, the argument suddenly shifts to a new level in the climax. The epigrammatic force of the final four lines seals the argument: law is not to be identified with anything specific; it is ultimately a mystery, but nonetheless, like love, it guides our lives, however inadequately we can define or live up to it. By placing law in a context of love ('If we, dear', 35 and the repeated 'like love we . . .' in lines 57–60), Auden may well be pointing to the 'law of love' of the New Testament.

In this brief sketch, we have seen how the form of the priamel has persisted throughout the poetic tradition and been used in very different contexts to espouse radically different ideas. Its longevity results from its protean adaptability to any subject or situation. It can be brief or long. As a species of enthymeme (rhetorical argument),[20] it has a philosophical dimension that appeals to the mind; by creating suspense and a sense of climax, it has a dramatic and rhetorical dimension that appeals to the emotions. We shall encounter many more examples in the following chapters.

Notes

1. This form, closely related to the catalogue, is a 'constructional type', of the kind sketched by A. Fowler, *Kinds of literature*, pp. 127–8. For a history of the term and a survey of Greek and Latin examples, see W.H. Race, *The Classical priamel from Homer to Boethius* (Brill, Leiden, 1982).

2. A good example of a summary priamel is the opening of the famous 'Ode to Man' in Sophocles' *Antigone* 332: '*Many* (II) are the *wonders* (I), *but* (III) *none is more wonderful than* (V) *man* (IV)'. Elements (II) and (I) before the comma are 'foil', while everything after 'but' (III) constitutes the 'climax'.

3. Although an adversative conjunction such as 'but' often occurs, the climax can just as well be indicated by a change of syntax or person, as also occurs in the example from Sappho: 'others . . . I' (οἱ μὲν . . . ἐγὼ δέ).

4. There is also a contrast between large groups ('arrays') of horses, men, ships and (later) chariots and the individual lover, as well as between the public and private realms. We have seen that the poem is also a *recusatio*.

5. For a good analysis, see M.S. Santirocco, *Unity and design in Horace's Odes* (University of North Carolina Press, Chapel Hill, 1986), pp. 15–19.

6. In Byron's *Don Juan*, Canto 1, stanzas 122–7, there is a long priamel on various things that are 'sweet' in life, culminating in: 'But sweeter still than this, than these, than all, / is first and passionate love'. It is fitting that a Romantic poet should single out this aspect of life as the most appealing, whereas Lucretius prefers serenity and wisdom.

7. Instead of adversatives such as 'but', colons frequently mark the transition from foil to climax. Cf. the priamel in Martial's *recusatio* (10.4.9–10, discussed on p. 21): 'Here you will not find Centaurs nor Gorgons / nor Harpies: man is the subject of my page.'

8. R.G. Austin, *Aeneidos Liber Sextus* (Oxford University Press, Oxford, 1977), pp. 260–1 has a very good analysis of the artistry of this priamel and notes: 'This epilogue to Anchises' prophecy is the most famous sustained passage in the whole *Aeneid*', a statement that reflects the ability of the priamel to make a memorable statement at important moments in longer works.

9. That the previous examples 'yield' to the climactic term is another way of saying that it surpasses them. This mode of expression became so commonplace during and after the time of Martial that it is called the 'out-doing' or 'cedat' formula by Curtius (*European literature*, pp. 162–4), many of whose examples are also priamels.

10. In ancient rhetorical treatises, *amplificatio* and *comparatio* are cited as the two chief means for praising a subject. The priamel is particularly well adapted to this purpose, for the climactic item is shown to surpass a multitude of other examples. For an adaptation of Martial's priamel, cf. Spenser's *Ruines of Rome*, Sonnet 2 ('Great Babylon her haughtie walls will praise').

11. For a list of priamels, see Race, *The Classical priamel*, pp. 161–71. There is scarcely an ancient author who does not use the form. The most sophisticated examples are found in Pindar and Horace, although Propertius and Ovid have the largest number.

12. The fifteenth-century Nuremberg poet, Hans Rosenplüt, was famous for his *priameln*, which consisted of a series of seemingly unrelated, often paradoxical statements that were cleverly brought together at the end of the poem. François Villon, the fifteenth-century French poet, has a number of priamels, including 'Ballade des Femmes de Paris' and 'Je Congnois Bien'.

13. As far as I know, Nisbet and Hubbard, in *A commentary on Horace: Odes Book I*, p. 3, were the first to call attention to this Shakespearean priamel.

14. Cf. *omnis labor* (7), 'all labour' in the example from Martial, and 'tout cela' in Baudelaire's 'Le Vin du Solitaire'.

15. Keats is using a standard topic here of indicating the magnitude of something by describing the reactions of beholders. The *locus classicus* is at *Iliad* 3.154–60, when Helen's beauty captivates (at least initially) even the wise elders of Troy. In Classical usage, the emotional reaction exists for the purpose of amplifying the subject (here Helen's great beauty): what makes Keats's use Romantic is the fact that the subject (reading Chapman's Homer) exists for the purpose of stimulating the emotion of the poet himself. This is a good example of Wordsworth's poetic aim in his 'Preface to lyrical ballads', where he states 'the feeling . . . gives importance to the action and situation, and not the action and situation to the feeling.'

16. Very often a demonstrative adjective ('this', 'that') emphasises a climactic term. Cf. the 'loe' in Spenser's Sonnet 15.5 (see p. 44).

17. The structure of the entire poem is that of a priamel. The speaker

journeys in search of ever-new experiences until he comes to the final one, death, which he accepts with the closing words of the poem: 'Au fond de l'Inconnu pour trouver du *nouveau*' (Into the depths of the Unknown to find something *new*).

18. Although there is no 'but' to signal the climax, the abrupt shift from negative to positive effectively underscores 'A lonely impulse' as the real reason for his action.

19. Although it is difficult to ascertain the precise nature of that 'impulse of delight', the condition of the speaker appears to be similar to that described in Baudelaire's 'Le Voyage', where the true voyager just goes for the sake of the journey in order to experience new pleasures. Of course, for an Irish volunteer in a war between other countries, the appeal of patriotism was diminished, but the final emphasis on 'waste of breath' and death suggests that some of the motivation may derive from personal ennui. In 'Reprisals', which he withheld from publication, Yeats provided bitter comments on Major Gregory's 'battle joy'.

20. See J.T. Kirby, 'Toward a general theory of the priamel', *Classical Journal*, vol. 80 (1985), pp. 142–4, who shows its relationship to an Aristotelian enthymeme.

3

Poetry and the Visual Arts:
The *Ekphrasis*

One of the standard writing exercises in rhetorical exercise books of late antiquity was the composition of a *descriptio* or ἔκφρασις (*ekphrasis*). These school texts, called *progymnasmata*, left their mark on medieval poetics,[1] and enjoyed a revival in Renaissance schools.[2] They defined *ekphrasis* as 'an expository speech which clearly brings the subject before our eyes', and among the topics they deemed appropriate for extended description were people, actions, places and seasons (including festivals). Aphthonius, for example, who composed one of the later *progymnasmata* (probably late fourth or early fifth century AD), provides a sample description of the acropolis at Alexandria, which he duly concludes with the following statement: 'Indeed, its beauty is greater than words can tell, and if anything has been omitted, it happened because of wonder' (θαύματος, 49.11 Sp.). As we shall see, Aphthonius was not being original in his appeal to wonder; it already existed in numerous examples of earlier poetry and prose that made up the tradition he was trying to pass on to schoolboys — 'wonder' was simply one of the standard topics of *descriptiones* from Homer on.[3]

There are hundreds of descriptions of all kinds in Graeco-Roman literature, some brief, some very long, in almost all genres of poetry and prose — epic, lyric, tragedy, history, philosophy and epigram.[4] Their history remains to be written. In this chapter we shall single out one strand of this complex tradition by restricting the discussion to examples that describe a work of art. In addition, even within this category, we shall concentrate on a few examples from the Classical, Hellenistic, Romantic and modern periods in which the style and content of the described work provide a kind of microcosm that reveals the author's own

56

poetic practice and captures the salient characteristics of his period.

As usual, Homer provides the starting-point. The most famous description in antiquity was that of Achilles' shield at *Iliad* 18.483–608. Since it is too long to quote here in its entirety, the following outline will reveal its very careful organisation.

(1) Earth and the heavenly bodies (483–9)

(2) Two cities (490–540)
    (a) a city at peace (490–508)
       (i) a marriage (491–6)
       (ii) a dispute in the marketplace (497–508)
    (b) a city at war: a description of an ambush (509–40)

(3) Rural scenes (541–606)
    (a) ploughing (541–9)
    (b) reaping (550–60)
    (c) harvesting grapes (561–72)
    (d) husbandry (573–89)
       (i) cattle herding: a description of lions attacking a bull (573–86)
       (ii) sheep pasture (587–9)
    (e) a rustic dance (590–606)

(4) Ocean running around the rim of the shield (607–8)

A remarkable feature of this *ekphrasis* is its comprehensiveness: the shield sketches the whole universe. Its emphasis, however, is decidedly on man. The only Olympian gods mentioned are Athene and Ares (516) and they are portrayed fighting among men. In that respect, the *ekphrasis* reflects the humanistic emphasis of the epic as a whole. The poet organises his array of material by means of subdivision, beginning with the heavens: the Sun, Moon, Pleiades, Orion and the Big Dipper. Then he portrays life in the *polis*, which he subdivides into activities of peace and war. The section on the peaceful city is further divided into scenes of a marriage and a lawsuit, while that on the city at war portrays the actions of both defenders and attackers. He then balances the activities of the city with a series of tableaux that depict rural life. First come the agricultural activities (in seasonal order): spring-time ploughing, then reaping and finally the grape harvest. These are followed by livestock herding, further specified as the herding of cattle and sheep. The human activities are completed with the rustic dance, and the entire shield is rounded off, so to speak, with Ocean. Thus, there is a clear movement from the heavens to cities, to fields and finally to the expanse of Ocean.[5]

Each of these tableaux is enlivened by descriptions of the human activities: the marriage, the dispute, the battle, a festival, singing, two lions attacking a bull as the men and dogs try to drive them off, and finally festive dancing, all of which work together to portray the grand sweep of human life as well as its details. And within each scene the poet takes care to make subtle contrasts. The city at peace, for example, is depicted by two panels: a marriage by torchlight in the evening (a happy occasion featuring young people and women) and a daytime quarrel in the market-place over a slain man, a scene of dissension involving men. Thus, even within the city there is a contrast between unity and strife, leisure and business, night and day, men and women, and the private realm (home) and the public (the forum).[6] The effect of this comprehensive survey of human activities within the epic as a whole is to remind Achilles (and the reader) of the entire context of human affairs within which the forthcoming battle takes place. It universalises the action.

We noted above that the expression of wonder is very frequent in *ekphraseis* and, as in the example from Aphthonius, it is often used to conclude a topic. Wonder appears in two places in the description of the shield. The marriage scene is completed with the sentence (495–6): 'The women stood before the doors of their houses and marvelled' (θαύμαζον), while at line 549 the word occurs again at the end of the ploughing scene to draw attention to the verisimilitude of the depiction: 'A great wonder (θαῦμα) of craftsmanship'. The two instances differ, however, in one important respect: the first passage refers to the wonder of characters within the work itself as they view the scene; the second refers to the wonder of external viewers as they marvel at the craftsmanship of the artist. The latter type becomes a favourite means of involving the reader in the process of visualising the scene, while at the same time reminding him that the depiction is, after all, only a work of art.

This Homeric example begins a long tradition of describing works of art. In epics, this often meant describing shields. Besides the shield of Achilles, there is the 'Shield of Heracles' (*Scutum*) attributed to Hesiod, which is much more diffuse and mannered than its Homeric predecessor, but which contains many correspondent scenes, the most interesting of which comes last. After describing the noise and rush of chariots in the midst of a race, the poet ends with a self-conscious remark that suddenly takes us outside the work (310–11): 'And so their labour was everlasting and never ended in victory; their contest was never decided.' As we shall see, Keats will exploit this device to great effect in his 'Ode on a Grecian Urn'. Ocean also frames this shield by running around its rim, and the entire description is completed with the 'wonder' motif (318): 'A wonder (θαῦμα) to behold, even for Zeus'.

However, the example that rivals the Homeric is Vergil's description of Aeneas' shield at *Aeneid* 8.626–731. The contrast between them is striking. Whereas Achilles' shield depicts a comprehensive range of human activities, the subject matter on Aeneas' shield is much more restricted (626–9):

> Illic res Italas Romanorumque triumphos
> haud vatum ignarus venturique inscius aevi
> fecerat Ignipotens, illic genus omne futurae
> stirpis ab Ascanio pugnataque in ordine bella.

> There on the shield were Italian deeds and Roman triumphs
> fashioned by the Fire-God, who was not ignorant of prophecy
> nor unaware of the coming age: on it was every generation
> to come
> in the line from Ascanius and the wars waged one after
> another.

The shield portrays scenes from Roman history from Ascanius to Augustus — in particular, the wars (*bella*, 629) and triumphs (*triumphos*, 626). Whereas Homer laid out his scenes by logical subdivisions, Vergil proceeds chronologically (*in ordine*, 629), selecting historical *exempla* which portray the triumph of Roman virtue (*virtus*). Also unique to Vergil is the sense of climax in his disposition of scenes, for all of these lead up (in priamel-like fashion) to the grand centre-piece, the Battle of Actium. Because Vergil saw all Roman history culminating in the Pax Augusta, the cumulative effect of all the scenes on the shield is one of preparation for the crowning event.

Vergil uses several formal means for making this last event

climactic. Firstly, he divides the previous scenes from the last one by placing a 'swelling sea' around them (671–4). Homer and the author of the *Scutum* had used Ocean to conclude their descriptions of the shields, but here Vergil uses the same motif to close off the group of examples before treating the most important. We have seen that in priamels a group of examples is frequently summed up before the climactic example is introduced. Here the sea not only sets the previous examples apart, but also serves as the setting of the Battle of Actium. Secondly, he devotes more verses to the battle itself than to all the other examples combined, a phenomenon that is also frequent in priamels, once the climactic term is reached. Thirdly, this scene occupies the place of honour: the middle (*in medio*, 675).

After the description of the actual battle, two briefer tableaux portray the peaceful effects of the victory. The first is Octavian's triple triumph with its festivity and rejoicing throughout the city (714–19); the last scene is of Octavian himself (*ipse*, 720) receiving the homage of all the subject nations.[7] Nor does Vergil omit the motif of wonder to complete the passage, for when Aeneas receives the shield, he 'admires' it (*miratur*, 730).[8]

Both shields are celebrations: Achilles' of human life in its daily activities in city and country; Aeneas' of the *virtus* of the Roman people that culminates in the civilising rule of Rome.[9] In a broad sense, both examples are in the Classical tradition, but with important differences. Homer sees reality as full and varied, and his depiction sketches that richness by means of subdivision and collocation: he does not try to evaluate or to provide any lesson. His scenes are completely generalised: no specific individual or place is named, for all proper names are reserved for divine or legendary beings. The world on his shield is timeless and universal: all levels of society — young and old, men and women, townsmen and rustics — are included. Vergil, however, selects the scenes on the shield to exemplify a specific theme — namely, Rome's historical mastery of the Mediterranean world.[10] The examples are historical events and are arranged chronologically. Even more important, however, is the fact that history, like a priamel, is seen to culminate in an epochal event: Octavian's victory at Actium.[11] In terms of chronology, all previous history leads up to it: in pictorial terms, the Battle of Actium and the ensuing Pax Augusta are the central focal points of all other events. Far from being merely decorative, these two *ekphraseis* vividly capture the world-views of their respective poems.

Hellenistic *ekphraseis* offer a marked contrast to those of Homer and Vergil. We have already noted the Hellenistic tendency to reject martial themes in favour of love, and in this little *recusatio* included in the *Anacreontea* (3.i West) the author does so by rejecting the type of *ekphrasis* associated with epic.

> When you emboss a work of silver,
> Hephaestus, make for me
> no suits of armour.
> What do battles have to do with me?
> 5 Rather, make me a hollow cup
> as deep as you can,
> but don't make on it
> either stars or Big Dippers
> or grim Orion.
> 10 What do I care about the Pleiades
> or the star Boötes?
> Put grapevines on it for me
> with clusters on them
> and make a wine-vat
> 15 with two golden figures
> treading grapes with handsome Bacchus:
> Eros and Bathyllos.

By requesting that Hephaestus, the divine smith who made Achilles' and Heracles' armour, make instead a cup for him, the speaker is in effect rejecting epic for symposiastic poetry. Typical of Hellenistic taste is the reduction from large things (suit of armour, stars) to small things (cup, grapevines), from fighting to drinking, from battle scenes to peaceful scenes, from war to love.[12] Fittingly, the most impressive Hellenistic *ekphrasis* is also of a cup. In the first *Idyll* of Theocritus, the goat herd describes the wooden cup which he promises to give to Thyrsis if he will sing his 'Lament for Daphnis' (27–60):

> καὶ βαθὺ κισσύβιον κεκλυσμένον ἁδέι κηρῷ,
> ἀμφῶες, νεοτευχές, ἔτι γλυφάνοιο ποτόσδον.
> τῶ ποτὶ μὲν χείλη μαρύεται ὑψόθι κισσός,
> 30 κισσὸς ἑλιχρύσῳ κεκονιμένος· ἁ δὲ κατ' αὐτόν
> καρπῷ ἕλιξ εἰλεῖται ἀγαλλομένα κροκόεντι.
> ἔντοσθεν δὲ γυνά, τι θεῶν δαίδαλμα, τέτυκται,
> ἀσκητὰ πέπλῳ τε καὶ ἄμπυκι· πὰρ δέ οἱ ἄνδρες

καλὸν ἐθειράζοντες ἀμοιβαδὶς ἄλλοθεν ἄλλος
35 νεικείουσ᾿ ἐπέεσσι· τὰ δ᾿ οὐ φρενὸς ἅπτεται αὐτᾶς·
ἀλλ᾿ ὄκα μὲν τῆνον ποτιδέρκεται ἄνδρα γέλαισα,
ἄλλοκα δ᾿ αὖ ποτὶ τὸν ῥιπτεῖ νόον· οἳ δ᾿ ὑπ᾿ ἔρωτος
δηθὰ κυλοιδιόωντες ἐτώσια μοχθίζοντι.
τοῖς δὲ μετὰ γριπεύς τε γέρων πέτρα τε τέτυκται
40 λεπράς, ἐφ᾿ ᾇ σπεύδων μέγα δίκτυον ἐς βόλον ἕλκει
ὁ πρέσβυς, κάμνοντι τὸ καρτερὸν ἀνδρὶ ἐοικώς.
φαίης κεν γυίων νιν ὅσον σθένος ἐλλοπιεύειν,
ὧδέ οἱ ᾠδήκαντι κατ᾿ αὐχένα πάντοθεν ἶνες
καὶ πολιῷ περ ἐόντι· τὸ δὲ σθένος ἄξιον ἄβας.
45 τυτθὸν δ᾿ ὅσσον ἄπωθεν ἁλιτρύτοιο γέροντος
περκναῖσι σταφυλαῖσι καλὸν βέβριθεν ἀλωά,
τὰν ὀλίγος τις κῶρος ἐφ᾿ αἱμασιαῖσι φυλάσσει
ἥμενος· ἀμφὶ δέ νιν δύ᾿ ἀλώπεκες, ἃ μὲν ἀν᾿ ὄρχως
φοιτῇ σινομένα τὰν τρώξιμον, ἃ δ᾿ ἐπὶ πήρᾳ
50 πάντα δόλον τεύχοισα τὸ παιδίον οὐ πρὶν ἀνησεῖν
φατὶ πρὶν ἢ ἀκράτιστον ἐπὶ ξηροῖσι καθίξῃ.
αὐτὰρ ὅγ᾿ ἀνθερίκοισι καλὰν πλέκει ἀκριδοθήραν
σχοίνῳ ἐφαρμόσδων· μέλεται δέ οἱ οὔτε τι πήρας
οὔτε φυτῶν τοσσῆνον ὅσον περὶ πλέγματι γαθεῖ.
55 παντᾷ δ᾿ ἀμφὶ δέπας περιπέπταται ὑγρὸς ἄκανθος,
αἰπολικὸν θάημα· τέρας κέ τυ θυμὸν ἀτύξαι.
τῶ μὲν ἐγὼ πορθμῆι Καλυδνίῳ αἶγά τ᾿ ἔδωκα
ὦνον καὶ τυρόεντα μέγαν λευκοῖο γάλακτος·
οὐδέ τί πω ποτὶ χεῖλος ἐμὸν θίγεν ἀλλ᾿ ἔτι κεῖται
60 ἄχραντον.

And [I will give you] a deep cup, washed with sweet wax,
two-handled, newly wrought, still smelling from the knife.
Around the lips on top runs ivy,
30 ivy dotted with golden clusters, and along it
winds the tendril glorying in its yellow fruit.
And inside (like a work of the gods) a woman is depicted,
wearing a cloak and headband. And beside her two men
with beautiful long hair dispute in turns from each side
35 with speeches, but they do not reach her thoughts.
Rather, she looks at one man with a smile,
and then turns her attention to the other; and they, long since
hollow-eyed from their love, waste their effort.
By these is depicted an old fisherman and a rugged rock
40 upon which the old man struggles to draw in a great net

for a cast, like a man toiling greatly.
You would say that he was fishing with all the might of his
    limbs,
for thus do the veins swell out all over his neck, although
his hair is grey, for his strength is that of a young man.
45 Not far from the sea-worn old man
is a vineyard beautifully loaded down with dark clusters,
guarded by a little boy, who sits on the stone
wall. Around him are two foxes; one roams up and down
    the rows
devouring the edible grapes, while the other uses all its
    craft
50 on his knapsack, resolved not to leave the child alone until
it has robbed him of his breakfast.
Meanwhile, the boy is making a pretty cricket-cage by
    weaving
stems and rushes together; his pack and the vine mean less
to him than his joy at weaving the cage.
55 And all around the cup winds smooth acanthus:
a wonder for goat herds, a marvel to amaze your heart.
For it I paid the ferryman at Calydna a goat
and a large cheese made of white milk;
it has never touched my lips and still remains
60 untainted.

In comparison with the descriptions in Homer and Vergil this one manifests a considerable reduction in scale. Not only is it of a small object and naturally much shorter, but also the scope of the description is much more limited. Gone are the heavens and Ocean; instead, ivy runs around the rim. Gone are the cities, warfare and gods. Instead, the poet depicts individuals, and even these, we shall see, are of restricted types.

There are three scenes on the cup: two men quarrelling in vain over a woman who coquettishly leads them on; an old man fishing with a net; and a little boy supposed to be guarding a vineyard, but so engrossed in plaiting a cricket-cage that he is oblivious to two foxes raiding the grapes and his pack. In the first and third tableaux, there is an elegant balance of three figures who are similarly balanced within each scene against the single fisherman in the second.

Theocritus' description is clearly indebted to Homer's. Like Homer, he pictures generalised scenes of a timeless quality: the figures have no names. The first scene on the cup even recalls the events in the city at peace on Achilles' shield, which depicted the marriages and the quarrel between the two men in the market-place. Theocritus has effectively combined these two scenes into one, where the two men quarrel over the favour of the girl, who refuses them both. A number of verbal resemblances show how closely Theocritus has imitated Homer. On the shield the two men are quarrelling (ἐνείκεον, 498), are both being led on by the crowd (502), and listen to judgements given in turn (ἀμοιβηδίς, 506). On the cup the two men are disputing (νεικείουσ᾽, 35), are both being led on by the girl (36–7), and speak in turn (ἀμοιβαδίς, 34).

In spite of these resemblances, however, the differences are even more striking and well illustrate the enormous changes that occurred between the Classical and Hellenistic periods. Homer depicted marriage as a public event in the context of the *polis*. Theocritus portrays frustrated courtship in a private context. The public quarrel over an important issue, a man's death, becomes a contest between two love-sick suitors. This scene clearly illustrates the shift from the Classical themes of public, political affairs to the private, amatory ones characteristic of the Hellenistic period. This is not to say that the theme of love is absent from the Classical period. On the contrary, *eros* is equally important in both periods; but in the Classical period *eros* has a political dimension. Paris' love for Helen, Clytemnestra's adultery with Aegisthus, Antigone's love for Haemon and Phaedra's love for Hippolytus all have political consequences, since they involve royalty and persons in power; whole cities are affected by them. In the Hellenistic period, personal love is valued as a theme for its own sake, particularly unrequited love and the psychological suffering that it causes.[13] The closing description of the two young men sums up the solitary world of Hellenistic frustrated love: 'and they, long since hollow-eyed from their love, waste their effort'.

The second tableau is a genre scene. An old man fishing from a rough rock is portrayed in the act of gathering a heavy net for a cast. There are several details that make this appropriately Hellenistic. The fisherman is at the bottom of society;[14] he is entirely alone;[15] he is unusual for his physical features, for he is an old man with youthful strength. In other words, he is interesting because of an incongruity. Hellenistic art delighted in portraying everyday activities by the lowest ranks of society, especially when they involved unusual postures and physical attributes. This is the period that mixed female and male qualities (the Hermaphrodite is an extreme example) and even turned the Cyclops into a pathetic lover.[16] Here the fisherman becomes 'interesting' to us because of his surprising features. And, finally, the poet singles out one visual detail: the swelling veins in his neck. This realistic detail that suggests physical strain (*pathos*) is a common feature of Hellenistic art.[17]

The last picture is the most fully developed. A little boy is so engrossed in making a cricket-cage that he not only neglects his duty of guarding the vineyard, but does not even notice that one fox is raiding his pack, presumably close by him. This climactic scene captures the precious, diminutive quality of much Hellenistic art and of Theocritus' own poetry. This little drama enclosed in a garden-like vineyard with a solitary small boy, two foxes and a cricket-cage effectively captures the spirit of Theocritus' new poetry.[18] The cricket-cage is a potent symbol of this diminished world in which nature is small enough for a child to capture it in an artfully 'pretty' (52) container while he pays no heed to practical affairs. This tableau vividly portrays the Hellenistic divorce of poetry from political life and the concomitant principle of art for art's sake;[19] it may even contain an anticipation of the much later Romantic glorification of the child.

Homer rounded off the shield with Ocean; Theocritus winds acanthus[20] around the cup. He also ends the description with the motif of wonder: 'a wonder (θάημα) for goat herds, a marvel (τέρας) to amaze your heart' (56). The goat herd then mentions that the cup has never touched his lips, and is still 'untainted' (ἄχραντον, 60). When we recall (see p. 4) that in his 'Hymn to Apollo' Callimachus compares good poetry with the droplet that is pure and 'untainted' (ἀχράαντος, 111), this last word (emphasised by enjambment) takes on special significance as a term describing the style of Theocritus' poetry. This 'newly wrought'[21] (νεοτευχές, 28) cup, covered with 'sweet' (ἁδέι, 27) wax, which is 'untainted', clearly embodies the traits of Theocritus' own poetic style, just as the scenes on it define the nature and scope of his subject matter.

Finally, it should be pointed out that Theocritus has organised the figures in his tableaux by age: adolescence, old age and childhood, thereby in spirit capturing 'everybody'. It is significant, however, that what is omitted is precisely the person of most concern to the Classical writers — namely, the mature,

serious (σπουδαῖος)[22] adult, who plays an active part in the
affairs of the *polis*, both in war and in peace. The world of
Theocritus (as depicted on this cup) is entirely removed from the
political life of the state;[23] instead, the emphasis is on the private
individual and the predominant mood is sentimentality.

These two traditions, the Classical and Hellenistic, continued
to exert their influence on Augustan authors. Vergil and Horace
were clearly heirs of both and their work exhibits a tension
between them. In the sixth book of his *Metamorphoses*, Ovid
strikingly juxtaposes these two influences when he relates the
contest between Minerva and Arachne to determine which was
the better weaver. Two *ekphraseis* describe the tapestries that
result.[24] Here (with some lines of description deleted) is the scene
Minerva weaves (6.70–102):

70 Cecropia Pallas scopulum Mavortis in arce
    pingit et antiquam de terrae nomine litem.
    bis sex caelestes medio Iove sedibus altis
    augusta gravitate sedent; sua quemque deorum
    inscribit facies: Iovis est regalis imago;
75 stare deum pelagi longoque ferire tridente
    aspera saxa facit, medioque e vulnere saxi
    exsiluisse fretum, quo pignore vindicet urbem;
    at sibi dat clipeum, dat acutae cuspidis hastam,
    dat galeam capiti, defenditur aegide pectus,
80 percussamque sua simulat de cuspide terram
    edere cum bacis fetum canentis olivae;
    mirarique deos: operis Victoria finis.
    ut tamen exemplis intellegat aemula laudis,
    quot pretium speret pro tam furialibus ausis
85 quattuor in partes certamina quattuor addit,
    clara colore suo, brevibus distincta sigillis . . .

    .   .   .   .

101 circuit extremas oleis pacalibus oras
     (is modus est) operisque sua facit arbore finem.

70 Pallas Athene depicts the Hill of Mars on Athens' citadel
    and the ancient dispute over the naming of the land.
    The twelve Olympians with Jove in the middle sit on lofty
       thrones

in august dignity. Each god is portrayed
with his own features: Jove's mien is regal,
75 while she makes the god of the sea stand and strike the
    rugged rock
with his long trident; and from the hole in the rock
springs up sea water, by which sign he claims the city for
    his own.
But to herself she gives a shield, sharp-pointed spear
and helmet for her head, while the aegis protects her
    breast.
80 She portrays the ground which she had struck with her
    spear-tip
sending forth a mature olive tree covered with berries;
The gods look on in wonder and Victory completes the
    work.
But to give her ambitious rival illustrations
of what reward to expect for her insane audacity,
85 she adds four contests in the four corners,
each brightly coloured and marked by miniature figures . . .

.   .   .   .

101 She winds olive leaves, the symbols of peace, around the
    borders;
thus ends her work, which she completes with her own tree.

The representation on Minerva's tapestry imitates Classical
style. It is laid out much like the sculptural scenes on the
Parthenon. Firstly, there are the seated gods, with Zeus in the
middle (one is reminded of the arrangement on the east pediment
of the Parthenon); then there are the two balanced figures of
Neptune and Minerva contending for patronage of Athens, much
as they are depicted on the west pediment. The motif of 'wonder'
(*mirarique deos*, 82) completes this portion of the tableau. In the
interests of space, I have omitted the description in lines 87–100
of the scenes in the four corners that depict the gods punishing
presumptuous mortals. The grand design is then completed with
a border of olive branches, the tree sacred to Minerva. Each
tableau occupies a clearly defined place in the overall scheme.

    The scenes on Arachne's tapestry are very different, both in
terms of subject and presentation. Here is a representative
sample (103–14, 127–8):

Maeonis elusam designat imagine tauri
Europam: verum taurum, freta vera putares;
105 ipsa videbatur terras spectare relictas
et comites clamare suas tactumque vereri
adsilientis aquae timidasque reducere plantas.
fecit et Asterien aquila luctante teneri,
fecit olorinis Ledam recubare sub alis;
110 addidit, ut satyri celatus imagine pulchram
Iuppiter inpulerit gemino Nycteida fetu,
Amphitryon fuerit, cum te, Tirynthia, cepit,
aureus ut Danaen, Asopida luserit ignis,
Mnemosynen pastor, varius Deoida serpens.

.   .   .   .

127 ultima pars telae, tenui circumdata limbo,
nexilibus flores hederis habet intertextos.

Arachne portrayed Europa cheated by Jove in the disguise
of a bull: you would think it a real bull, real waves;
105 the girl herself seemed be looking at the shore she had left,
calling to her companions and, fearing the touch
of the lapping water, she draws back her feet in fright.
And she showed Asterie in the grip of the struggling eagle;
and Leda lying back under the wings of the swan;
110 she added how Jupiter, concealed in the guise of a satyr,
impregnated the beautiful Antiope with twin offspring,
how he became Amphitryo when he took you in, Alcmena,
how he deceived Danaë as gold, Aegina as a flame,
Memory as a shepherd, Persephone as a spotted snake . . .

.   .   .   .

127 the edge of her tapestry, surrounded by a thin border,
contains flowers mixed with twining ivy.

Arachne's tapestry not only contains very different subjects; it is
also based on a different theory of art — it is much more
Hellenistic. The contrast is apparent in the first scene, which
depicts the rape of Europa.[25] The first difference is its realism:
'you would think (*putares*) it a real (*verum*) bull, real (*vera*) waves'
(104).[26] The second is the posture and situation of Europa: as she

looks back to the land and calls to her companions, she pulls back her feet in fear of the threatening waves. This dainty, realistic touch, combined with the sentimental *pathos* of the grief-stricken young girl, especially in an erotic context, is a Hellenistic theme *par excellence*.[27]

Another striking feature is the fact that the 21 scenes listed on Arachne's work have no clear spatial arrangement. They presumably were jumbled together, as they appear to be in the poem. Here again we have a technique of episodic arrangement that was in vogue among Hellenistic authors (e.g. in Callimachus' *Aetia*) and, indeed, is the arrangement of Ovid's own *Metamorphoses*, a series of loosely connected thematic episodes.

In addition, the central action depicted on Minerva's tapestry is a Classical theme. It is set in Athens and is political, for it concerns the patronage of a *polis*; and Minerva is appropriately dressed in battle gear for this great contest. The scenes on Arachne's tapestry are typical of the Hellenistic interest in the distraught *amata*: all depict defenceless women being raped by gods. In Minerva's tapestry all the figures are solidly stationary, while those in Arachne's are in awkward positions as they are assaulted by disguised gods. There is even a contrast with respect to the borders of the two tapestries. Arachne fills her 'thin' (*tenui*, 127) one with intertwined ivy and flowers, complex decoration typical of more refined Hellenistic taste.[28]

These two types of artistic representation occur in a larger context in the *Metamorphoses*, for Minerva and Arachne are competing to determine which is the better artist. Of course the god traditionally wins such competitions, but Ovid has deliberately added a twist, for he places Arachne's work last, and according to the convention by which the second contestant outdoes the first (see p. 102), he creates the expectation that Arachne's tapestry will win. Indeed, Minerva cannot fault the workmanship — a remarkable vindication of Hellenistic art[29] — but she does destroy it because of its immoral subject matter and turns Arachne into a spider (*arachne* is the Greek word for spider), a fitting symbol of the fine-spinning Hellenistic artist. In these tableaux Ovid presents the two major artistic and poetic traditions to which he was heir. The tension between the two of them (and Ovid's ultimate preference for the Hellenistic) is apparent throughout the *Metamorphoses* and accounts to a great extent for the ambivalence so many readers detect in it.

Before turning to Romantic and modern *ekphraseis*, we shall look at one more Latin example. We have noted the shift in interest from Classical *eros* (desire in the large sense, often for power) to Hellenistic eroticism (frustrated sexual desire). A famous *ekphrasis* in Latin with roots in this Hellenistic tradition is the description of the tapestry that covered the wedding bed of Peleus and Thetis in Catullus' most ambitious poem, *Carmen* 64. The *ekphrasis* itself is too long and complicated to quote at length,[30] so I have selected one passage (60–70) that describes Ariadne, who has just awakened on the island of Naxos to see Theseus sailing off and stranding her.

> 60 quem procul ex alga maestis Minois ocellis,
>   saxea ut effigies bacchantis, prospicit, eheu,
>   prospicit et magnis curarum fluctuat undis,
>   non flavo retinens subtilem vertice mitram,
>   non contecta levi velatum pectus amictu,
> 65 non tereti strophio lactentes vincta papillas,
>   omnia quae toto delapsa e corpore passim
>   ipsius ante pedes fluctus salis alludebant.
>   sed neque tum mitrae neque tum fluitantis amictus
>   illa vicem curans toto ex te pectore, Theseu,
> 70 toto animo, tota pendebat perdita mente.

> 60 As Theseus sails far from the seaweed-strewn shore, Ariadne,
>   with grief-filled eyes, like a marble statue of a bacchant, gazes
>   toward him, alas, gazes and is tossed on great waves of sorrow,
>   no longer wearing the fine-spun scarf on her lovely head,
>   nor clothed in the lightweight gown that covered her bosom,
> 65 nor wearing the smooth brassière that bound her swelling breasts —
>   all these have fallen here and there from her whole body
>   and at her feet the salt waves played with them.
>   But at that point she cared nothing for her head-dress or floating
>   gown, but she hung on you, Theseus, with all her heart,
> 70 with all her spirit, with all her mind — desperately in love.

This is a sophisticated *ekphrasis* within an *ekphrasis*, for this figure, portrayed on the tapestry, is in turn 'like a marble statue of a bacchant'. The description could well be of a statue of a woman whose garments have slipped down, a theme common in Hellenistic statuary.[31] In describing Ariadne, Catullus follows the 'head to toe' procedure,[32] beginning with her headband, proceeding to her torso and bare breasts. The eye follows the path of the garments that have fallen down (*delapsa*, 66) from her body, and which the waves continue to play with (*alludebant*, 67) at her feet (*ante pedes*, 67). It masterfully depicts every detail. Jenkyns rightly notes the 'sensuous delight' in this description.[33] I would go even further and say that it is a fine example of Hellenistic eroticism; the description exists for the sake of arousing feeling in the reader. We are meant to see the expression of despair in her 'grief-filled eyes' and in her pose as a 'bacchant'. Ariadne herself is totally oblivious to everything but Theseus: Catullus has frozen her in a moment of complete absorption in passion; and 'with all her heart' (*toto ex pectore*), 'with all her spirit' (*toto animo*), 'with all her mind' (*tota . . . mente*) she is 'desperately in love' (*perdita*).

Ariadne is not a grand tragic figure, however: by means of his description Catullus has reduced the emotional response from tragic grief to sentimentalism. The first indication of this is the diminutive *ocellis* (60), '(little) eyes', but the effect is continued through the adjectives that describe her articles of clothing: 'fine-spun' (*subtilem*, 63), 'lightweight' (*levi*, 64), and 'smooth' (*tereti*, 65), all of which connote tenderness — and, incidentally, describe the refined style of Hellenistic poetry. Line 62 seems to portray grand emotion ('tossed on great waves of sorrow'), but it is undercut at 67 by the detail of the waves playing (*alludebant*) with her fallen garments, a particularly tender touch — and the type of technical challenge typical of Hellenistic sculpture.[34]

Although there is an erotic scene on Theocritus' cup, its detail is very sketchy; the young men are merely said to be 'hollow-eyed from their love', and they are portrayed objectively. Catullus' *descriptio*, however, is carefully designed to arouse a very specific emotion of tender sympathy. Theocritus' art still retains much of its Classical heritage; Catullus combines the Hellenistic interest in frustrated love with a sentimental sympathy for the distraught figure. This sympathy is expressed at two points where the author intrudes, firstly with the exclamation 'alas' (*eheu*, 61), and with the apostrophe 'you, Theseus' (*te . . . Theseu*, 69). Fordyce points out that 'the apostrophe was developed by Hellenistic poetry as a device to give a subjective, personal quality to the narrative, and thence was adopted by the *neoterici*.'[35] The apostrophe and the exclamation *'eheu'* effectively collapse the distance between the viewer and the scene, putting the poet (and by extension, us), for a moment, in Ariadne's position.

In this poem the intrusion of the author is slight, but by the time of the Romantic poet John Keats, the reaction of the poet as viewer takes on much greater importance.[36] His 'Ode on a Grecian Urn' is one of the best-known examples of *ekphrasis* in English poetry.[37]

I

Thou still unravished bride of quietness,
   Thou foster-child of silence and slow time,
Sylvan historian, who canst thus express
   A flowery tale more sweetly than our rhyme:
5 What leaf-fringed legend haunts about thy shape
   Of deities or mortals, or of both,
     In Tempe or the dales of Arcady?
   What men or gods are these? What maidens loth?
What mad pursuit? What struggle to escape?
10   What pipes and timbrels? What wild ecstasy?

II

Heard melodies are sweet, but those unheard
   Are sweeter; therefore, ye soft pipes, play on;
Not to the sensual ear, but, more endeared,
   Pipe to the spirit ditties of no tone:
15 Fair youth, beneath the trees, thou canst not leave
   Thy song, nor ever can those trees be bare;
     Bold lover, never, never canst thou kiss,
Though winning near the goal — yet do not grieve:
   She cannot fade, though thou hast not thy bliss,
20   For ever wilt thou love, and she be fair!

III

Ah, happy, happy boughs! that cannot shed
   Your leaves, nor ever bid the Spring adieu;
And, happy melodist, unwearièd,
   For ever piping songs for ever new;
25 More happy love! more happy, happy love!

For ever warm and still to be enjoyed,
    For ever panting, and for ever young;
All breathing human passion far above,
    That leaves a heart high-sorrowful and cloyed,
30   A burning forehead, and a parching tongue.

IV

Who are these coming to the sacrifice?
    To what green altar, O mysterious priest,
Lead'st thou that heifer lowing at the skies,
    And all her silken flanks with garlands dressed?
35 What little town by river or sea shore,
    Or mountain-built with peaceful citadel,
        Is emptied of this folk, this pious morn?
And, little town, thy streets for evermore
    Will silent be; and not a soul to tell
40   Why thou are desolate, can e'er return.

V

O Attic shape! Fair attitude! with brede
    Of marble men and maidens overwrought,
With forest branches and the trodden weed;
    Thou, silent form, dost tease us out of thought
45 As doth eternity: Cold Pastoral!
    When old age shall this generation waste,
        Thou shalt remain, in midst of other woe
Than ours, a friend to man, to whom thou say'st,
    'Beauty is truth, truth beauty, — that is all
50   Ye know on earth and all ye need to know.'

One salient characteristic of Keats's ode is our constant awareness of the speaker's presence, from the opening of the poem, through the devices of question and apostrophe: 'Thou still unravished bride of quietness . . . what . . . what . . . what?' (1–10). Like Catullus, Keats uses exclamations, but with an important difference. Catullus (or more precisely, the narrator) was reacting to the emotion of the scene depicted; his *eheu* was an extension of Ariadne's emotion. Keats's exclamations, however, such as 'Ah' (21) and 'O Attic shape!' (41) arise in the poet's own mind as he contemplates the vase rather than in the minds of the figures on it. And the address 'Cold Pastoral!' (45) even more clearly indicates the poet's private response to the scene before him; another viewer, presumably, would have a very different reaction. Thus, the *ekphrasis* actually serves as a springboard for an impassioned meditation by the poet.[38] Instead of letting the scene speak for itself, as Catullus does, the poet becomes an interpreter, and in the case of an imaginary work of art the only interpreter.

No known Greek vase served as a model for the poem, but from the description of the imagined scene, we can extrapolate one important observation: the style and subject matter are Hellenistic. When the nineteenth-century Romantics looked to Graeco-Roman antiquity for models, they generally found the Hellenistic tradition the most congenial, and this preference is reflected in Keats's ode.[39] The setting is pastoral (cf. 'Cold Pastoral!', 45) and all the events take place outdoors. The depiction of a lone piper sitting under a tree is a typical Hellenistic scene as is the pursuit of a maiden by a youth. We have seen in Ovid the Hellenistic delight in portraying women in awkward positions of struggle or flight as they are pursued by amorous young men. Even the decoration on the vase ('leaf-fringed', 5) suggests elaborate Hellenistic borders such as those on the cup of Theocritus and the tapestry of Arachne.

The fourth stanza, whose primary rhetorical function in the poem is to provide some relief from the emotional intensity of the previous stanza before the apostrophes of the final stanza, portrays another scene, also outdoors. This scene (presumably on the other side of the vase) is a Romanticised version of Greek religion, presumably inspired by the Panathenaic procession depicted in the Elgin marbles, but carefully removed by Keats from any city and put into a rural setting ('green altar', 32). The poet depicts a kind of natural piety ('this folk', 37; 'this pious morn', 37) that leaves the diminutive city ('little town', 35, 38) forever 'desolate' (40). Unlike the Panathenaic procession depicted on the Parthenon's monumental frieze, which took place in the heart of Athens and celebrated the grandeur and might of the city, this sacrifice leaves its nameless town deserted.

Far from a mere description of the vase, the poem is in fact a record of the poet's *process* of understanding the meaning of the scenes before him. The poem began with a list of specific questions that proved impossible to answer concretely, for the urn remains silent. In the fifth stanza the poet reveals a further stage in his attempt to understand the urn's meaning, one that goes far beyond the earlier questions that sought mere information, for when he says of the urn, 'Thou, silent form, dost tease us out of thought / As doth eternity' (44–5), he appears to apprehend intuitively the meaning and value of the urn through a leap reminiscent of his famous doctrine of 'negative capability', an experience that takes place 'out of thought' and is similar to the experience of 'eternity'. From that point on, he can confidently let the urn speak ('thou say'st', 48) its eternal message to mankind. The ode is a remarkably sophisticated example of adapting Hellenistic materials to Romantic poetic and epistemological concerns.

In the twentieth century, descriptive poems, particularly *ekphraseis* of paintings, have been very popular and constitute a flourishing subgenre.[40] Keats found the sensuous, amatory ambience of Hellenistic art congenial to his nostalgic vision of the past, but the poets of the mid-twentieth century turned to art that reflected their more 'objective', less sentimental view of reality. A favourite has been the sixteenth-century Flemish painter Pieter Brueghel.[41] We shall conclude with two modern poems on his works. One of the best-known *ekphraseis* of this century, and one which helped establish the subgenre is W.H. Auden's 'Musée des Beaux Arts'.

> About suffering they were never wrong,
> The Old Masters: how well they understood
> Its human position; how it takes place
> While someone else is eating or opening a window or just
>   walking dully along;
> 5 How, when the aged are reverently, passionately waiting
> For the miraculous birth, there always must be
> Children who did not specially want it to happen, skating
> On a pond at the edge of the wood:
> They never forgot
> 10 That even the dreadful martyrdom must run its course
> Anyhow in a corner, some untidy spot
> Where the dogs go on with their doggy
>   life and the torturer's horse
> Scratches its innocent behind on a tree.
>
> In Brueghel's *Icarus*, for instance: how everything turns away
> 15 Quite leisurely from the disaster; the ploughman may

Have heard the splash, the forsaken cry,
But for him it was not an important failure; the sun shone
As it had to on the white legs disappearing into the green
Water; and the expensive delicate ship that must have seen
20 Something amazing, a boy falling out of the sky,
Had somewhere to get to and sailed calmly on.

Although this poem is in the tradition we have been following, it departs in some important ways from the examples we have examined. Firstly, it is the only one that describes actual works of art that are available to anyone who wishes to see them or a copy of them.[42] In fact, Auden even gives the location in the title and names one of the paintings in the poem. Secondly, its main purpose is to *interpret* the scene. Unlike Vergil, who created the shield of Aeneas to demonstrate the march of Roman history, Theocritus, who captured the diminished Hellenistic world in his cup, Catullus, who tried to convey pitiful emotions of frustrated love through a vivid description of a distraught figure, and unlike Keats, who used a description to evoke his own sympathetic meditation on the meaning of the work, Auden describes details from three Brueghel paintings in order to illustrate a general point, which he attributes to the artists themselves ('the Old Masters'): that the world is indifferent to suffering. Although less passionately involved, the speaker in this poem is as much in evidence as the one in Keats's, but his interpretations of the scenes are more like the observations of an art historian or an ethical philosopher than personal meditation.

The structure of the poem is very rhetorical. It begins with a statement of the poem's subject ('About suffering') and attributes the correct thesis concerning it to a group of artists, 'the Old Masters'. The rest of the poem consists of illustrative examples in support of the thesis, and they are arranged in the form of a priamel. Although some of the details do not square with the actual paintings, Auden is probably referring to Brueghel's *The Numbering at Bethlehem* in verses 5–8 and to *The Massacre of the Innocents* in verses 10–13. There is no doubt, however, when he comes to the climactic example, emphatically set off by the break after verse 13. The specification of 'Old Masters' (2) with the particular painter Brueghel and the actual name of the painting, *Icarus*, clearly mark this as the crowning example, as does the greater elaboration and precision of detail in its description. The sense of arrival is also reinforced, however, by a greater regularity of style. We had seen in Auden's 'Law Like Love' (see p. 52) that once the priamel finally arrived at the correct view ('Like love I say', 56), the metre and rhyme became very regular. Although less striking, the same trend can be seen in lines 14–21, in comparison with the irregularities of verses 1–13.[43] Much of the poem's effect lies in its understatement and bathos, especially when it is describing brutality (10–13). Even the closing motif of wonder, 'something amazing' (20) is undercut by the description of the ship that 'sailed calmly on' (21).[44]

In an interview called 'Speaking straight ahead', William Carlos Williams discussed his lifelong interest in painting, and added:[45]

> The design of the painting and of the poem I've attempted to fuse. To make it the same thing. And sometimes when I write I don't want to say anything. I just want to present it. Not a didactic meaning. I don't care about the didactic meaning — the moral. To add some tag is absolutely repulsive to me.

Williams had long been an admirer of Brueghel, and the painter's concern for depicting homely details of everyday life reminded the poet of his own 'objectivist' goals. The last volume of his poetry, published just after his death in 1963, featured a sequence of twelve poems on paintings by (or attributed to) Brueghel, entitled *Pictures from Brueghel*. Here is his 'Landscape with the Fall of Icarus':

> According to Brueghel
> when Icarus fell
> it was spring
>
> a farmer was ploughing
> 5 his field
> the whole pageantry
>
> of the year was
> awake tingling
> near
>
> 10 the edge of the sea

    concerned
    with itself

    sweating in the sun
    that melted
15 the wings' wax

    unsignificantly
    off the coast
    there was

    a splash quite unnoticed
20 this was
    Icarus drowning

Each of the *ekphraseis* we have so far examined has been part of a larger whole and has served to illustrate or vivify a theme, the traditional role of the topic. In this concluding case, however, Williams has (in his own words) fused the poem and the painting, thereby establishing a subgenre, the ekphrastic poem, which exists in its own right and serves no overt didactic purpose, as do Auden's 'Musée des Beaux Arts' and 'The Shield of Achilles'. Williams's goal of capturing a visual scene as in a snapshot is apparent from earlier poems such as 'The Red Wheelbarrow' (1923), and the paintings of Brueghel provided what he felt to be a close analogue to his own procedures. Indeed, the sequence of *ekphraseis* in *Pictures from Brueghel* is manifestly a demonstration of his own poetic principles.[46]

Whereas Auden enters into his *ekphrasis* by attributing thoughts and motives to the characters ('the ploughman may / have heard the splash . . . but for him it was not an important failure', 15–17), Williams intrudes only slightly with the word 'unsignificantly' (16). His poem is trimmed of lengthy reportage (the entire poem consists of only 56 words), so that he can thereby concentrate on the essential points. The organisation of the poem is modelled on that of a priamel. The phrase 'whole pageantry' (6) sketches the various springtime activities of which the ploughman is one example: this background is obviously foil for the specific event of real interest, the 'splash' (19), prepared for by the pivotal word 'unsignificantly', which itself sums up the point that Auden had made at considerable length.

This is not the only poem in the series that is arranged as a priamel.[47] Another notable example is 'The Hunters in the Snow', which contains a detailed description of the painting and then concludes (17–21):

> Brueghel the painter
> concerned with it all has chosen
>
> a winter-struck bush for his
> 20 foreground to
> complete the picture. .

Out of all the details mentioned in the first 16 lines (summed up with 'it all', 18), Brueghel (note the proper name to indicate the climactic term) chooses to emphasise the bush in the foreground of the picture, which 'completes' the painting just as it completes the priamel and the poem.[48] Although he avoids the didactic element in Auden's poetry, Williams's formal concerns and poetic theory are just as much in evidence as Auden's. Williams's 'objectivism' is far from absolute.

In these examples *ekphrasis* has served a variety of purposes in various genres and in recent times has become a flourishing subgenre. Here we have confined the discussion to descriptions of works of art, but the same principles of composition apply generally, and in the following chapters we will encounter more examples in laments, *carpe-diem* poems, hymns and eulogies,[49] whenever a poet wishes to hold our attention and — as one of the *progymnasmata* puts it — 'tries to make his listeners spectators'.[50]

Notes

1. Priscian translated Hermogenes' *Progymnasmata* into Latin about 500 AD, thus making it part of the later Latin tradition. For a translation, see J.M. Miller, M.H. Prosser and T.W. Benson (eds), *Readings in Medieval rhetoric* (Indiana University Press, Bloomington, 1973), pp. 52–68. The first part of Matthew of Vendôme's *Ars Versificatoria* deals with descriptions (in the broadest sense) and Geoffrey of Vinsauf devotes lines 554–667 of his *Poetria Nova* (c. 1210 AD) to composing *descriptiones*. For the text, see E. Faral, *Les arts poétiques du XIIᵉ et du XIIIᵉ siècle* (Edouard Champion, Paris, 1923), pp. 214–17. For a translation of the *Ars Versificatoria*, see A.E. Galyon, *Matthew of Vendôme: the art of versification* (Iowa State University Press, Ames, 1980) and of the passage from the

Poetria Nova, see J.J. Murphy (ed.), *Three Medieval rhetorical arts* (University of California Press, Berkeley, 1971), pp. 53–7.

2. Four *progymnasmata* (in Greek) have survived and are attributed to Theon, Hermogenes, Nicolaus and Aphthonius. They range in date from the second (possibly late first) to fifth century AD. For the texts, see L. Spengel, *Rhetores Graeci*, 3 vols (Teubner, Leipzig, 1853–6); for translations of Hermogenes, see C.S. Baldwin, *Medieval rhetoric and poetic* (Macmillan, New York, 1928), pp. 23–38 and for Aphthonius, see R. Nadeau, 'The *Progymnasmata* of Aphthonius in translation', *Speech Monographs*, vol. 19 (1952), pp. 264–85. For an overview, see G. Kennedy, *Greek rhetoric under Christian emperors* (Princeton University Press, Princeton, 1983), pp. 54–73. For the place of *descriptiones* in Roman education, see S.F. Bonner, *Education in ancient Rome* (University of California Press, Berkeley, 1977), p. 270. For their use in Renaissance schools, see D.L. Clark, *John Milton at St Paul's School: a study of ancient rhetoric in English Renaissance education* (Columbia University Press, New York, 1948), pp. 244–5.

3. For example, after the description of the wild area around Calypso's cave (*Od.* 5.63–75), even Hermes is said to have marvelled, while Odysseus 'wondered in his heart' (*Od.* 7.135) at Alcinous' palace and grounds.

4. The standard treatment of *ekphrasis* in antiquity remains that of P. Friedländer, *Johannes von Gaza und Paulus Silentiarius: Kunstbeschreibungen Justinianischer Zeit* (Teubner, Leipzig and Berlin, 1912), pp. 1–103. For a brief overview, see G. Downey, 'Ekphrasis', in *Reallexikon für Antike und Christentum* (Hiersemann, Stuttgart, 1960), vol. IV, cols 922–43.

5. Here we have the traditional divisions of sky, earth and sea. We also begin at the height and end at the depth. The *progymnasmata* will later recommend describing a statue from head to feet, a commonplace that has a long history from the Latin poets (e.g. Catullus and Ovid) to Renaissance descriptions of the beloved (*blasons*), variations of which include Du Bellay's *Regrets* 91, Robert Herrick's 'To Julia' (H–88) and Thomas Carew's 'The Complement'. The anti-Petrarchan *blason* in Shakespeare's Sonnet 130 begins with 'My mistress' eyes are nothing like the sun' and ends with 'My mistress, when she walks, treads on the ground.'

6. Polar doublets (e.g. gods–men, land–sea, men–women, old–young) are a regular feature of Classical style (although certainly not restricted to it), and are often equivalent to 'everyone' or 'everything' or 'everywhere'. They are also a common feature of hymnal style (see p. 147.

7. As we shall see in the chapter on eulogy, deeds of war are regularly followed by those of peacetime.

8. The Latin *admiratio* is a synonym of the Greek θαῦμα (*thauma*). In another important *ekphrasis* in the first book of the *Aeneid*, when Vergil describes the scenes from the Trojan War depicted on the temple at Carthage, Aeneas is repeatedly said to 'admire' (*miratur*) them (419, 420, 456 and 494).

9. The central portion of the shield, which portrays Octavian's victory at Actium, his triple triumph at Rome and his reviewing the

subject peoples, dramatically illustrates the exhortation of Anchises to Aeneas at 6.851–3: 'you, Roman, remember to rule the nations with your empire / (this will be your art), to enforce the rule of peace, / to spare the humbled and to battle down the haughty'. For an analysis of this passage as a priamel, see p. 40.

10. The description also reveals that the *Aeneid* is to a degree a *genus mixtum*, composed of epic and history, a combination already established in Roman poetry by Ennius. With respect to the historical aspect of his work, Vergil's intention is similar to that of Polybius' *History* (1.1.5): to show 'how . . . the Romans gained control of nearly the whole world . . . and placed it under their sole rule — something that had never happened before'.

11. Vergil is not alone in his view: Horace and Propertius also stress the importance of Actium and the reign of Octavian (later called Augustus).

12. See pp. 12–13. Note the sense of climax with the last two figures mentioned in the poem: Eros (Love) and the poet's favourite, Bathyllos.

13. Later in Theocritus' poem, Thyrsis sings about the 'agonies' (19) of Daphnis, who is 'most unhappy in love and helpless' (85). This theme bulks large in the Theocritean corpus: cf. *Idylls* 2, 3, 6, 10, 11, 14 and 23. A famous example in Hellenistic epic is the treatment of Medea's love in the third book of Apollonius' *Argonautica*, which greatly influenced Vergil's depiction of Dido.

14. Although there are many characters from the lower levels of society in Classical works such as the *Odyssesy*, an interest in shepherds and lower-class individuals for their own sake is particularly prominent in Hellenistic poetry, as, for example, in many of Theocritus' *Idylls* and in Herodas' *Mimes*. For a good account of Theocritus' interest in little people and of the programmatic function of the *ekphrasis*, see D.M. Halperin, *Before pastoral: Theocritus and the ancient tradition of bucolic poetry* (Yale University Press, New Haven, 1983), pp. 161–89. For a good overall view, see G. Zanker, 'The everyday and the low in Alexandrian poetry' in *Realism in Alexandrian poetry: a literature and its audience* (Croom Helm, London, 1987), pp. 155–227.

15. The isolated individual, whose activity has no other reference but itself, is also a characteristic concern of Hellenistic thought, which tended to separate man from his *polis* and placed great emphasis on individual character. Cynicism, Epicureanism and Stoicism all show this tendency.

16. In Theocritus' *Idyll* 11, Homer's ferocious Cyclops is transformed into a lonely, love-sick swain.

17. See J.J. Pollitt, *Art and experience in Classical Greece* (Cambridge University Press, Cambridge, 1972), pp. 136–94. Classical sculptors knew how to portray such *pathos*, but they generally reserved it for sub-human subjects, such as the Centaurs on the west pediment of the Temple of Zeus at Olympia. A subtle visual touch is provided by the rock from which the old man fishes, whose 'rugged' (40) texture (emphasised by enjambment) highlights the figure of the fisherman.

18. The poetry, that is, in some of his 'pastoral' poems. He also wrote mythological narratives (*Idylls* 13, 24 and 25), a hymn (22), an

epithalamium (18), and two public encomia (16 and 17). However, coming as this poem does at the beginning of his collection, a traditional place for programmatic poems, the world depicted on the cup advertises that aspect of Theocritus' art which is truly new, and on which his subsequent reputation mainly rested.

19. It should be noted that the cricket (or cicada) is regularly a symbol of poetry. The *locus classicus* is Plato, *Phaedrus* 258E ff. Cf. also the epigrams on cicadas at *Anthologia Palatina* 7.192–8.

20. Even this detail is telling, for acanthus leaves decorate the Corinthian capital, which made its appearance shortly before the Hellenistic period and became a favourite during it. Also cf. Ovid, *Metamorphoses* 13.761, in which he concludes his *ekphrasis* of the drinking bowl by describing the acanthus that runs around the rim.

21. As we saw in the first chapter, newness is often stressed in *recusationes*. Catullus was known as one of the 'new poets' and in the opening poem of his collection, he announces the fresh (*modo*) newness (*novum*) of his work.

22. The word σπουδαῖος covers both of these meanings. Aristotle defines the subject of tragedy as a 'serious' action. For a discussion of the importance of the *spoudaioi* ('mature men') in Aristotle's ethical philosophy, see E. Voegelin, *Plato and Aristotle* (= *Order and History*, vol. 3) (Louisiana State University Press, Baton Rouge, 1957), pp. 303–36. G. Braden, *The Classics and English Renaissance poetry: three case studies* (Yale University Press, New Haven, 1978), pp. 210–12, shows that adult sexuality is absent from the *Anacreontea*.

23. Undoubtedly the most important factor in creating the Hellenistic world view was the disappearance of the Classical city-state (*polis*) as an independent political and cultural unit. Absorbed into vast kingdoms in the years following Alexander's conquest and death (323 BC), the *polis*, whose intense political life had formed such a large part of Classical poetry and philosophy, gave way to great urban centres such as Alexandria. The tremendous change is clear if one compares the comedies of Aristophanes and Menander. Those of Aristophanes are full of political references, for the characters are intimately bound up in the full life of Athens. In Menander's *Dyscolus*, his only surviving complete play, there are no references to politics, for the characters have no share in running the State. The setting is realistic and the plot concerns a lovesick boy who finally wins his girl, the daughter of a cranky old misanthrope. It is a charming, elegant play that pleases with its artistry, while it instructs by portraying human social graces and foibles. In comparison with Aristophanes' plays, it displays an extreme reduction of scope with a corresponding increase of polish, the same two traits advocated by Callimachus.

24. For stimulating discussions of these *ekphraseis* in the context of Ovid's own poetics, see E.W. Leach, 'Ekphrasis and the theme of artistic failure in Ovid's *Metamorphoses*', *Ramus*, vol. 3 (1974), pp. 102–42 and D. Lateiner, 'Mythic and non-mythic artists in Ovid's *Metamorphoses*', *Ramus*, vol. 13 (1984), pp. 1–30.

25. This subject is a favourite of Hellenistic art and poetry. Cf. the *Idyll* of Moschus on Europa, which itself contains an *ekphrasis* of her basket in

lines 43–62.

26. Note the direct appeal to the reader (as viewer) that underscores the realism of the art. Although this topic can be traced to the shield of Achilles (see pp. 57–8), the direct appeal to the viewer (*putares*) with the insistence on realism (*verum*) are characteristic of the Hellenistic period (even though here Ovid provides an ironic twist because the bull is really Jove in disguise). The poet also reveals his involvement with the direct addresses to the figures (e.g. 'when he took you in, Alcmena', 112), more of which occur in the following lines not quoted. For an excellent discussion of pictorial realism in Hellenistic poetry, see G. Zanker, *Realism in Alexandrian poetry*, pp. 39–112.

27. We shall see another instance of a distraught maiden in the following example from Catullus.

28. For the word *tenuis* as a mark of Hellenistic style, see p. 9. Acanthus leaves also decorate the rim of Theocritus' cup: see p. 65 with Note 20.

29. W.S. Anderson, *Ovid's Metamorphoses, Books 6–10* (University of Oklahoma Press, Norman, 1972), p. 160, well summarises the qualities of the two works:

> The composition of the goddess' work is flawlessly Classical, perfectly centered, balanced and framed, highly moral and didactic in content. It is not unlike certain surviving examples of Augustan classicistic art. Inasmuch as Ovid refuses to give it the victory, he may . . . be suggesting the value of Arachne's kind of composition: freer, more mannered, more dramatic and distorted, less specifically didactic.

30. For a close, sensitive analysis of the poem, see R. Jenkyns, *Three Classical poets: Sappho, Catullus, and Juvenal* (Harvard University Press, Cambridge, 1982), pp. 98–150.

31. An example is the Aphrodite from Melos. For a picture and discussion, see J.J. Pollitt, *Art in the Hellenistic age* (Cambridge University Press, Cambridge, 1986), pp. 167–8. The trend had begun much earlier, at the end of the fifth century. In Euripides' *Hecuba* 558–61, as Polyxena is about to be sacrificed, she bares her torso and breasts that are 'most beautiful, like those of a statue'.

32. See above, Note 5 and cf. the playful example of Ovid at *Amores* 1.5.17–22, where he describes his naked mistress — although he never gets past her thigh.

33. Jenkyns, *Three Classical poets*, p. 117.

34. The last piece of clothing mentioned, *strophio* (brassière), also adds a realistic touch. If one compares the attitudes of Theocritus' fisherman, Ovid's Europa, and Catullus' Ariadne, one could conclude that a favourite scene in Hellenistic art must have been that of a figure caught in a dramatic gesture at the edge of water.

35. C.J. Fordyce, *Catullus: a commentary* (Oxford University Press, Oxford, 1961), p. 288.

36. For another example of Keats's interest in the reactions of the speaker, cf. 'On First Looking into Chapman's Homer' (discussed on pp. 45–6). In his sonnet, 'On Seeing the Elgin Marbles', there is no

description at all, merely his own reaction to those 'wonders' (11).

37. This is hardly the place to discuss the vexed details of its interpretation, especially the problems raised by the various versions and analyses of its closing two lines. I follow the text defended by W.J. Bate, *John Keats* (Oxford University Press, Oxford, 1966), pp. 516–20. For a helpful discussion of the poem, see L.T. Lemon, *Approaches to literature* (Oxford University Press, Oxford, 1969), pp. 38–65.

38. For a similar procedure, cf. the doubloon in Melville's *Moby Dick*, which is first described objectively. Then each crew member reports his subjective reactions to it. There is a long tradition behind Keats's procedure that can only be mentioned in passing here — namely, the description of a setting followed by a meditation on its meaning. The topic is fully developed in Horace's *carpe-diem* poems (e.g. 1.4, 1.9 and 4.7) and in the sixteenth century it receives a new impetus from the practice of religious meditation, particularly from the exercise of picturing a setting (*compositio loci*). See L.L. Martz, *The poetry of meditation: a study in English religious literature of the seventeenth century* (Yale University Press, New Haven, 1954). W.J. Bate, *John Keats*, p. 512, notes of Keats's 'Ode on a Grecian Urn': 'He adopts . . . the conventional romantic form of the *ut pictura poesis* tradition, in which the poet contemplates the work of art, often while directly addressing it, and derives from it a subject for meditation.'

39. In 'The dawn of romanticism in Greek poetry', the final chapter of *Some aspects of the Greek genius* (Macmillan, London, 1904), pp. 245–324, S.H. Butcher argues that Hellenistic poetry most clearly anticipates the Romantic feeling for nature.

40. See the list of poems on paintings and painters by Americans in E.L. Huddleston and D.A. Noverr (eds), *The relationship of painting and literature: A guide to information sources* (Gale Research Co., Detroit, 1978), pp. 61–101. For a brief sketch of the subgenre, see A. Fowler, *Kinds of literature: an introduction to the theory of genres and modes* (Harvard University Press, Cambridge, Mass., 1982), pp. 115–18. For an analysis of three examples from Randall Jarrell and brief references to examples by other poets, see J. Meyers, 'Randall Jarrell: the paintings in the poems', *Southern Review*, vol. 20, 2 (1984), pp. 300–15.

41. Fowler, *Kinds of literature*, p. 115, notes that 'nearly 12 per cent of the American poems on paintings listed [in Huddleston and Noverr's survey] refer to works by Brueghel.'

42. Interpretative poems on known works of art have been very popular in the twentieth century and have a distant counterpart in the numerous Greek epigrams that describe and interpret paintings or statues. Although they began to be written in the Classical period as inscriptions for actual statues, they eventually became a minor genre with many representatives in the *Palatine anthology*, and were very popular in the Renaissance (e.g. Marino, *La Galeria*). There are prose examples by the two Philostrati and Callistratus in the third century AD, collected and translated by A. Fairbanks, *Philostratus Imagines* (Harvard University Press, Cambridge, Mass., 1931). The history of this subgenre remains to be written.

43. Auden frequently reinforces a sense of arrival in his poetry by

shifting to a more regular metre and rhyme. We shall encounter another example in his 'In Memory of W.B. Yeats'; see p. 110.

44. Auden also ends his description in 'The Shield of Achilles' with the motif of 'wonder', but he there converts it to horror, for Thetis 'Cried out in dismay / At what the god had wrought / To please her son' (63–5).

45. L.W. Wagner (ed.), *Interviews with William Carlos Williams* (New Directions, New York, 1976), p. 53.

46. For a recent study of Williams's use of the visual arts in his poetry, see H.M. Sayre, *The visual text of William Carlos Williams* (University of Illinois Press, Urbana, 1983). For a more detailed discussion of the Brueghel sequence in light of Williams's poetics, see B. Duffey, *A poetry of presence: the writing of William Carlos Williams* (University of Wisconsin Press, Madison, 1986), pp. 215–23.

47. Likewise, 'The Adoration of the Kings' ends with the detail of 'the downcast eyes of the Virgin'; the 'Peasant Wedding' with 'a spoon in his hatband'; and 'Children's Games I' with 'one leans / hollering / into / an empty hogshead'.

48. The semi-ellipsis at the end of this poem is probably intended to cancel some of the effect of closure and send the reader/viewer back to the painting/poem. See Sayre, *The visual text*, p. 139.

49. There is also a whole tradition of *ekphraseis* of private buildings, beginning with the description of Alcinous' palace and garden at *Odyssey* 7.84–132 and continuing through Ovid, Statius and Martial to the country house poems of the seventeenth and eighteenth centuries, including Jonson's 'To Penshurst'. For references, see 'Additional Examples'. Another favourite theme for description is the *locus amoenus* (pleasant place). The prototype is the description of the area around Calypso's cave at *Odyssey* 5.63–75. An early example in drama occurs in Sophocles' *Oedipus at Colonus* 688–93. For a brief survey of this topic, see E.R. Curtius, *European literature*, pp. 195–202 and for a bibliography, see R.G.M. Nisbet and M. Hubbard, *A commentary on Horace: Odes Book II* (Oxford University Press, Oxford, 1978), pp. 52–3.

50. Nicolaus Sophistes in L. Spengel, *Rhetores Graeci III* (Teubner, Leipzig, 1856), p. 491.

4

The Rhetoric of Lament and Consolation

Expressions of grief and condolence occur throughout Graeco-Roman poetry in many genres: epic, tragedy, elegy, lyric and pastoral poetry. They take many forms and the relative emphasis on lament or consolation varies greatly from poem to poem.[1] Although they generally occur together, we shall separate *lamentatio* and *consolatio* in the following discussion in order to identify recurrent topics.[2] When combined, they respond as two voices: one of emotion (πάθος) and one of reason (λόγος). In the *lamentatio*, the passions hold sway; the language is contorted to reflect the intense emotion and hyperbole is the dominant mode; frequently there are rhetorical questions and bitter reproaches. In the *consolatio*, the appeal is to the mind: the language is more straightforward and its intention is to calm the passions and to instruct the intellect. In the first two sections of this chapter we shall isolate standard topics of lament and consolation by a close analysis of selected poems. In the third part we shall briefly examine poems by Milton and Auden to see how effectively English poets have adapted these strategies to the specific occasion of their poems.

The topics of *lamentatio*

One of the best ways of isolating generic features of poetry is to examine parodies. In order to illustrate the topics of *lamentatio*, we shall begin with two Latin poems on the death of pet birds. The first is the lament (or more exactly, monody) by Catullus on the death of his mistress' sparrow (*Carm.* 3):

Lugete, o Veneres Cupidinesque,

86

et quantumst hominum venustiorum!
passer mortuus est meae puellae,
passer, deliciae meae puellae,
5 quem plus illa oculis suis amabat:
nam mellitus erat suamque norat
ipsam tam bene quam puella matrem,
nec sese a gremio illius movebat,
sed circumsiliens modo huc modo illuc
10 ad solam dominam usque pipiabat.
qui nunc it per iter tenebricosum
illuc, unde negant redire quemquam.
at vobis male sit, malae tenebrae
Orci, quae omnia bella devoratis:
15 tam bellum mihi passerem abstulistis.
o factum male, quod, miselle passer,
tua nunc opera meae puellae
flendo turgiduli rubent ocelli!

Mourn, you Venuses and Cupids,
and all you more charming men!
My girlfriend's sparrow is dead,
the sparrow that was my girl's delight,
5 which she loved more than her own eyes:
for it was a sweetheart and knew its
mistress as well as a girl knows her own mother;
it never left her lap,
without hopping here and there,
10 constantly chirping only for its mistress.
But now it travels down the dark road
to that place from which no one is said to return.
But curses upon you, evil shades
of Orcus, who devour everything pretty:
15 such a pretty sparrow have you taken from me.
Ah cruel deed, poor sparrow, that
because of your doing, my girlfriend's little eyes
are red and puffy from weeping.

In his prescriptions for writing a monody, Menander Rhetor
(434.10 ff.) suggests using several topics: apostrophes, descriptions
of the deceased, contrasts of past achievements or future hopes
with the present disappointment, and complaints (σχετλιασμοί)
against unjust fate. He also points out that in a monody praise

must not exist for its own sake, but must serve as a motive for lament. All of these topics occur in Catullus' parody.

The first two lines issue a call to mourning, in which there is a play on the name Venus and the word *venustus*, 'charming', which applies not only to the mourners, but also those readers who would appreciate the poet's own charm in composing this parody. The pet sparrow[3] is duly eulogised for its exemplary past life in lines 6–10, but this praise, as Menander Rhetor recommends, merely points up the harshness of the present (*nunc*) reality: *qui nunc it* ... ('But now it travels ...' 11).[4] The euphemism for death ('the dark road', 11) is particularly charming, and the phrase 'from which no one is said to return' (12) adds a fitting note of pathos by emphasising the finality of death. At 13 the complaint marks the emotional high point of the lament: 'But curses upon you, evil shades of Orcus, who devour everything pretty.'[5] This heightened emotion continues with the apostrophe to the dead sparrow (16). All this bravado, however, is neatly undercut by the last two lines, which ostensibly develop the conventional topic of the mourner's disfigurement, but imply that the worst result of the poor sparrow's fate was that it upset Catullus' mistress. Particularly charming is the specific detail (expressed by two diminutives) of her 'puffy little eyes' (*turgiduli ... ocelli*, 18).

Catullus' poem parodies the monody. At *Amores* 2.6 Ovid outdoes Catullus' performance with a full-scale lament and consolation for the pet parrot of his mistress Corinna:

> Psittacus, Eois imitatrix ales ab Indis,
>   occidit: exsequias ite frequenter, aves;
> ite, piae volucres, et plangite pectora pinnis
>   et rigido teneras ungue notate genas;
> 5 horrida pro maestis lanietur pluma capillis,
>   pro longa resonent carmina vestra tuba.
> quod scelus Ismarii quereris, Philomela, tyranni,
>   expleta est annis ista querela suis;
> alitis in rarae miserum devertere funus:
> 10   magna sed antiqua est causa doloris Itys.
> omnes, quae liquido libratis in aere cursus,
>   tu tamen ante alios, turtur amice, dole.
> plena fuit vobis omni concordia vita
>   et stetit ad finem longa tenaxque fides.
> 15 quod fuit Argolico iuvenis Phoceus Orestae,

hoc tibi, dum licuit, psittace, turtur erat.
quid tamen ista fides, quid rari forma coloris,
    quid vox mutandis ingeniosa sonis,
quid iuvat, ut datus es, nostrae placuisse puellae?
20   infelix avium gloria nempe iaces.
tu poteras fragiles pinnis hebetare zmaragdos
    tincta gerens rubro Punica rostra croco.
non fuit in terris vocum simulantior ales;
    reddebas blaeso tam bene verba sono.
25 raptus es invidia: non tu fera bella movebas;
    garrulus et placidae pacis amator eras.
ecce, coturnices inter sua proelia vivunt,
    forsitan et fiant inde frequenter anus.
plenus eras minimo, nec prae sermonis amore
30   in multos poteras ora vacare cibos:
nux erat esca tibi causaeque papavera somni,
    pellebatque sitim simplicis umor aquae.
vivit edax vultur ducensque per aera gyros
    milvus et pluviae graculus auctor aquae;
35 vivit et armiferae cornix invisa Minervae,
    illa quidem saeclis vix moritura novem.
occidit ille loquax humanae vocis imago
    psittacus, extremo munus ab orbe datum.
optima prima fere manibus rapiuntur avaris;
40   implentur numeris deteriora suis:
tristia Phylacidae Thersites funera vidit
    iamque cinis vivis fratribus Hector erat.
quid referam timidae pro te pia vota puellae,
    vota procelloso per mare rapta Noto?
45 septima lux venit non exhibitura sequentem,
    et stabat vacuo iam tibi Parca colo;
nec tamen ignavo stupuerunt verba palato:
    clamavit moriens lingua 'Corinna, vale'.
colle sub Elysio nigra nemus ilice frondet
50   udaque perpetuo gramine terra viret.
si qua fides dubiis, volucrum locus ille piarum
    dicitur, obscenae quo prohibentur aves:
illic innocui late pascuntur olores
    et vivax phoenix, unica semper avis;
55 explicat ipsa suas ales Iunonia pinnas,
    oscula dat cupido blanda columba mari.
psittacus has inter nemorali sede receptus

89

convertit volucres in sua verba pias.
ossa tegit tumulus, tumulus pro corpore magnus,
60   quo lapis exiguus par sibi carmen habet:
COLLIGOR EX IPSO DOMINAE PLACVISSE
SEPULCRO.
ORA FVERE MIHI PLVS AVE DOCTA LOQVI.

Parrot, the talking bird from the far East,
    has died: come flocking to his funeral, you birds;
come, faithful birds, beat your wings upon your breasts
    and scratch your soft cheeks with a hard claw.
5 Tear your ruffled plumage instead of hair,
    and in lieu of the long trumpet let your songs ring out.
The crime of the tyrant Tereus which you bemoan,
    Philomela —
    all the years you have been at it have finished that
        complaint;
turn now to the sad funeral of a rare bird:
10   yes, Itys was a great source of grief, but that was long
        ago.
Mourn, all of you who balance your flight in the liquid air,
    but you before all others, dear turtle-dove:
your life together was filled with complete accord
    and your long fidelity stood firmly to the end;
15 What Phocaean Pylades was to Spartan Orestes,
    turtle-dove was to you, Parrot, as long as fate allowed.
But of what avail was your friendship, your body of rare
    colours,
    your voice so talented at changing sounds?
what good was the joy you gave my girl from the day she
    got you?
20   Unlucky glory of birds — yes, you lie low.
Your wings could outshine brittle emeralds
    and your beak was purple with yellow spots.
No bird on earth was a better mimic of speech:
    how well you could lisp back words.
25 Envy carried you off; you stirred up no fierce wars,
    for you were a talker and a lover of restful peace.
Just look at the quails, who fight each other all their lives —
    maybe that is why they often live so long.
Your needs were minimal; because you loved to talk so
    much

30   your mouth had little time for very much food:
    a nut provided your meal and poppy seeds helped you
      sleep;
      a single drop of water quenched your thirst.
    But yet the greedy vulture goes on living, as does the hawk
      that circles in the air and the daw that announces
      rainstorms.
35 yet the raven goes on living, and although armed Minerva
     hates it,
      it will probably outlive nine generations.
    But dead lies that loquacious echo of the human voice,
      Parrot, a gift from the furthest east.
    Greedy hands almost always seize the best first,
40   while inferior things live out their lives.
    Thersites watched the sad funeral of Protesilaus;
      Hector's brothers lived to see his ashes.
    Why tell of my worried girlfriend's solemn prayers for you,
      prayers carried out to sea by the storm-wind?
45 The seventh day came — none was to follow —
      and there stood your Fate with her empty spindle:
  and yet your palate never faltered in speaking
      and your dying tongue cried out, 'Corinna, farewell!'
    At the foot of a hill in Elysium flourishes a grove of dark ilex
50   and the moist ground forever sprouts a crop of grass;
    If one can trust uncertain reports, there is said to exist a place
      for decent birds, where no nasty fowl are permitted:
    there range harmless swans
      and the immortal phoenix, ever unique;
55 Juno's peacocks spread their tail-feathers
      and amorous doves kiss their mates.
    Parrot joins them in their woodland abode
      and captivates these good birds with his words.
    His bones are covered by a mound that fits his small body,
60   on which a little matching tombstone bears the inscription:
    FROM THIS GRAVE YOU CAN JUDGE THAT I
    PLEASED MY MISTRESS;
      I LEARNED HOW TO SAY MORE THAN ANY
      BIRD.

The rhetorical flourishes begin with the enjambment of *occidit* ('has died') in the second line. Catullus had summoned Venuses, Cupids and charming men to mourn the sparrow; Ovid's list of mourners consists of 'faithful' (*piae*, 3) birds, who are duly summoned to disfigure themselves in grief. Even Philomela, the proverbial mourner who was changed into a nightingale, is requested to cease lamenting the outrage of Ismarus and the death of Itys and turn now to the funeral of a 'rare bird' (*alitis . . . rarae*, 9), since, Ovid slyly intimates, her story is getting old (if not hackneyed).[6] By means of a summary priamel, lines 11–12 single out of all the mourners the parrot's special friend, the turtle-dove,[7] and in grand fashion compares their friendship with that of Orestes and Pylades.

The following section (17–42) intersperses eulogy of the parrot with outbursts of indignation (σχετλιασμοί).[8] The first complaint questions the point of goodness in the face of death with the 'what boots it' formula:[9] *Quid tamen . . . iuvat* (17–19) and concludes with the pathetic *nempe iaces* ('yes, you lie low', 20). The second complaint elaborates the topic of 'the good die, while the unworthy survive'. The parrot was a 'lover of restful peace' (*placidae pacis amator*, 26), yet he died young, while pugnacious quails live to old age; he was abstemious, yet those greedy vultures, kites and ravens live on. Ovid then rounds off this section with a generalisation and two epic examples (39–42): 'Greedy hands almost always seize the best first': witness Protesilaus, survived by Thersites, and Hector, survived by his brothers.[10] Then, after a delightful portrayal of the parrot's final day and his parting words to Corinna (45–8), comes the consolation (to be discussed more fully in the following section): the parrot will join the 'faithful' (*piarum*, 51) birds in a grove somewhere in Elysium (off limits to 'nasty fowl'), where he will continue to impress everyone with his gift of speech. The poem ends with a description of his little tomb and his epitaph.[11]

From these two examples, we can single out most of the standard topics of lament:

    (1) a list of mourners (often summoned in a 'call')
    (2) disfigurement (of mourners or the corpse)[12]
    (3) praise of the deceased
    (4) a contrast of past and present ('but now')
    (5) a description of the last day
    (6) the finality of death
    (7) complaints:
        (a) 'what boots it?'
        (b) 'the good die, the unworthy survive'

In general the *lamentatio* tries as much as possible to immerse the audience in particulars, and thereby to arouse the emotion (*pathos*) of pity through a vivid portrayal of details. When it contains a eulogy of the deceased, it does so for the purpose of arousing greater pain at the loss of such a person. Likewise, by portraying the large number of those who mourn his death, the poet amplifies the importance of the loss. Also, the theme of disfigurement (whether of the speaker, the mourners, or the corpse) provides visual proof of the horror of the situation, while the speaker's helplessness in the face of the catastrophe calls forth a disjointed style full of rhetorical questions, anaphora, apostrophes and (at its most intense) outbursts of indignation.[13]

Although there are many other laments we could analyse, each with its distinct emphasis, most are combined with consolation and better reserved for the following discussion. There is, however, a modern lament which eschews all consolation. It is in the Romantic tradition and counsels complete abandonment to the 'complaint', the villanelle by Dylan Thomas: 'Do Not Go Gentle Into That good Night'.

> Do not go gentle into that good night,
> Old age should burn and rave at close of day;
> Rage, rage against the dying of the light.
>
> Though wise men at their end know dark is right,
> 5 Because their words had forked no lightning they
> Do not go gentle into that good night.
>
> Good men, the last wave by, crying how bright
> Their frail deeds might have danced in a green bay,
> Rage, rage against the dying of the light.
>
> 10 Wild men who caught and sang the sun in flight,
> And learn, too late, they grieved it on its way,
> Do not go gentle into that good night.
>
> Grave men, near death, who see with blinding sight
> Blind eyes could blaze like meteors and be gay,
> 15 Rage, rage against the dying of the light.
>
> And you, my father, there on the sad height,
> Curse, bless, me now with your fierce tears, I pray.

Do not go gentle into that good night.
Rage, rage against the dying of the light.

The poem is formally a priamel, in which the poet gives instances of the kinds of men who 'do not go gentle into that good night' — wise men, good men, wild men and grave men — in order to apply their examples to the real subject of the poem, his dying father ('And you, my father', 16), reserved for the concluding quatrain. The poem rejects all forms of Graeco-Roman and Christian consolation, advising instead intense emotional reaction ('rage') to the coming of death. In that sense it is a reversal of traditional advice as presented, for example, in Boethius' *Consolation of Philosophy*, since for Thomas there is no consolation through wisdom ('wise men', 4), morality ('good men', 7), or stoic endurance ('grave men', 13). Fittingly, this reversal of Classical norms is reinforced by the fact that a young man instructs his father, rather than the other way round.[14] The poem depicts the loss of meaning that issues in unmitigated indignation: it is a continuous complaint.

The topics of *consolatio*

The topics of consolation are more varied than those of lament, since there is a multitude of ways for assuaging grief.[15] For that reason, we shall survey more examples before arriving at a comprehensive overview. We have already seen two consolatory topics in Ovid's lament for the parrot: burial rites and translation to the Isles of the Blessed, but there are other strains as well. At the beginning of *Hamlet* (I.ii.70–5), Gertrude tries to persuade Hamlet to stop mourning for his father.

> QUEEN
> 70 Do not for ever with thy vailèd lids
>   Seek for thy noble father in the dust.
>   Thou know'st 'tis common. All that lives must die,
>   Passing through nature to eternity.
> HAMLET
>   Ay, madam, it is common.
> QUEEN
>   If it be,
> 75 Why seems it so particular with thee?

Hamlet's mother uses one of the commonest topics of consolation: the universality of death. Whereas lament appeals to the emotions by emphasising the particularity of death, consolation often appeals to the mind by recalling that death is universal ("'tis common', 72). By showing that an individual is part of a whole, consolation seeks to assuage one's suffering by diminishing its particularity. If all men must die, then (so runs the argument) a person has no exceptional complaint about his own (or a loved one's) death: 'Why seems it so particular with thee?' asks the Queen. A principal means of consolation consists of lifting the bereaved from his immersion in particulars to a contemplation of universal principles.[16] When Hamlet rejects the Queen's consolation, Claudius continues with arguments to the effect that Hamlet's grief is 'unmanly' (94) and 'unprevailing' (107) — that is, futile. These topics are part of a long tradition which we shall call 'manly' consolation.

The first fully developed example of these consolatory topics is in Book 24 of the *Iliad*, when Achilles entertains Priam and consoles him for the loss of his son Hector. After inviting the old man to sit down, he enjoins him to restrain his grief 'since nothing is accomplished by grim lamentation' (οὐ γάϱ τις πϱῆξις πέλεται κϱυεϱοῖο γόοιο, 524). Achilles then uses a series of arguments to placate Priam's grief. First, he universalises human suffering through the parable of the two urns from which Zeus gives men good and evil (527–33). The point is that no man is without suffering; the most that one can hope for is a mixture of good and evil. He then gives the particular example of his own father, Peleus, who reached the pinnacle of fortune by marrying the goddess, Thetis, but who suffers, nonetheless, through his son's absence and imminent death (534–40).[17] Having moved from principle to example, Achilles then turns to Priam himself (543–8): 'And you too, old man, were formerly (τὸ πϱίν) reputed to be fortunate . . .' and offers Priam this consolatory advice (549–51):

> ἄνσχεο, μηδ᾽ ἀλίαστον ὀδύϱεο σὸν κατὰ θυμόν·
> 550 οὐ γάϱ τι πϱήξεις ἀκαχήμενος υἷος ἑῆος,
> οὐδέ μιν ἀνστήσεις, πϱὶν καὶ κακὸν ἄλλο πάθῃσθα.

> Endure! and do not sorrow endlessly in your heart,
> 550 for you will accomplish nothing by grieving for your son,
> nor will you bring him back before you suffer yet another evil.

The main point, expressed at the beginning and end of Achilles' speech, is that excessive lamentation is futile.[18] The other point, brought home by the parable of the two jars and the example of his own father, is that suffering is universal: Achilles observes that Priam may have lost his son in war, but so will Achilles' own father. The logical conclusion is then formulated in one word of manly advice which echoes throughout the entire tradition: 'Endure!'

Another example of manly consolation occurs in an elegiac poem by the early Greek lyric poet, Archilochus (*fr.* 7, 13 West).

κήδεα μὲν στονόεντα, Περίκλεες, οὔτε τις ἀστῶν
μεμφόμενος θαλίῃς τέρψεται οὐδὲ πόλις·
τοίους γὰρ κατὰ κῦμα πολυφλοίσβοιο θαλάσσης
ἔκλυσεν· οἰδαλέους δ᾽ ἀμφ᾽ ὀδύνῃς ἔχομεν
5 πνεύμονας. ἀλλὰ θεοὶ γὰρ ἀνηκέστοισι κακοῖσιν,
ὦ φίλ᾽, ἐπὶ κρατερὴν τλημοσύνην ἔθεσαν
φάρμακον. ἄλλοτέ τ᾽ ἄλλος ἔχει τάδε· νῦν μὲν ἐς ἡμέας
ἐτράπεθ᾽, αἱματόεν δ᾽ ἕλκος ἀναστένομεν,
ἐξαῦτις δ᾽ ἑτέρους ἐπαμείψεται. ἀλλὰ τάχιστα
10 τλῆτε γυναικεῖον πένθος ἀπωσάμενοι.

No citizen will enjoy the feast, Pericles, by blaming
the woeful sorrows, — neither will the city:
such were the men the wave of the resounding sea
washed down, while our lungs are swollen
5 with grief. But the gods, my friend, have provided
steadfast endurance as a remedy for incurable
ills, which afflict different men at different times: now evil
has turned to us and we bemoan our bloody wound;
but in time it will change over to others. So, men,
10 quickly shake off this effeminate grief and endure!

With this poem we turn from an epic context to life in the *polis*, but the consolatory message is essentially the same. Instead of saying that 'grief accomplishes nothing', Archilochus says that continued lamentation will keep the city from enjoying the feast (2). In the face of grief and helplessness, the remedy is 'endurance' (τλημοσύνην, 6), along with the recognition that everyone has his share of troubles and that the present ones will pass in time. Once again, consolation consists of universalising experience, of accepting the flux of the human condition, what in another poem (67a, 128 West) Archilochus calls the 'rhythm' (ῥυσμός) of life. 'In time' (ἐξαῦτις, 9) things will be different and the 'now' (νῦν, 7) of mourning will pass, when Zeus will give evils to others (cf. Achilles' parable of the two urns). Then comes the conclusion, expressed as usual in the imperative: 'endure' (τλῆτε, 10). The consolation moves through logical steps toward practical advice. It is, in Aristotelian terms, an enthymeme, a rhetorical argument.

Another example of this manly consolation is Horace, *Odes* 1.24, addressed to Vergil on the death of a dear friend and critic, Quintilius Varus:

> Quis desiderio sit pudor aut modus
> tam cari capitis? praecipe lugubres
> cantus, Melpomene, cui liquidam pater
>   vocem cum cithara dedit.
>
> 5 ergo Quintilium perpetuus sopor
> urget? cui Pudor et Iustitiae soror,
> incorrupta Fides, nudaque Veritas,
>   quando ullum inveniet parem?
>
> multis ille bonis flebilis occidit,
> 10 nulli flebilior quam tibi, Vergil.
> tu frustra pius heu non ita creditum
>   poscis Quintilium deos.
>
> quid? si Threicio blandius Orpheo
> auditam moderere arboribus fidem,
> 15 num vanae redeat sanguis imagini,
>   quam virga semel horrida,
>
> non lenis precibus fata recludere,
> nigro compulerit Mercurius gregi?
> durum: sed levius fit patientia,
> 20   quicquid corrigere est nefas.

What moderation or limit could there be to grief
for one so dear? Teach me a song of mourning,
Melpomene, whom Father Jupiter gave a liquid
    voice and accompanying lyre.

5 So then, does eternal sleep oppress Quintilius?
   when will Moderation, when will firm Loyalty,
     the sister of Justice, and naked Truth ever find
       another to equal him?

   Many good men wept at his death,
10 but none, Vergil, wept more than you.
   Useless are your devoted appeals to the gods for Quintilius'
     return; alas, he was not lent you on such terms.

   What is the point of it? Even if you played the lyre
     more compellingly than Orpheus did when trees obeyed,
15 do you really think that blood could ever return to an empty
       shade once Mercury with his dread wand,

   a god not disposed to granting prayers that change fate,
     has driven it into his dark flock?
   Hard it is: but endurance lightens
20   whatever it is sinful to correct.

In spite of the poet's tight control of form and diction, the opening question about 'moderation or limit' (1) and the appeal to the Muse for a dirge indicate the depth of grief that the speaker feels at the loss of his friend. The word *ergo* (5) 'so then'[19] suggests the reluctant acceptance of Quintilius' death, while *perpetuus* (5) drives home its finality. By putting these facts in a question, the speaker suggests his shocked disbelief of the fact of his friend's death. The following brief but spirited eulogy (6–8) emphasises the loss of Quintilius' rare qualities.[20]

Of the many mourners, Vergil is singled out as the saddest.[21] It is to him that Horace addresses the consolation, as Archilochus did to Pericles. The word *frustra* (11) indicates the uselessness of Vergil's refusal to accept the human condition and of his continued desire for the impossible, while the *heu* (11) expresses the speaker's sympathy. To make his point, Horace uses an *argumentum a fortiori*:[22] not even if Vergil (a poet) could sing more sweetly than Orpheus could he win back Quintilius once (*semel*, 16) Mercury has included him among the dead.[23] The single word *durum* ('hard', 19) sums up the painful helplessness of Vergil's condition. This argument is followed by the same consolatory remedy we saw in Homer and Archilochus: 'endurance' (*patientia*, 19). The poem is remarkable for the tension (typical in Horatian lyric) between its dignified restraint and the *pathos* that emerges only occasionally from the 'alas' (11) and from the rhetorical questions that comprise the argument of the poem.

Lament and consolation are very common in tragedy. Euripides' *Alcestis* is a veritable compendium of topics. At 872–1005, the chorus tries to console Admetus as he grieves for his dead wife, Alcestis. At first they tell him, as Achilles did Priam, that his grief does not help the deceased, and remind him that he will never see her again (875–7). When that fails, they continue (889–94):

> τύχα τύχα δυσπάλαιστος ἥκει·
> 890 πέρας δέ γ᾿ οὐδὲν ἀλγέων τίθης.
> βαρέα μὲν φέρειν, ὅμως δὲ . . .
> τλᾶθ᾿· οὐ σὺ πρῶτος ὤλεσας . . .
> γυναῖκα· συμφορὰ δ᾿ ἑτέρους ἑτέρα
> πιέζει φανεῖσα θνατῶν.

> Fortune, overpowering fortune, has come.
> 890 And yet you set no limit to your grief.
> Your troubles are heavy to bear, but nevertheless,
> endure! You were not the first to lose
> a wife: different disasters come
> to oppress different mortals.

Here, as in the poems of Archilochus and Horace, the chorus admits that Admetus' grief is great; *yet* (ὅμως δέ),[24] they enjoin him to 'endure' (τλᾶθ᾿, 892). Like Archilochus, they remind the sufferer that disaster is part of the flux of human life.

Still unsuccessful, they try an example *a fortiori* (903–11). They recall a man who lost his only child, an exemplary boy, *but nevertheless* (ἀλλ᾿ ἔμπας, 906) his father bore up, even though he was old. Admetus, however, remains inconsolable. The following choral ode to Necessity (962–83) stresses her tremendous power and implacable nature, against which no science, prayer or sacrifice can avail. The chorus then applies these reflections to the situation at hand: Necessity holds Admetus in her grip and he will never bring his wife back by crying, for even the sons of the gods cannot escape death (984–94). They then conclude the ode with the fame that her tomb will enjoy and predict that she will be apotheosised and worshipped as a 'blessed spirit' (995–1005):

995 μηδὲ νεκρῶν ὡς φθιμένων χῶμα νομιζέσθω
    τύμβος σᾶς ἀλόχου, θεοῖσι δ' ὁμοίως
    τιμάσθω, σέβας ἐμπόρων.
1000 καί τις δοχμίαν κέλευθον
    ἐκβαίνων τόδ' ἐρεῖ·
    Αὕτα ποτὲ προύθαν' ἀνδρός,
    νῦν δ' ἐστὶ μάκαιρα δαίμων·
1005 χαῖρ', ὦ πότνι', εὖ δὲ δοίης. τοιαί νιν προσεροῦσι
    φῆμαι.

995 Let no one think that your wife's tomb is merely
    a mound to cover men dead and gone, but let it receive
    divine-like honours and veneration from travellers;
1000 and when someone walks along the
    winding road he will say:
    'This woman died for her husband,
    and now she is a blessed spirit.
1005 Hail, mistress, be gracious to me.' Such will be the words
    addressed to her.

This apotheosis is the ultimate consolation:[25] it is the best that
the chorus (and the Graeco-Roman world view) can offer. In the
action of the play, however, this consolation is spoken just as
Heracles is bringing back Alcestis, whom he has miraculously
rescued from Death.

In order to explore more thoroughly the topic of apotheosis and
to complete this survey of consolatory topics, we shall take an
example from a genre in which lament and consolation
flourished: pastoral. In Vergil's *Eclogue* 5, two shepherds, Mopsus
and Menalcas, sing a pair of songs about Daphnis, a cowherd
who has died. These two songs beautifully portray the movement
from lament to consolation in the Graeco-Roman tradition. In
the song of Mopsus lament predominates.

20 Exstinctum Nymphae crudeli funere Daphnin
    flebant (vos coryli testes et flumina Nymphis),
    cum complexa sui corpus miserabile nati
    atque deos atque astra vocat crudelia mater.
    non ulli pastos illis egere diebus
25 frigida, Daphni, boves ad flumina; nulla neque amnem
    libavit quadrupes nec graminis attigit herbam.
    Daphni, tuum Poenos etiam ingemuisse leones

interitum montesque feri silvaeque loquuntur.
Daphnis et Armenias curru subiungere tigres
30 instituit, Daphnis thiasos inducere Bacchi
et foliis lentas intexere mollibus hastas.
vitis ut arboribus decori est, ut vitibus uvae,
ut gregibus tauri, segetes ut pinguibus arvis,
tu decus omne tuis. postquam te fata tulerunt,
35 ipsa Pales agros atque ipse reliquit Apollo.
grandia saepe quibus mandavimus hordea sulcis,
infelix lolium et steriles nascuntur avenae;
pro molli viola, pro purpureo narcisso
carduus et spinis surgit paliurus acutis.
40 spargite humum foliis, inducite fontibus umbras,
pastores (mandat fieri sibi talia Daphnis),
et tumulum facite et tumulo superaddite carmen:
'Daphnis ego in silvis, hinc usque ad sidera notus,
formosi pecoris custos, formosior ipse.'

20 The Nymphs lamented Daphnis, destroyed by a cruel
death,
(you hazels and rivers will vouch for the Nymphs),
when, as she embraced her poor son's corpse,
his mother charged both the gods and stars with cruelty.
During those days no one fed his cattle
25 or drove them, Daphnis, to the cool rivers: no livestock
would drink from a stream or touch a blade of grass.
Daphnis, the wild mountains and the forests tell
that even African lions bemoaned your death.
Daphnis taught how to yoke Armenian tigers
30 to a cart, Daphnis taught how to worship Bacchus in revels
and to weave soft leaves around tough spears.
As the vine adorns trees, as grapes adorn the vines,
as bulls adorn herds and grain fertile fields,
you are the total glory of herdsmen. But when fate took you,
35 the very gods Pales and Apollo left the fields.
The furrows in which we often planted large barley grains
produce dreary darnel and sterile wild oats;
in place of the soft violet and the colourful narcissus
thistles spring up and bushes with sharp thorns.
40 Scatter the ground with leaves, shepherds, shade over
the springs (such are the rites Daphnis prescribes for
himself),

101

and make a mound and place over it this verse:
Daphnis am I, known in the forests and from there to the stars,
guardian of a handsome flock, handsomer myself.

The first word *exstinctum* ('destroyed') immediately sets the tone
of lament. The complaint is vividly placed in the mouth of
Daphnis' mother as she clasped his body. Indeed the line: *atque*
deos atque astra vocat crudelia mater' ('his mother charged both the
gods and the stars with cruelty', 23) could serve as a model
complaint. The following lines portray the topic of mourning
nature, especially common in pastoral poetry, whose setting is
outdoors.[26] In lines 26–8, the animals, both domestic and wild,
are portrayed as mourning. Lines 29–34 praise Daphnis for
instituting Bacchic rites in the countryside and conclude with a
priamel: 'As the vine adorns trees, as grapes adorn the vines, /
bulls adorn herds and grain fertile fields, / you are the total glory
of herdsmen.' This priamel rises to a triumphant boast, but in
mid-line the poet suddenly introduces the contrast with the
present: 'But when fate took you . . .' (34). Whereas in lines 26–8
the animals mourned, in lines 35–9 plant life suffers blight, a
topic neatly anticipated by choice of foil in the priamel (32–3).
This sympathy of nature, expressed as reversals of her customary
laws (*impossibilia* or *adynata*), is a frequent feature of pastoral
lament.[27] The final five lines of consolation partially relieve the
sorrow by a description of the funerary rites and of the tomb that
will bear a laudatory inscription. Although dead, Daphnis will
live in memory; his fame will reach the stars. The consolation has
reached a first stage, commemoration through fame. The
following song will proceed a step further.

It is a convention of pastoral poetry that the answering song
outdo its predecessor (see p. 69). The epitaph in Mopsus' song
had claimed that Daphnis would be 'known . . . to the stars' (43).
Menalcas, the elder singer, says that in his song he proposes to
'raise Daphnis himself to the stars' (*Daphnin ad astra feremus*, 52).

> Candidus insuetum miratur limen Olympi
> sub pedibusque videt nubes et sidera Daphnis.
> ergo alacris silvas et cetera rura voluptas
> Panaque pastoresque tenet Dryadasque puellas.
> 60 nec lupus insidias pecori, nec retia cervis
> ulla dolum meditantur; amat bonus otia Daphnis.
> ipsi laetitia voces ad sidera iactant

intonsi montes; ipsae iam carmina rupes,
ipsa sonant arbusta: 'deus, deus ille, Menalca!'
65 sis bonus o felixque tuis! en quattuor aras:
ecce duas tibi, Daphni, duas altaria Phoebo.
pocula bina novo spumantia lacte quotannis
craterasque duo statuam tibi pinguis olivi,
et multo in primis hilarans convivia Baccho,
70 (ante focum, si frigus erit; si messis, in umbra)
vina novum fundam calathis Ariusia nectar.
cantabunt mihi Damoetas et Lyctius Aegon,
saltantis Satyros imitabitur Alphesiboeus.
haec tibi semper erunt, et cum sollemnia vota
75 reddemus Nymphis, et cum lustrabimus agros.
dum iuga montis aper, fluvios dum piscis amabit,
dumque thymo pascentur apes, dum rore cicadae,
semper honos nomenque tuum laudesque manebunt.
ut Baccho Cererique, tibi sic vota quotannis
80 agricolae facient: damnabis tu quoque votis.

Radiant Daphnis admires the unfamiliar threshold of
    Olympus
and beneath his feet sees the clouds and stars.
As a result, keen delight grips the forests and countryside,
as well as Pan, the shepherds and Dryad maidens.
60 The wolf plots no ambush for the flock nor net
any snare for deer, for beneficent Daphnis loves peace.
Even the woodland mountains raised their cry in joy
to the stars; the very rocks and orchards
burst into song: 'He is a god, a god, Menalcas!'
65 Be bountiful and gracious to your people. Here are four
    altars.
See, Daphnis, two are for you and two high ones for
    Phoebus.
Every year I shall set out two goblets frothing with fresh
    milk
and two bowls of rich olive oil for you;
and best of all, to enliven the festivities with lots of wine,
70 (before the hearth in winter, in summer under the shade),
I shall pour the fresh nectar of Arusian wine from bowls.
Damoetas and Cretan Aegon will sing for me,
while Alphesiboeus imitates dancing Satyrs.
These will always be your offerings, both when we pay

103

75 the regular vows to the Nymphs and when we purify the
   fields.
   So long as boars love mountain peaks and fish the rivers,
   so long as bees feed on thyme, and crickets on dew,
   for all time will your honour, name and praises endure.
   As farmers make vows each year to Bacchus and Ceres,
80 So will they to you, and you will see that they fulfil them.

The contrasting mood of Menalcas' song is apparent from the
first word. Mopsus had begun with *exstinctum*; Menalcas answers
with *candidus* ('radiant').[28] Mopsus had ended with Daphnis'
tomb; Menalcas begins in heaven with his apotheosis. As his
departure from the countryside had caused blight, now his
beneficent influence as a god gladdens it. Instead of funeral rites,
he now will enjoy annual celebrations. In contrast to the reversal
of nature in Mopsus' song, Menalcas stresses its continuity in a
priamel that culminates in Daphnis' praises (76–8): 'So long as
boars love mountain peaks and fish the rivers, / so long as bees
feed on thyme, and crickets on dew, / for all time will your
honour, name and praises endure.'

On the basis of these examples, we can now list some of the
major topics that recur in poetic *consolationes*.[29]

(1) Manly consolation
      (a) death is common to all men (even Heracles had to
   die)
      (b) grief is futile
      (c) time will cure (things will change)
      (d) one must endure (what is beyond our power)

(2) Commemoration through
      (a) funeral rites and tomb
      (b) memorialisation in poetry

(3) Apotheosis through
      (a) translation to heaven (the Elysian Fields)
      (b) deification (as a guardian divinity or 'genius')

Two examples of *lamentatio* and *consolatio* in English

We shall complete this survey with a brief analysis of two major

English poems, Milton's 'Lycidas' and W.H. Auden's 'In Memory of W.B. Yeats'. Milton's 'Lycidas' is a compendium of the topics of lament and consolation which we have discussed.[30] After an introduction and an address to the Muse (1–24), Milton portrays the idyllic life that he and Edward King enjoyed together as students at Cambridge (25–36). As is customary in laments, however, this happiness is suddenly contrasted with the present (*nunc*) reality (37–49):

> But O the heavy change, now thou art gone,
> Now thou art gone, and never must return!
> Thee, shepherd, thee the woods and desert caves,
> 40 With wild thyme and the gadding vine o'ergrown,
> And all their echoes mourn.
> The willows and the hazel copses green
> Shall now no more be seen,
> Fanning their joyous leaves to thy soft lays.
> 45 As killing as the canker to the rose,
> Or taint-worm to the weanling herds that graze,
> Or frost to flowers that their gay wardrobe wear,
> When first the white thorn blows;
> Such, Lycidas, thy loss to shepherd's ear.

'But O the heavy change' vividly portrays the shock of loss. The repeated 'now thou art gone' drives home the fact of King's death, while 'and never must return' expresses its finality. The list of mourners begins with the flora (39–44), while lines 45–9 are a priamel (like that in Mopsus' song at 32–4) that introduces the last (and most important) mourners, the shepherds, and whose foil also indirectly portrays the topic of the blight on nature.

In the following lines, the speaker complains that the Nymphs were not there to save his friend, but recognises (*a fortiori*, see p. 98 with Note 22) that even the Muse herself could not have saved him, since she was unable to save her own son Orpheus. These references to the Muse and Orpheus lead to a stronger complaint that calls into question the point of writing poetry at all.

> Alas! What boots it with incessant care
> 65 To tend the homely slighted shepherd's trade,
> And strictly meditate the thankless Muse?
> Were it not better done as others use,

105

> To sport with Amaryllis in the shade,
> Or with the tangles of Neaera's hair?
> 70 Fame is the spur that the clear spirit doth raise
> (That last infirmity of noble mind)
> To scorn delights, and live laborious days;
> But the fair guerdon when we hope to find,
> And think to burst out into sudden blaze,
> 75 Comes the blind Fury with th' abhorrèd shears,
> And slits the thin spun life.

In its most intense forms, the complaint raises the issue of theodicy. Daphnis' mother calls the gods and stars cruel. When a loved one dies, particularly a young person whose talents have never had a chance to come to fruition, the universe appears irrational and unjust: human life seems to lose its purpose. 'What boots it?',[31] asks the speaker, if the Muse is 'thankless'(66) and all that effort to gain fame is suddenly cut short by a 'blind Fury' (75), a vindictive spirit with no regard for merits. In his grief, the speaker even indulges the thought of lowering his ideals to the level of living merely for pleasure. Like Job, he flings his challenge at the gods; the answer comes as suddenly to him.

At *Eclogue* 5.34 Vergil had effectively emphasised the contrast of Daphnis' past glory with the blight that followed his death by introducing it in mid-line: 'You are the total glory of herdsmen. But when fate took you . . .' Here the full stop in mid-line (76) not only imitates the Fury's sudden curtailment of life, but also permits the startling appearance of Apollo, who rebukes the poet for his shortsightedness.

>   'But not the praise,'
> Phoebus replied, and touched my trembling ears;
> 'Fame is no plant that grows on mortal soil,
> Not in the glistering foil
> 80 Set off to th' world, nor in broad rumour lies,
> But lives and spreads aloft by those pure eyes,
> And perfect witness of all-judging Jove;
> As he pronounces lastly on each deed,
> Of so much fame in Heaven expect thy meed.'

The poet had complained that King did not live long enough to gain the 'fair guerdon' (73) of fame. Apollo answers that earthly fame is not real fame, but rather the 'fame in Heaven' (84) is the true reward.[32] Critics have long argued whether this is 'pagan' or 'Christian' consolation. It is clearly a mixture of Greek (Phoebus Apollo), Roman (Jove), and Christian ('Heaven', 84) theology, a combination that reflects Milton's schooling in the Christian-Humanist tradition. More important, however, is the issue: fame. The first consolation offered by the poem, like that in Mopsus' song, involves fame (*hinc usque ad sidera notus*, 43). However, fame as conceived in merely human terms is inadequate: survival through fame must yield to a greater consolation.

Probably the most striking section of 'Lycidas' is the diatribe of St Peter that begins at 113. It is a digression — 'by occasion', as Milton puts it in the headnote — but it is generically appropriate. For one thing, St Peter caps the priamel of mourners (89–109) consisting of Triton, who represents the Graeco-Roman tradition, and Camus, who represents King's humanist education. Furthermore, his speech is essentially an elaboration of the complaint 'the good die, while the unworthy survive'.[33]

> 'How well could I have spared for thee, young swain,
> Enow of such as for their bellies' sake,
> 115 Creep and intrude, and climb into the fold!'

Finally, in terms of rhetoric, the elevated style of the passage ('the dread voice', 133) is warranted by the emotion of wrath that motivates a *schetliasmos*. Ovid spent eight couplets (27–42) complaining of the vile birds that live long lives, whereas the good parrot died young. Here St Peter complains of the unworthy who remain among the clergy. This complaint is an intensification of its companion at (64–76): these two complaints take up, in order of importance, the two goals of King's study at Cambridge: poetry and holy orders.

After continued lament for the 'hapless youth' (134–64) comes the final consolation, the apotheosis of Lycidas (165–85):

> 165 Weep no more, woeful shepherds, weep no more,
> For Lycidas your sorrow is not dead,
> Sunk though he be beneath the watery floor,
> So sinks the day-star in the ocean bed,
> And yet anon repairs his drooping head,
> 170 And tricks his beams, and with new-spangled ore,
> Flames in the forehead of the morning sky:
> So Lycidas sunk low, but mounted high,

Through the dear might of him that walked the waves,
Where other groves, and other streams along,
175 With nectar pure his oozy locks he laves,
And hears the unexpressive nuptial song,
In the blest kingdoms meek of joy and love.
There entertain him all the saints above,
In solemn troops and sweet societies
180 That sing, and singing in their glory move,
And wipe the tears forever from his eyes.
Now, Lycidas, the shepherds weep no more;
Henceforth thou art the genius of the shore,
In thy large recompense, and shalt be good
185 To all that wander in that perilous flood.

By combining pagan consolation, such as that in Menalcas' song, with the Christian idea of heaven, Milton provides Lycidas with the ultimate consolation: he dwells in Heaven and is a 'genius',[34] whose beneficence aids others.

The poem's promise of apotheosis is in the Christian–Humanist tradition: the modern example we shall examine is far more reserved, as one would expect of a poem from the sceptical twentieth century. W.H. Auden's 'In Memory of W.B. Yeats (d. Jan. 1939)' is one of the best-known tributes to a fellow poet of the twentieth century.[35] Since it contains subtle reworkings of many of the topics we have covered, we shall treat it in its entirety. The first section opens with a variation of the theme of 'nature mourns'.

I

He disappeared in the dead of winter:
The brooks were frozen, the air-ports almost deserted,
And snow disfigured the public statues;
The mercury sank in the mouth of the dying day.
5 O all the instruments agree
The day of his death was a dark cold day.

Far from his illness
The wolves ran on through the evergreen forests,
The peasant river was untempted by the fashionable
quays;
10 By mourning tongues
The death of the poet was kept from his poems.

But for him it was his last afternoon as himself,
An afternoon of nurses and rumours;
The provinces of his body revolted,
15 The squares of his mind were empty,
Silence invaded the suburbs,
The current of his feeling failed: he became his admirers.

Now he is scattered among a hundred cities
And wholly given over to unfamiliar affections;
20 To find his happiness in another kind of wood
And be punished under a foreign code of conscience.
The words of a dead man
Are modified in the guts of the living.

But in the importance and noise of to-morrow
25 When the brokers are roaring like beasts on the floor of the
Bourse,
And the poor have the sufferings to which they are fairly
accustomed,
And each in the cell of himself is almost convinced of his
freedom;
A few thousand will think of this day
As one thinks of a day when one did something slightly
unusual.

30 O all the instruments agree
The day of his death was a dark cold day.

Although the 'instruments' (5, 30) give this opening description
an air of objectivity, the 'dead' (1) of winter and the 'dying' (4)
day suggest that nature somehow sympathised with the poet's
death. Even the theme of disfigurement is apparent in the snow
that 'disfigured' (3) the public statues, as if they were mourners.
These disfigured 'public statues' also suggest the political
bankruptcy that is taken up in the third section of the poem. In
the first stanza Auden adapts the topic of the 'blight on the
countryside' we have seen in pastoral poetry by applying it to an
urban landscape, and in the second stanza gives the parallel topic
of 'nature mourns' a twist. As we saw in Vergil's *Eclogue*, the wild
animals mourned the dead man and nature was upset, but here
the wolves are said to be unaffected, while nature maintains her
customary laws ('The peasant river was untempted by the

fashionable quays', 9). Indeed, it is only the mourners' tongues that kept his poems alive. Auden has effectively undercut the traditional topics while yet retaining them.

In keeping with the tendency of monodies to fix attention on the details of death, the third stanza turns to the very afternoon when Yeats died.[36] In order to avoid maudlin detail, Auden resorts to vivid metaphors to portray the last moments, when 'The current of his feeling failed' (17). The last words of the stanza hint at a kind of apotheosis ('he became his admirers', 17), but in fact, by an ironic twist of the topic of 'living in fame', Auden identifies the poet with his poems that now take on life in the 'guts of the living' (23), where they are no longer in control of their meaning, but subject to strange modifications. By alluding to Dante's *selva oscura* with the phrase 'another kind of wood' (20) and by choosing the word 'punished' (21), Auden hints that the poet is undergoing a kind of purgatorial experience.

The fifth stanza takes up the topic of the mourners. Instead of providing a roll call of those afflicted with grief in order to amplify the stature of the deceased, Auden uses a priamel to single out a 'few thousand' (28), who, against the background of everyday life, will recall the day of Yeats's death as one on which they did something 'slightly unusual' (29). This extreme understatement serves two purposes: on the one hand, it criticises modern society's disregard for poetry; and on the other, it implies that Yeats's prestige among those few thousand is so considerable that the poet does not need to amplify their grief, or belabour Yeats's virtues. The 'few' carries the satire, for the mourners are few in proportion to the rest of mankind portrayed in the foil: the 'thousand' carries the praise, for within the poetic community, that is a considerable number. This first section is remarkably free of direct praise: the words 'the poet' in line 11 carry enormous weight.

This first section, which consists mainly of lament, is fittingly composed in free verse. We noted at the beginning of the chapter that the style of lament was generally irregular[37] and in an earlier chapter (see p. 77) observed that Auden had a penchant for regularising his versification once he had arrived at the subject of interest. These two tendencies work together in this poem as it progresses from lament to consolation. The transition is apparent in the second part. Whereas the first part consistently referred to the poet in the third person, the second opens by addressing Yeats and is composed in iambic pentameters and hexameters with near rhymes (except for 'south' and the final, emphatic word 'mouth').

II

You were silly like us: your gift survived it all;
The parish of rich women, physical decay,
Yourself; mad Ireland hurt you into poetry.
35 Now Ireland has her madness and her weather still,
For poetry makes nothing happen: it survives
In the valley of its saying where executives
Would never want to tamper; it flows south
From ranches of isolation and the busy griefs,
40 Raw towns that we believe and die in; it survives,
A way of happening, a mouth.

These lines begin the consolation, as the repetition of the word 'survive' (32, 36, 40) indicates. The theme is remembrance in verse, which outlives the imperfections of the individual ('You were silly like us', 32). Although poetry does not effect great political or social changes (as Yeats had at times hoped), nonetheless, it does survive — as, of course, this very poem demonstrates. Once again, Auden is deliberately understating the power of poetry: he is reluctant to blow any trumpets.

The final section consists of regular trochaic couplets.

III

Earth, receive an honoured guest;
William Yeats is laid to rest:
Let the Irish vessel lie
45 Emptied of its poetry.

Time that is intolerant
Of the brave and innocent,
And indifferent in a week
To a beautiful physique,

50 Worships language and forgives
Everyone by whom it lives;
Pardons cowardice, conceit,
Lays its honours at their feet.

Time that with this strange excuse
55 Pardoned Kipling and his views,
And will pardon Paul Claudel,
Pardons him for writing well.

In the nightmare of the dark
All the dogs of Europe bark,
60 And the living nations wait,
Each sequestered in its hate;

Intellectual disgrace
Stares from every human face,
And the seas of pity lie
65 Locked and frozen in each eye.

Follow, poet, follow right
To the bottom of the night,
With your unconstraining voice
Still persuade us to rejoice;

70 With the farming of a verse
Make a vineyard of the curse,
Sing of human unsuccess
In a rapture of distress;

In the deserts of the heart
75 Let the healing fountain start,
In the prison of his days
Teach the free man how to praise.

The first stanza, which reads like an epitaph, finally gives the
poet's name. The theme of the next three stanzas (46–57),
omitted in Auden's later revision, is that Yeats's excellent use of
language will assure the survival of his poetry in spite of the views
it espouses. The next two memorable stanzas (58–65) describe
the tense situation in 1939 before the Second World War, a
variation of the motif, 'blight on the countryside', with which the
poem began. In these lines the focus narrows from nations (60),
to 'every human face' (63), to 'each eye' (65). The final three
stanzas consist of an apostrophe to the poet, and, as if he were a
'genius' such as Lycidas, the speaker requests him to exert his
beneficent influence during the present crisis: 'Teach the free
man how to praise' (77).

In much the same way that Milton's 'Lycidas' summed up the whole tradition of lament and consolation for the seventeenth century, so Auden's poem does for the twentieth. Although its tone is far more ironic and understated than Milton's, it contains almost all the topics of genre we have identified and gives them a new application. Even St Peter's condemnation of the clergy and the spectre of the 'grim wolf' in 'Lycidas' is paralleled in Auden's stanzas on the 'dogs of Europe'.

Notes

1. In his instructions on how to compose occasional speeches, Menander Rhetor, the third-century AD rhetorician, discusses three types that concern death: the monody (μονῳδία), the funeral speech (ἐπιτάφιος λόγος), and the speech of consolation (παραμυθητικὸς λόγος). The monody consists entirely of lament, and its purpose is to arouse pity in the audience: the funeral speech may also contain lamentation, but stresses the element of encomium; its main purpose is commemorative. The consolatory speech begins with lament, but turns to the consolatory topics of philosophy and religion and ends on a note of hope. These three types also help to define the range of poems in terms of their relative emphasis on the *lamentatio*, eulogy, or *consolatio*. Thus, for example, Ben Jonson's 'To the Immortal Memory of that Noble Pair, Sir Lucius Cary and Sir H. Morison' contains both lament and consolation, whereas his 'To the Memory of My Beloved, The Author, Mr William Shakespeare, And What He Hath Left Us', is mainly eulogy. Likewise, lament predominates in Auden's 'In Memory of W.B. Yeats', eulogy in his 'In Memory of Sigmund Freud'.
2. In the following discussion, the terms *lamentatio* and *consolatio* do not refer to genres, but to specific poems and to passages in longer works where the intention to lament or console is clear. I have concentrated on poems that lament death, but the topics easily apply to 'complaints' in Graeco-Roman love poetry, to the Medieval *contemptus mundi*, and to Renaissance 'complaints'. For an overview of these, see M. Donker and G.M. Muldrow, *Dictionary of literary-rhetorical conventions of the English Renaissance* (Greenwood Press, Westport, CT, 1982), pp. 48–51 and 74–7.
3. Sparrows were considered particularly randy birds in antiquity. In Sappho's 'Hymn to Aphrodite' (see p. 148) they pull Aphrodite's (Venus') chariot.
4. The word 'now' (*nunc*, νῦν) regularly marks the contrast between the past and present. Cf. *Il.* 22.436 and 24.757 in Hecuba's laments and 22.482, 505 and 508 in Andromache's lament, and Statius, *Silvae* 2.4.8 (*at nunc*), also a lament on a dead parrot.
5. As we shall see in the next example, this complaint càn easily be expanded to include a corollary: The good die . . . while the base survive.
6. This allusion is also a clever adaptation of the 'out-doing' motif

(see p. 54, Note 9), since even Philomela, the proverbial mourner, now has (supposedly) found an even greater tragedy to mourn.

7. We shall see both Horace and Auden use priamels to single out the most important mourners (see pp. 98 and 110).

8. The Latin equivalent of σχετλιασμός is *querel(l)a* or *querimonia* ('complaint'). For many examples in Graeco-Roman poetry, see F. Cairns, *Generic composition in Greek and Latin poetry* (University of Edinburgh Press, Edinburgh, 1972), index, s.v. *schetliasmos*.

9. The expression comes from Milton's 'Lycidas', 64.

10. The fact that noble Greeks died at Troy while the vile Thersites still survived was a standard topic of complaint about the justice of the gods as early as Sophocles' *Philoctetes* 446–52. Catullus touches on half of this topic with his curse of the shades of Orcus 'who devour everything pretty' (14).

11. Statius also wrote a mock-lament for a friend's parrot (*Silvae* 2.4) with delightful rhetorical flourish that contains many of the same topics. John Skelton's 'Philip Sparrow' is a rambling Renaissance adaptation.

12. In pastoral poetry this topic often takes the form of 'nature mourns' or 'a blight on the countryside'.

13. Besides the complaint (13–14), Catullus' lament contains several examples of anaphora (e.g. *passer . . . passer*, 3–4), exclamation (*o factum male*, 16), and apostrophe (e.g. *malae tenebrae Orci*, 14–15).

14. This is an extreme application of Wordsworth's famous dictum, 'the child is father of the man'. For the normal situation, cf. Plato, *Republic* 412C: 'Is it not obvious that the elders ought to rule and the younger to be ruled?'

15. A very brief bibliography on the topics of consolation would include the following ancient sources: Seneca, *Ep.* 63; Plutarch, *Consolatio ad Apollonium*; Menander Rhetor on 'The Consolatory Speech', 'The Funeral Speech' and 'The Monody' and pseudo-Dionysius of Halicarnassus on 'Funeral Speeches' (included in D.A. Russell and N.G. Wilson (eds), *Menander Rhetor* (Oxford University Press, Oxford, 1981)). Some modern studies include: T.C. Burgess, *Epideictic literature*, pp. 155–7; G. Norlin, 'The conventions of the pastoral elegy', *American Journal of Philology*, vol. 32 (1911), pp. 294–312; E.R. Curtius, *European literature and the Latin Middle Ages*, trans. W.R. Trask (Princeton University Press, Princeton, 1973), pp. 80–2; R. Kassel, *Untersuchungen zur Griechischen und Römischen Konsolationsliteratur* (Beck'sche Verlagsbuchhandlung, München, 1958); R. Lattimore, *Themes in Greek and Latin epitaphs* (University of Illinois Press, Urbana, 1962); G. Davis, '*Ad Sidera Notus*: strategies of lament and consolation in Fortunatus' *De Gelesuintha*', *Agon*, vol. 1 (1967), pp. 118–34; and C.E. Manning, 'The consolatory tradition and Seneca's attitude to the emotions', *Greece and Rome*, vol. 21 (1974), pp. 71–81. For the influence of the consolatory topics of rhetorical handbooks (chiefly Wilson's) on sixteenth-century English lyric poetry, see D.L. Peterson, *The English lyric from Wyatt to Donne: a history of the plain and eloquent styles* (Princeton University Press, Princeton, 1967), pp. 62–9.

16. The lament at the beginning of Boethius' *Consolation of Philosophy* (Book 1, metron 2), contrasts the former (*quondam*, 6) elevation of the prisoner's mind, when he explored the secrets of nature, with his present

fallen state (*nunc iacet*, 24), when he 'is compelled, alas, to contemplate the stolid ground' (*cogitur, heu, stolidam cernere terram*, 27). Dame Philosophy's mission in the rest of the work is to raise his mind back to the contemplation of universals. Because consolation appeals to reason, it became a major topic of philosophical schools.

17. It is a truism of Greek ethical thought that no man is completely happy. Although he may enjoy personal well-being, he can suffer through the misfortunes of his loved ones. This is a lesson that both Achilles in the *Iliad* and Admetus in Euripides' *Alcestis* learn.

18. This topic is commonplace in Greek poetry and drama: cf. Bacchylides 5.162–3, Sophocles, *Electra* 137–9, and Euripides, *Alcestis* 985–6, 1078 and 1091 for a few of many examples.

19. For a good appreciation of this word in laments (with many examples), see R.G.M. Nisbet and M. Hubbard, *A commentary on Horace: Odes Book I* (Oxford University Press, Oxford, 1970), p. 283.

20. This is a good example of the use of eulogy as an occasion for lament. Cf. Milton's 'Lycidas' 9: 'and hath not left his peer'.

21. Lines 9–10 are a brief summary priamel along the lines of that at Sophocles, *Antigone* 332 (see p. 53, Note 2). The word *multis* (9) could easily have been expanded into a list (cf. the list of birds in Ovid's lament).

22. The argument *a fortiori* states that if even x could (or could not) do something, then certainly y could (or could not) do it. This kind of persuasion is very common in consolatory admonitions, for by reminding the bereaved of others' suffering, it universalises his own and helps him accept it. At *Il*. 18.117–18 Achilles consoles himself with the thought that even Heracles had to die. Milton uses a similar argument in 'Lycidas', when he observes that if the Muse could not even save Orpheus (her own son), she certainly could have done nothing for Lycidas.

23. The word *semel* regularly drives home the point that death occurs once and for all. Mercury is described as 'not disposed' (*non lenis*) to make exceptions, an example of Horatian *litotes* (understatement). Death is inexorable.

24. The transition from lament to consolation is often marked by an adversative, as in the example from Archilochus (ἀλλὰ . . . γάρ, 5) and Horace (*sed*, 19).

25. From the earliest times, dead heroes were considered able to become protective divinities (δαίμονες) and receive regular rites. Heracles and the Dioscuri (Castor and Pollux) are well-known examples, and the apotheosis of Oedipus is familiar from Sophocles' *Oedipus at Colonus*. Another form of consolation consists of translation after death to the Isles of the Blessed (the Elysian Fields). We know from fragments that this topic appeared in Pindar's dirges and we have seen it in Ovid's parody. Menander Rhetor prescribes it as a standard topic of consolatory speeches (cf. 414.16–27) and of funeral orations (cf. 421.16–17).

26. The topic begins with the lament for Daphnis in Theocritus, *Idyll* 1.71–5 and 7.74–7, and continues in the laments of Bion and pseudo-Moschus.

27. For discussions and examples of this very common topic, see

Curtius, *European literature*, pp. 95–7; and A. Preminger, F.J. Warnke, and O.B. Hardison, Jr. (eds), *The Princeton encyclopedia of poetics* (Princeton University Press, Princeton, 1965), p. 5.

28. There is a play on the meanings of 'extinguished' and 'bright', reinforced by the contrast between the *umbras* (40) associated with the funeral rites for Daphnis and the splendour of heaven. There is also a contrast between the passivity of the accusative case (*exstinctum*) and the active nominative *candidus*. In Menalcas' song, Daphnis becomes an active force.

29. Another important topic is the fact that death releases us from the ills of this life, but it mainly occurs in philosophical prose. It finds its full expression in Plato's *Phaedo*, where Socrates must paradoxically console his friends for having to go on living, while he finds his joyful release in a death for which philosophy has been preparing him all his life. The topic was also a favourite of the Epicureans and Stoics. Much later, Robert Garnier uses it extensively in his 'Elégie Sur le Trespas de Pierre de Ronsard' and it reappears in A.E. Housman's ironic 'To an Athlete Dying Young'.

Another consolatory topic, the enjoyment of the present, which appears in the *Iliad* and in the example from Archilochus, will be treated fully in the following chapter on *carpe-diem* poems. For yet others, cf. the exhaustive examples of 'comforting' in T. Wilson's *Arte of rhetorique*, ed. G.H. Mair (Oxford University Press, Oxford, 1909), pp. 66–85, conveniently summarised in O.B. Hardison, *The enduring monument* (University of North Carolina Press, Chapel Hill, 1962), p. 118; and R. Lattimore, *Themes in Greek and Latin epitaphs*, pp. 172–265.

30. The main Graeco-Roman models for 'Lycidas' are Theocritus, *Idyll* 1, Bion's 'Lament for Adonis', pseudo-Moschus, 'Lament for Bion', Vergil's *Eclogues* 5 and 10, and Ovid's 'Lament for Tibullus' (*Amores* 3.9). For surveys of the models that influenced 'Lycidas', see Norlin, 'The conventions of the pastoral elegy' *American Journal of Philology*, vol. 32 (1911), pp. 294–312 and T.G. Rosenmeyer, *The green cabinet: Theocritus and the European pastoral lyric* (University of California Press, Berkeley, 1969). For a convenient collection of the relevant generic materials, see S. Elledge, *Milton's 'Lycidas'* (Harper and Row, New York, 1966).

31. 'What boots it?' is Milton's equivalent for the Latin *quid iuvat*, a formula which Ovid has parodied in his elegy on the parrot (*Amores* 2.6.17–20). Ovid also uses it in a more intense complaint in the elegy on his fellow poet Tibullus, undoubtedly one of the models for 'Lycidas' (*Amores* 3.9.35–6): 'When evil fate snatches away good men — forgive me for saying so — / I am tempted to doubt that any gods exist'.

32. Milton is contrasting the 'guerdon' (73) of earthly fame with the 'meed' (84) of heavenly fame. As we have seen, Milton had precedents in Vergil, Horace and Propertius for the sudden appearance and admonition of Apollo, especially when the topic involves poetic fame.

33. It is also a species of 'blight on the countryside' now that the 'dearest pledge' (107) is gone. Part of the strategy of praise is to show how deficient things are since the subject's departure, a topic Carew uses extensively in his elegy on Donne.

34. This 'genius' is the equivalent of the 'blessed spirit' that Alcestis is

said to become. Both protect wayfarers. Ovid also ends his 'Lament for Tibullus' (*Amores* 3.9.59–68) with a Vision of Tibullus in the Elysian Fields, where he is greeted by his fellow poets Calvus, Catullus and Gallus. In this way, he combines the motifs of fame through poetry and a blessed afterlife. John Donne also has a witty treatment of these themes in the last two stanzas of his 'Canonization'.

35. I am using the unrevised version. Auden's poem is in a long line of laments (called 'elegies') for fellow poets, which are numerous from the Hellenistic period on, especially in the Renaissance. Cf. pseudo-Moschus, 'Lament for Bion', Ovid, 'Lament for Tibullus' (*Amores*, 3.9), Robert Garnier, 'Elégie Sur le Trespas de Pierre de Ronsard', Ben Jonson, 'To the Memory of My Beloved, the Author Mr William Shakespeare', Thomas Carew, 'An Elegie upon the Death of the Dean of Paul's, Dr John Donne', and, of course, Milton's 'Lycidas'.

36. For Menander Rhetor's prescriptions for the monody, cf. p. 87. The first section of García Lorca's famous 'Llanto por Ignacio Sánchez Mejías', concentrates on the very moment of the bullfighter's death with the constantly recurring refrain 'a las cinco de la tarde' ('at five in the afternoon').

37. Menander Rhetor (437.4) observes that the style of the monody should be 'relaxed' (ἄνετος) in the sense of not overly refined. Although he is discussing prose style, the same applies to poetic style. Milton's 'Lycidas' is a good example, for it contains many anomalies: half lines, an irregular rhyme scheme, false starts and sudden shifts of argument.

5

The Argument of *Carpe-diem* Poems

A recent handbook defines 'carpe diem' as 'the theme of poems urging a young woman to live and love, since time is short and youth fleeting'.[1] This is a standard meaning the term has taken in lyric poetry since the Renaissance, but as we shall see, this definition is too narrow, both for Graeco-Roman and English poetry, for sexual enjoyment is but one feature of a more general theme. In fact, the *carpe-diem* poem is a highly developed subgenre of consolatory and didactic poetry with a well-defined form and vocabulary that is not confined to lyric poetry, but occurs in epic and tragedy as well.

In the last chapter we traced the theme of manly consolation to the 24th book of the *Iliad*, in which Achilles urges Priam to bear up under his grief for his slain son. Fifty lines later, after preparing Hector's body for return, Achilles invites Priam to stay and eat supper with him, and in order to persuade the reluctant old man, he briefly recalls the story of Niobe, who, even though she had lost all twelve of her children at once, remembered to eat in the midst of her great grief. After relating this example, he draws the conclusion (618–9):

> ἀλλ' ἄγε δὴ καὶ νῶϊ μεδώμεθα, δῖε γεραιέ,
> σίτου· ἔπειτά κεν αὖτε φίλον παῖδα κλαίοισθα.

Come then, noble old man, let us also take thought of food; then afterwards you may lament your dear son.

This is the first occurrence in Greek of a theme which became so frequent in later Graeco-Roman poetry that it constitutes a subgenre commonly known as *carpe diem* ('pluck the day').[2] Three features of Achilles' speech are noteworthy: the context, the content and the form. Firstly, his speech takes place in a setting of death and lamentation. Secondly, the message — enjoying what is at hand while one is able — is the burden of all *carpe-diem* poetry and is essentially consolatory. Finally, the speech contains a formal argument. Achilles uses the example of Niobe (an *argumentum a fortiori*)[3] to substantiate his conclusion, which is stated as an injunction: 'Come then . . .' (ἀλλ᾽ ἄγε . . .). As we shall see, the spectre of death (or old age) and a didactic argument leading to an exhortation are regular features of this subgenre.

Alcaeus, a lyric poet of the early sixth century, wrote many *carpe-diem* poems, but unfortunately only scraps of his poetry have survived. One reasonably well-preserved fragment (38A), however, contains a good example:

πῶνε [καὶ μέθυ᾽ ὦ] Μελάνιππ᾽ ἄμ᾽ ἔμοι· τί [φαῖς
†ὄταμε[. . . .]δινάεντ᾽† Ἀχέροντα μεγ[

ζάβαι[ς ἀ]ελίω κόθαρον φάος [ἄψερον
ὄψεσθ᾽; ἀλλ᾽ ἄγι μὴ μεγάλων ἐπ[ιβάλλεο·

5 καὶ γὰρ Σίσυφος Αἰολίδαις βασίλευς [ἔφα
ἀνδρῶν πλεῖστα νοησάμενος [θανάτω κρέτην·

ἀλλὰ καὶ πολύιδρις ἔων ὐπὰ κᾶρι [δὶς
δινάεντ᾽ Ἀχέροντ᾽ ἐπέραισε, μ[

αὔτῳ μόχθον ἔχην Κρονίδαις βα[σίλευς κάτω
10 μελαίνας χθόνος· ἀλλ᾽ ἄγι μὴ τά[δ᾽ ἐπέλπεο·

θᾶς] τ᾽ ἀβάσομεν αἴ ποτα κἄλλοτα . [
. . .]ην ὄττινα τῶνδε πάθην τά[χα δῷ θέος.

Drink and get drunk with me, Melanippus. Why do you
    think
that once you have crossed wide eddying Acheron

you will again see the clear light of the sun?
Come then, do not aim for graet things:

5 for example, King Sisyphus, Aeolus' son, who knew more
    than any man, thought that he could overcome death,

but in spite of his intelligence fate made him twice
cross eddying Acheron . . .

and King Zeus, son of Cronus, made him toil
10 under the black earth. Come then, do not hope for these
    things:

now, if ever, while we are young, [let us] endure
any of these sufferings the god may give.

It is not certain whether we have the entire poem or just its
beginning, but as it stands it provides some standard topics of the
carpe-diem theme. The first is the inevitability of death, which lies
behind all *carpe-diem* poems. There are various ways for the poet
to point up this topic. Here, Alcaeus, like Homer's Achilles, uses
an *argumentum a fortiori*: if even Sisyphus, that shrewd man who
tricked the gods into letting him return from death, could not
escape his eventual fate, how could anyone hope to do so? As in
the passage from the *Iliad*, this example is followed by an
injunction ('Come then', ἀλλ᾽ ἄγι, 10) to bear up under life's
hardships and enjoy what is at hand. In both examples, the
enjoyment is intimately bound up with manly consolation, just as
in Archilochus, *fr.* 13 (West), where Pericles is urged to bear up
in order to enjoy the city's feasting (see p. 96).

While it shares themes and topics with lament and consolation,
particularly with manly consolation, the *carpe-diem* poem is also a
species of didactic poetry, for it gives advice on how to live. For
that reason, it often depicts a setting in which an older (or at least
more experienced) person counsels another.[4] Such is the situation
in Euripides' *Alcestis*, 779–802, when Heracles gives advice to a
slave who is grieving for his mistress' death.

δεῦρ᾽ ἔλθ᾽, ὅπως ἂν καὶ σοφώτερος γένῃ.
780 τὰ θνητὰ πράγματ᾽ οἶδας ἣν ἔχει φύσιν;
οἶμαι μὲν οὔ· πόθεν γάρ; ἀλλ᾽ ἄκουέ μου.
βροτοῖς ἅπασι κατθανεῖν ὀφείλεται,
κοὐκ ἔστι θνητῶν ὅστις ἐξεπίσταται
τὴν αὔριον μέλλουσαν εἰ βιώσεται·
785 τὸ τῆς τύχης γὰρ ἀφανὲς οἷ προβήσεται,
κἄστ᾽ οὐ διδακτὸν οὐδ᾽ ἁλίσκεται τέχνῃ.
ταῦτ᾽ οὖν ἀκούσας καὶ μαθὼν ἐμοῦ πάρα,
εὔφραινε σαυτόν, πῖνε, τὸν καθ᾽ ἡμέραν

βίον λογίζου σόν, τὰ δ᾽ ἄλλα τῆς τύχης.
790 τίμα δὲ καὶ τὴν πλεῖστον ἡδίστην θεῶν
Κύπριν βροτοῖσιν· εὐμενὴς γὰρ ἡ θεός.
τὰ δ᾽ ἄλλ᾽ ἔασον ταῦτα καὶ πιθοῦ λόγοις
ἐμοῖσιν, εἴπερ ὀρθά σοι δοκῶ λέγειν.
οἶμαι μέν. οὔκουν τὴν ἄγαν λύπην ἀφεὶς
795 πίῃ μεθ᾽ ἡμῶν τάσδ᾽ ὑπερβαλὼν τύχας,
στεφάνοις πυκασθείς; καὶ σάφ᾽ οἶδ᾽ ὁθούνεκα
τοῦ νῦν σκυθρωποῦ καὶ ξυνεστῶτος φρενῶν
μεθορμιεῖ σε πίτυλος ἐμπεσὼν σκύφου.
ὄντας δὲ θνητοὺς θνητὰ καὶ φρονεῖν χρεών·
800 ὡς τοῖς γε σεμνοῖς καὶ συνωφρυωμένοις
ἅπασίν ἐστιν, ὥς γ᾽ ἐμοὶ χρῆσθαι κριτῇ,
οὐ βίος ἀληθῶς ὁ βίος, ἀλλὰ συμφορά.

Come here and learn something to make you wiser.
780 Do you know the nature of the human condition?
I doubt it. How could you? Well then, listen to me.
Death is a debt all mortals must pay
and there is no man who knows for certain
if he will be alive tomorrow,
785 for the outcome of fortune is uncertain
and cannot be learned or mastered by study.
Now that you have heard and understood what I have said,
enjoy yourself, drink, and reckon that your life today
is all you own — the rest belongs to fortune.
790 Then too, pay homage to mankind's sweetest goddess,
Aphrodite, for she is a gracious god.
Drop all these other considerations and do what I say,
if you believe I am telling the truth.
I for one think so. Therefore, shake off your excessive grief,
795 overcome these misfortunes, put garlands on your head
and drink with me. I am certain that
wine splashing in a cup will set you free
from these present scowls and gloomy thoughts.
We are only human and ought to think like humans.
800 As for all those sombre and scowling
folks, as far as I can judge,
theirs is not really a life but a disaster.

This example is a full expression of the theme. When Heracles
says: 'Come here and learn something to make you wiser' (779),

he assumes the typical didactic stance of one who delivers the *carpe-diem* message. The subject is, appropriately, the nature of the human condition (τὰ θνητὰ πράγματα, 780), and the first topic is the inevitability of death (782), followed by the uncertainty of life (783–4). Of great importance is the word 'tomorrow' (αὔριον, 784), for the notion of the day as the critical length of time available to a human pervades Greek thought.[5] We have daily needs and must live each day as it comes, for tomorrow is beyond our control (hence, the *diem* part of *carpe diem*). Having thus instructed the servant about the uncertainty of the human condition, Heracles issues the injunction, expressed as an imperative (hence the *carpe* part of *carpe diem*), to enjoy life today (καθ' ἡμέραν, 788), which, he adds, includes sex. Like Alcaeus, Heracles concludes with an exhortation from the tradition of manly consolation: in order to enjoy the present, the servant must cease from his excessive grief and overcome his sadness, lest he become like those 'scowling' (800) cynics who reduce life to a 'disaster' (802).

From these two examples we can isolate some basic features of *carpe-diem* poems. First of all, they contain (implicitly or explicitly) a rhetorical argument — in Aristotelian terms, an *enthymeme*. Four major premisses concerning life underlie all of them:

(I) that death is irrevocable ('Why do you think that once you have crossed wide eddying Acheron you will again see the clear light of the sun?' Alcaeus, *fr.* 38A.1–3);

(II) that death is inevitable ('Death is a debt all mortals must pay', *Alcestis*, 782);

(III) that the immediate future is beyond our control ('Fortune is uncertain', *Alcestis*, 785); and

(IV) that life is transient ('while we are young', Alcaeus, *fr.* 38A.11).[6]

In each *carpe-diem* poem the speaker demonstrates one or more of these premisses and expresses the logical conclusions as an injunction binding on the addressee. The following outline sketches some of the common arguments and includes terms used in advancing them that we shall encounter in the Latin tradition, one which is especially rich in *carpe-diem* poems.

    (I) Death is irrevocable[7]
        (a) examples, often *a fortiori* (e.g. not even Sisyphus

could escape it)
(b) key terms: *semel* 'once and for all', *perpetuus* 'ever-lasting'

(II) Death is inevitable
    (a) examples
       (i) from nature (e.g. everything passes)
       (ii) from legend, often *a fortiori* (e.g. even Heracles died)
       (iii) from history (e.g. *ubi sunt* . . . 'where are . . .?')[8]
    (b) tokens (e.g. tombs, skulls)[9]
    (c) there are no exemptions (e.g. 'everybody', 'rich and poor')
    (d) nothing avails against it (e.g. Sisyphus' intelligence, piety)

(III) The immediate future is uncertain
    (a) only 'today' (i.e., the immediate present) is in our control
    (b) 'tomorrow' cannot be known by any means
    (c) long-range hopes are useless
    (d) key terms: *spes longa* 'far-reaching hope'; *dum licet* 'while we may'

(IV) Life is transient
    (a) examples from nature
       (i) by analogy (e.g. flowers, seasons)
       (ii) by contrast (e.g. unlike the sun, moon, etc.)
    (b) youth passes (and old age approaches) quickly
    (c) key terms: *mox* 'soon'; *brevis* 'short'; *tempus fugit* 'time flees'; *senecta* 'old age'

The conclusion to be drawn from the first three propositions is that the present existence is all that we have to work with: indeed, today is the longest period of time that is reasonably under our control. The conclusion drawn from the fourth proposition is that we are progressing rapidly toward death and that it is urgent to make the best possible use of the fleeting moment (*tempus fugit*). In almost all cases the conclusion is expressed syntactically as an imperative, whether it precedes the demonstration of the thesis or follows it. With this scheme in mind, we can turn to some examples from Latin literature.

One of the most celebrated poems of Catullus is a *carpe-diem* poem addressed to his lover Lesbia (5).

> Vivamus, mea Lesbia, atque amemus,
> rumoresque senum severiorum
> omnes unius aestimemus assis.
> soles occidere et redire possunt:
> 5 nobis, cum semel occidit brevis lux,
> nox est perpetua una dormienda.
> da mi basia mille, deinde centum,
> dein mille altera, dein secunda centum.
> deinde usque altera mille, deinde centum.
> 10 dein, cum milia multa fecerimus,
> conturbabimus illa, ne sciamus,
> aut nequis malus invidere possit,
> cum tantum sciat esse basiorum.

> Let us live, my Lesbia, and let us love,
> and all the gossip of stern old men
> let us value at one penny.
> Suns can set and rise again:
> 5 but we, once our brief light has set,
> must sleep one everlasting night.
> Give me a thousand kisses, then a hundred more,
> then another thousand, then a second hundred,
> then yet another thousand, then a hundred.
> 10 Then, after many thousands,
> we will confuse the record to lose count
> and prevent envious harm from some evil person
> who knows the number of our kisses.

The 'stern old men' in the poem are similar to the 'scowling folks' in the passage from Euripides' *Alcestis*, and are foil for the youthful enjoyment of life characteristic of the *carpe-diem* injunction. To emphasise the finality of death, Catullus uses an example from nature: in contrast to the continual rising and setting of the sun, human existence has a linear quality marked by the irrevocability (*perpetua*) of our once-and-for-all (*semel*) death, which in comparison with the seemingly endless cycles of nature is very brief (*brevis*). Catullus even puns on the verb *occidere*, which means 'to set' but also 'to die'. Then follows the injunction, with the prominent imperative: *da* (7). The exaggeration of the number of kisses completes the poem with a fittingly youthful enthusiasm, which will baffle any 'evil person' (*malus*, 12) who would set a limit to their enjoyment out of sheer envy.

The Latin poet who used *carpe-diem* themes with the greatest skill and inventiveness was Horace. It is his *Odes* 1.11 that gives the genre its name.

> Tu ne quaesieris — scire nefas — quem mihi, quem tibi
> finem di dederint, Leuconoë, nec Babylonios
> temptaris numeros. ut melius, quicquid erit, pati!
> seu plures hiemes, seu tribuit Iuppiter ultimam,
> 5 quae nunc oppositis debilitat pumicibus mare
> Tyrrhenum. sapias, vina liques, et spatio brevi
> spem longam reseces. dum loquimur, fugerit invida
> aetas: carpe diem, quam minimum credula postero.

> Do not seek to know, Leuconoë (for such knowledge is
>   forbidden),
> what end the gods have determined for you and me, nor
>   consult
> Babylonian horoscopes. How much better to endure
>   whatever comes,
> whether Jupiter has allotted many winters or just this final
>   one,
> 5 which now wears down the Tuscan Sea against the opposing
> cliffs. Be sensible: strain the wine, and prune back within
>   brief
> limits long-range hope. Even while we are speaking
>   envious time
> has sped. Pluck the day; trust as little as possible in the
>   future.

In his address to an otherwise unknown woman, the speaker concentrates on premisses (III) and (IV): the uncertainty of the immediate future and the brevity of life. Since she is overly anxious about knowing when she and Horace will die, there is no need for him to demonstrate the inevitability of death (II). The Babylonian astrology represents worthless attempts to know the future. The word 'endure' (*pati*, 3) clearly places this poem in the Latin tradition of manly consolation (cf. *patientia* at *Odes* 1.24.19, discussed on p. 98). The mention of winter (seasonal change in Horace's *carpe-diem* poems is frequently a reminder of the transience of human life) and the fact that it 'wears down' (*debilitat*, 5) the sea serves as a subtle reminder that time is progressing and human life too is wearing out;[10] and to demonstrate how urgent the matter is, Horace points out that even while they talk time will have fled (*fugerit*, 7). Metaphors drawn from gardening underlie his injunctions to 'prune back' (*reseces*, 7) long-range hope (*spem longam*, 7) and to 'pluck' (*carpe*, 8) the day, as if it were fruit. The final piece of advice to trust as little as possible in the future neatly brings the argument around to that of the poem's beginning.[11]

Since Horace, *Odes* 1.4 includes all four of the premisses covered on pp. 122–3, I have for convenience inserted references to them in the discussion of the poem.

> Solvitur acris hiems grata vice veris et Favoni,
>   trahuntque siccas machinae carinas,
> ac neque iam stabulis gaudet pecus aut arator igni,
>   nec prata canis albicant pruinis.
>
> 5 iam Cytherea choros ducit Venus imminente luna,
>   iunctaeque Nymphis Gratiae decentes
> alterno terram quatiunt pede, dum graves Cyclopum
>   Volcanus ardens visit officinas.
>
> nunc decet aut viridi nitidum caput impedire myrto
> 10   aut flore, terrae quem ferunt solutae;
> nunc et in umbrosis Fauno decet immolare lucis,
>   seu poscat agna sive malit haedo.
>
> pallida Mors aequo pulsat pede pauperum tabernas
>   regumque turres. o beate Sesti,
> 15 vitae summa brevis spem nos vetat incohare longam.
>   iam te premet nox fabulaeque Manes
>
> et domus exilis Plutonia; quo simul mearis,
>   nec regna vini sortiere talis,
> nec tenerum Lycidan mirabere, quo calet iuventus
> 20   nunc omnis et mox virgines tepebunt.
>
> Bitter winter is softening with the pleasant change of spring
>   breezes, and tackles are drawing dry hulls to the water;

no longer do the animals enjoy the barn or the ploughman
   his hearth,
     nor are the meadows white with morning frost.

5 Already Cytherean Venus leads her moonlit dances
   and the lovely Graces join the Nymphs
in beating the earth with dancing feet, while blazing
   Vulcan
     frequents the massive workshop of the Cyclopes.

Now it is proper to crown glistening hair with green myrtle
10   or flowers which the softened earth is sprouting;
now it is proper to sacrifice in shady groves to Faunus
   whether he wishes a lamb or prefers a kid.

Pallid Death knocks with an impartial foot at paupers'
   hovels
   and at kings' towers. O prosperous Sestius,
15 life's brief sum keeps us from embarking on long-range
   hope:
     soon night will oppress you, as will the legendary shades

and Pluto's dismal abode; as soon as you go there,
   you will not win the toss to become king of the drinking
nor admire tender Lycidas, whom all the boys
20   now adore, but soon will inflame the girls.

The poem plunges us *in medias res*, at the point of 'pleasant change' (*grata vice*, 1) from winter to spring, thereby introducing the theme of transition that dominates the poem. The following verses (2–12) provide an *ekphrasis* that sketches the effects of spring's approach,[12] which by its extensive use of doublets recalls the organisation of scenes on Achilles' shield. The first indication of spring's arrival is the opening of the Mediterranean sailing season: Horace captures the point of transition as the tackles are hauling the dry hulls to the shore. In the rest of the stanza he switches from the sea (sailing) to land (farming), and in the latter he depicts the reaction of animals (husbandry) and the ploughman (agriculture). The syntactical switch to the negative ('no longer, *neque iam*, 3) underscores the change from one state to another. The second stanza, which begins with the emphatic 'already' (*iam*, 5), turns from human activities during the day to those of the gods at night: Venus, the Graces, and Nymphs now dance while Vulcan is busy forging thunderbolts,[13] thus providing more doublets — men and gods, day and night, female and male, play and work.

The third stanza begins with the even more emphatic 'now it is proper' (*nunc decet*, 9), repeatd at line 11, and depicts the springtime activities of ordinary people at leisure: donning floral garlands and enjoying a sacrifice in a shady grove, thus ending this broad survey in the manner of a priamel with the kind of activity appropriate to a *carpe-diem* poem.

Horace has consciously crafted this *ekphrasis* to lull the reader into a sense of complacency, for the following lines contain one of his most dramatic passages. Without any warning Death suddenly appears (III); the alliteration of the p's vividly portrays his knocking (actually kicking) on the door. The doublet paupers and kings (*pauperum . . . regumque*, 13–14) is a poetic way of saying 'everybody', but it also serves as a reminder that wealth and power cannot ward off death (II). The unexpected, startling arrival of Death is imitated in the very form of the poem.

After this striking demonstration of the uncertainty of life and of the inevitability of death, Horace turns to his addressee to draw the conclusion: 'life's brief (*brevis*, 15) sum (IV) keeps us from embarking on long-range hope' (*spem . . . longam*, 15) (III). This is simply the *carpe-diem* injunction stated negatively. Although Sestius may be very well off, his present good is all that he can be certain of enjoying. The following lines drive home the point: soon (*iam*, 16) night will oppress him (IV), and as soon as (*simul*, 16) he dies he will forever (I) lose what he now enjoys: presiding over drinking parties and admiring the youthful Lycidas. The idea of time and change have dominated the poem,[14] and the final example illustrates it one more time. The homosexual admiration that Lycidas now enjoys will soon pass as he matures and girls take an interest in him. The pointed contrast of *nunc* and *mox* in the last line shows that Lycidas' passage into adulthood, like death, is being considered as one of the ravages of time that enjoins us to seize the present good, which in this case is the favour of Lycidas.[15]

Horace effectively exhausted the *carpe-diem* theme in lyric poetry for the remainder of the Latin tradition, until, as we shall see, a late author gave the theme a twist that proved influential in the Renaissance. In the Middle Ages, however, there is very little *carpe-diem* poetry, perhaps because this was the Age of Faith;[16] but

one short example in the Goliardic secular songs continues the
tradition:

> Gaudeamus igitur,
> iuvenes dum sumus;
> post molestam senectutem
> nos habebit tumulus.
> 5 Ubi sunt, qui ante nos
> in mundo vixere?
> Abeas ad tumulos
> si vis hos videre.
> Vita nostra brevis est,
> 10 breve finietur:
> venit mors velociter,
> neminem veretur.

> Let us make merry, therefore,
> while we are young;
> after troublesome old age
> the grave will have us.
> 5 Where are those who lived
> in the world before us?
> Go to their tombs
> if you wish to see them.
> Our life is short,
> 10 and will end quickly:
> death comes swiftly;
> it respects no man.

The erotic side of the *carpe-diem* tradition was the most
appealing to the Renaissance, and foremost in this tradition
is Pierre de Ronsard's 'Mignonne, Allons Voir Si la Rose':

> Mignonne, allons voir si la rose
> Qui ce matin avait déclose
> Sa robe de pourpre au soleil,
> A point perdu cette vêprée
> 5 Les plis de sa robe pourprée,
> Et son teint au vôtre pareil.
> Las! voyez comme en peu d'espace,
> Mignonne, elle a dessus la place

Las! las! ses beautés laissé choir!
10 O vraiment marâtre Nature,
Puisqu'une telle fleur ne dure
Que du matin jusques au soir!
Donc, si vous me croyez, mignonne,
Tandis que votre âge fleuronne
15 En sa plus verte nouveauté,
Cueillez, cueillez votre jeunesse:
Comme à cette fleur, la vieillesse
Fera ternir votre beauté.

My dear, let us go and see if the rose,
which opened this morning
its purple gown to the sun,
has this evening lost
5 the folds of its purple gown
and its colour just like yours.
Alas, see how quickly
my dear, it has shed its beauty,
alas, alas, on the ground!
10 O truly cruel Nature,
for such a flower to last
only from morning to evening!
Therefore, if you will heed me, my dear,
while your years are blossoming
15 in their green freshness,
pluck your youth, pluck it:
as with this flower, old age
will tarnish your beauty.

Much of the poem's appeal lies in its simplicity of form and logic. The poet invites the beloved to go and see if the morning rose still blooms. The exclamations 'Alas . . . alas' ('Las! . . . Las! las!') mark the discovery of the transience of beauty in nature. Then the logical conclusion ('So', 'Donc', 13) is drawn. The poem clearly exhibits the didactic strain of the genre ('heed me'), as well as its syllogistic form, for it begins with an observation of nature, derives a principle, and then applies it to human life.[17] The injunction 'gather, gather' ('cueillez, cueillez', 16) descends from Horace's 'carpe', but is also influenced by the late fourth-century AD poem attributed to Ausonius, 'De Rosis Nascentibus', in which the poet describes in great detail roses blooming at Paestum, and draws the conclusion:

> collige, virgo, rosas, dum flos novus et nova pubes,
> 50   et memor esto aevum sic properare tuum.

> Gather, maiden, roses, while the bloom is fresh and fresh is youth,
> 50   And remember that your lifetime hastens thus.

The *carpe-rosam* motif, which became very popular in French poetry,[18] opens Robert Herrick's well-known poem 'To the Virgins, to Make Much of Time'.

> Gather ye rosebuds while ye may,
>   Old time is still a-flying;
> And this same flower that smiles today
>   Tomorrow will be dying.

> 5 The glorious lamp of heaven, the sun,
>   The higher he's a-getting,
> The sooner will his race be run,
>   And nearer he's to setting.

> That age is best which is the first,
> 10   When youth and blood are warmer;
> But being spent, the worse, and worst
>   Times still succeed the former.

> Then be not coy, but use your time,
>   And, while ye may, go marry;
> 15 For, having lost but once your prime,
>   You may forever tarry.

Although the injunction 'Gather ye rosebuds' is inspired by the *carpe-rosam* poems of Ausonius and Ronsard, the rest of the poem owes much more to the earlier Latin tradition. The line 'Old time is still a-flying' recalls Horace's *fugerit . . . aetas* at *Odes* 1.11.7–8 (and *fugaces . . . anni* at 2.14.1–2), while the example of the setting sun neatly reverses Catullus' use of it in *Carm.* 5. Whereas Catullus had contrasted linear human time with the constant return of the sun by emphasising *redire* ('rise again'), Herrick uses the course of the sun as an analogy for human life. The third stanza elaborates the 'while we are young' topic: 'worse and worst' are euphemisms for old age and death (cf. *senectae . . . morti* at Horace, *Odes* 2.14.3–4). The last stanza, which draws the conclusion ('Then be not coy'), is full of echoes of the Latin tradition. 'Use your time' (13) is a variation of *carpe diem*; 'while ye may' (14) parallels *dum licet* in numerous Horatian passages;[19] 'but once' (15) is equivalent to *semel* at Catullus 5.5 and Horace, *Odes* 4.7.21, while 'forever' (16) is reminiscent of Catullus' *nox perpetua* (5.6).

In this poem Herrick combines Catullan and Horatian elements, but in fact two strains of *carpe-diem* poems stem from these two Latin poets: one, the Catullan, urges erotic enjoyment; the other, the Horatian, counsels the wise use of the present in the tradition of manly consolation. Ben Jonson provides extreme examples of each kind. Volpone's adaptation of Catullus, *Carm.* 5 becomes, in its context (*Volpone*, III.vii.166–83), a sinister poem of seduction couched in traditional *carpe-diem* terms.[20]

> Come, my Celia, let us prove,
> While we can, the sports of love;
> Time will not be ours forever;
> He, at length, our good will sever;
> 170 Spend not then his gifts in vain.
> Suns that set may rise again;
> But if once we lose this light,
> 'Tis with us perpetual night.
> Why should we defer our joys?
> 175 Fame and rumour are but toys.
> Cannot we delude the eyes
> Of a few poor household spies?
> Or his easier ears beguile,
> Thus removed by our wile?
> 180 'Tis no sin love's fruit to steal,
> But the sweet thefts to reveal:
> To be taken, to be seen,
> These have crimes accounted been.

The other strain is evident in his Epigram 70: To William Roe, which is in the Horatian, didactic tradition.

> When Nature bids us leave to live, 'tis late

Then to begin, my Roe; he makes a state
In life that can employ it, and takes hold
On the true causes ere they grow too old.
5 Delay is bad, doubt worse, depending worst;
Each best day of our life escapes us first.
Then, since we (more than many) these truths know,
Though life be short, let us not make it so.

Although they are formally similar by the fact that both offer advice to another person, derive their arguments from the limitations imposed by nature and time and draw logical conclusions with the word 'then', these two poems mark the two poles of *carpe-diem* poetry: the first espouses sensualism as an end in itself, the latter rational use of opportunities.

The poem that came to sum up the *carpe-diem* poem of seduction and even extended its limits was Andrew Marvell's 'To His Coy Mistress'.

Had we but world enough, and time,
This coyness, Lady, were no crime.
We would sit down and think which way
To walk and pass our long love's day.
5 Thou by the Indian Ganges' side
Shouldst rubies find: I by the tide
Of Humber would complain. I would
Love you ten years before the Flood,
And you should, if you please, refuse
10 Till the conversion of the Jews.
My vegetable love should grow
Vaster than empires, and more slow;
An hundred years should go to praise
Thine eyes and on thy forehead gaze;
15 Two hundred to adore each breast;
But thirty thousand to the rest;
An age at least to every part,
And the last age should show your heart;
For, Lady, you deserve this state,
20 Nor would I love at lower rate.
But at my back I always hear
Time's winged chariot hurrying near;
And yonder all before us lie
Deserts of vast eternity.

25 Thy beauty shall no more be found,
   Nor, in thy marble vault, shall sound
   My echoing song: then worms shall try
   That long preserved virginity,
   And your quaint honour turn to dust,
30 And into ashes all my lust:
   The grave's a fine and private place,
   But none, I think, do there embrace.
     Now therefore, while the youthful hue
   Sits on thy skin like morning dew,
35 And while thy willing soul transpires
   At every pore with instant fires,
   Now let us sport us while we may,
   And now, like amorous birds of prey,
   Rather at once our time devour
40 Than languish in his slow-chapt power.
   Let us roll all our strength and all
   Our sweetness up into one ball,
   And tear our pleasures with rough strife
   Thorough the iron gates of life:
45 Thus, though we cannot make our sun
   Stand still, yet we will make him run.

The syllogistic basis of the *carpe-diem* genre is clearly articulated in this poem, whose three parts represent a logical argument consisting of an hypothesis, objection and conclusion.[21] If we had endless time at our disposal, then this coyness would be appropriate; but we do not. *Ergo*. The hypothesis projects what life would be like if we did indeed have Horace's *spem longam* (1.4.15). It consists of a delightful catalogue of what the lovers would do if there were no limits on human life, in which Marvell cleverly inserts a conventional *ekphrasis* of the beloved's beauties (13–17) that follows the head-to-toe procedure of the *blason* (see p. 80 with Note 5) and is in the form of a priamel that singles out her 'heart' (18) as the last item, just as Spenser's praise in *Amoretti* 15 ended with the beloved's 'mind' (see p. 45). However, the subjunctives that propose this hypothesis ('had we', 'would', 'should') are suddenly cut short by an indicative statement of fact (21–4):

   But at my back I always hear
   Time's winged chariot hurrying near;

And yonder all before us lie
Deserts of vast eternity.

These famous lines come with all the sudden power of Horace's
pallida mors at *Odes* 1.4.13, vividly capturing the rush of time (IV)
and the endlessness of death (I). The following lines demonstrate
the inevitability (II) and privations of death through a forceful,
yet witty depiction of conditions that await the couple in the
grave. The conclusion of the argument comes with the emphatic
'Now therefore' (33). The 'now' (cf. *nunc* and *iam*, which mark the
conclusion of the argument and the injunction to seize the day in
the Latin poets) brings us to the actual present, while the
'therefore' applies the logic of the argument. The repeated 'while
. . . while' (33–6)[22] and 'now . . . now . . . now' (33–8) suggest the
urgency of seizing the day while there is still time (III). In his
injunctions (37–46), however, Marvell goes further than any
previous writer of *carpe-diem* poems in depicting the violence with
which the couple are to enjoy their pleasure. Catullus had
amplified his and Lesbia's pleasure by counting up thousands of
kisses, but Marvell's comparison of the lovers to 'amorous birds
of prey' that 'devour' their time and the command to 'tear our
pleasures with rough strife' go far beyond the conventional 'sport'
of lovers and suggest a deadly earnestness. Even the closing
reference to the sun, which recalls the suns in Catullus' and
Herrick's poems, turns their flat comparisons into a defiant
challenge. Marvell's poem definitively sums up the tradition and
even goes beyond it by mixing the seriousness generally associated with manly consolation (cf. Jonson's 'Though life be short,
let us not make it so') with the frivolity of the seduction poem.[23]

The *carpe-diem* genre languishes in the two centuries following
Marvell's brilliant performance, but re-emerges (often tinged
with irony or cynicism) in the nineteenth century in some of
Baudelaire's poems,[24] in Edward FitzGerald's popular *Rubáiyát of
Omar Khayyám*, and in many of A.E. Housman's poems (see
'Additional Examples'), including his sophisticated little poem,
'Loveliest of Trees, the Cherry Now':

Loveliest of trees, the cherry now
Is hung with bloom along the bough,
And stands about the woodland ride
Wearing white for Eastertide.

5 Now, of my threescore years and ten,
   Twenty will not come again,
   And take from seventy springs a score,
   It only leaves me fifty more.

   And since to look at things in bloom
10 Fifty springs are little room,
   About the woodlands I will go
   To see the cherry hung with snow.

The poem reproduces the logical form of most *carpe-diem* poems. The first stanza is a description of nature at the present time ('now', 1); typically, it is springtime and the subject of interest is a flower — in this subgenre always a reminder of transience.[25] Since Horace was a favourite of his, Housman may well have been following the Latin poet's procedure of opening with an *ekphrasis* of the season that leads to a meditation on change and then to an exhortation to action. The 'now' (5) that introduces the meditation of the second stanza has both logical and temporal force, as the speaker contrasts linear human life with the cyclical return of spring by means of a deceptively toneless calculation. The third stanza summarises the results of this observation ('since', 9) and draws the conclusion: 'About the woodlands I will go / To see the cherry hung with snow.' The verb 'will' (11) is not a simple future but expresses resolve and corresponds to the imperatives often present in other *carpe-diem* poems when the speaker is addressing someone else. It is precisely the recognition of our finite condition that prompts the urge to enjoy what the present offers, here reduced, however, to a Romantic appreciation of nature. In this otherwise very Horatian poem that emphasises seasonal change, the final word 'snow' (12) cannot help but be a reminder that winter (and by extension, death) is sure to come.

We shall conclude this survey with two twentieth-century examples. The first is John Crowe Ransom's 'Blue Girls'.

   Twirling your blue skirts, travelling the sward
   Under the towers of your seminary,
   Go listen to your teachers old and contrary
   Without believing a word.

5 Tie the white fillets then about your hair

And think no more of what will come to pass
Than bluebirds that go walking on the grass
And chattering on the air.

Practise your beauty, blue girls, before it fail;
10 And I will cry with my loud lips and publish
Beauty which all our power shall never establish,
It is so frail.

For I could tell you a story which is true;
I know a woman with a terrible tongue,
15 Blear eyes fallen from blue,
All her perfections tarnished — yet it is not long
Since she was lovelier than any of you.

The 'teachers old and contrary' are like the 'stern old men' (*senum severiorum*) in Catullus 5, who would inhibit the enjoyment of youth. Here 'think no more of what will come to pass' corresponds to *spem longam reseces* at Horace, *Odes* 1.11.7, and enjoins devotion to the present moment, vividly symbolised by the carefree bluebirds. By urging the girls to 'practise' their beauty, the speaker neatly appropriates a word that would more fittingly apply to their lessons. The rhyme of 'fail' (9) and 'frail' (12), along with the abrupt ending of line 12, 'It is so frail', reinforces the sense of urgency against the ravages of time.[26] The last stanza substantiates his advice with an example *a fortiori*. The image of the old crone who was once lovelier than any of the girls, however, adds a sardonic tone not encountered in any of the previous examples by suggesting that these girls in their blue school uniforms face similar disillusionment when their beauty is gone.

The final example is an early poem of Adrienne Rich's, 'Versailles: Petit Trianon'.

Merely the landscape of a vanished whim,
An artifice that lasts beyond the wish:
The grotto by the pond, the gulping fish
That round and round pretended islands swim,
5 The creamery abandoned to its doves,
The empty shrine the guidebooks say is love's.

What wind can bleaken this, what weather chasten

Those balustrades of stone, that sky stone-pale?
A fountain triton idly soaks his tail
10 In the last puddle of a drying basin;
A leisure that no human will can hasten
Drips from the hollow of his lifted shell.

When we were younger gardens were for games,
But now across the sungilt lawn of kings
15 We drift, consulting catalogues for names
Of postured gods: the cry of closing rings
For us and for the couples in the wood
And all good children who are all too good.

O children, next year, children, you will play
20 With only half your hearts; be wild today.
And lovers, take one long and fast embrace
Before the sun that tarnished queens goes down,
And evening finds you in a restless town
Where each has back his old restricted face.

The speaker begins in the Horatian manner with an *ekphrasis*. The first two stanzas describe the bleak artificiality of the landscape around the Petit Trianon, the chateau and park that was a favourite haunt of Marie Antoinette — whose own fate lends urgency to the poem's *carpe-diem* argument. The third stanza reflects on the scene by recalling the past, when 'gardens were for games' (13), and contrasts it ('But now', 14) with the aimlessness ('we drift', 15) and second-hand experience ('consulting catalogues', 15) of the sightseers. Suddenly, in mid-line, like the appearance of Death in Horace's poems, 'the cry of closing rings' (16). The final stanza contains the conventional *carpe-diem* injunction. The children are urged to 'be wild today' (20), since within a year they will lose their present enthusiasm; the lovers are to 'take one long and fast embrace' (21). The poem closes with the analogy of the setting sun and with euphemisms for the old age and death ('tarnished', 22; 'evening', 23; 'old', 24) that await the children and the lovers.[27] The desolate grounds of the pleasure palace that once delighted their 'tarnished queen' (22) fittingly symbolise the loss of life's vitality, and provide the warning (cf. *monet* at Horace, *Odes* 4.7.7) intrinsic to the subgenre.

Notes

1. N. Frye, S. Baker and G. Perkins (eds), *The Harper handbook to literature* (Harper and Row, New York, 1985), p. 89.

2. The 'eat, drink, and be merry' theme commonly associated with *carpe-diem* poetry is much older than Homer. It is already fully developed in the Egyptian 'Song of the Harper', which dates from the Middle Kingdom, perhaps as early as 1800 BC; see J.B. Pritchard, *Ancient Near Eastern texts* (Princeton University Press, Princeton, 1969), p. 467. There is also the famous *carpe-diem* speech of Siduri, the ale-wife, to Gilgamesh, when he goes in quest of immortality (see Pritchard, *Ancient Near Eastern texts*, p. 90).

3. An argument *a fortiori* is a frequent feature of consolatory poetry. See p. 115, Note 22.

4. Robert Frost observes in 'Carpe Diem': 'The age-long theme is Age's. / 'Twas Age imposed on poems / Their gather-roses burden'. In Horace, *Odes* 1.9, for example, the speaker addresses a young man (*puer*) and advises him to enjoy his youth while he can.

5. For a discussion and many examples, see H. Fränkel, 'Man's "Ephemeros" nature according to Pindar and others', *Transactions of the American Philological Association*, vol. 77 (1946), pp. 131–45. In *Poetics* 5 Aristotle observes that tragedy endeavours as much as possible to keep the action within 'a single circuit of the sun' (1449b13).

6. Three of the four propositions appear in stanza 63 of FitzGerald's *Rubáiyát of Omar Khayyám* (the numbers refer to the theses):

O threats of Hell and Hopes of Paradise!   (III)
One thing at least is certain — *This* Life flies;   (IV)
    One thing is certain and the rest is Lies —
The Flower that once has blown forever dies.   (I)

7. It is over this premiss that the basic *carpe-diem* philosophy is inimical to Christianity, where everything of this world must be directed to the afterlife. Cf. 1 Corinthians 15.32: 'If the dead are not raised, "Let us eat and drink, for tomorrow we die."' Cf. Mark 12.19 and Wisdom of Solomon 2.1–9; the latter is a full exposition of the topic.

8. This is a frequent motif in medieval poetry, as in the Goliardic song quoted on p. 129 and in François Villon's 'Mais Ou Sont les Neiges d'Antan?'

9. At Petronius, *Satyricon* 34.8 a slave displays a silver skeleton to the guests and the host recites the following couplet: *Sic erimus cuncti, postquam nos auferet Orcus. / Ergo vivamus, dum licet esse bene.* 'Thus shall we all be, once Death has taken us off. / Therefore let us live, while we can live well.' For another example, cf. Byron's 'Lines Inscribed upon a Cup Formed From a Skull', and below, Note 17.

10. R.G.M. Nisbet and M. Hubbard, *A commentary on Horace: Odes Book I* (Oxford University Press, Oxford, 1970), p. 140, also see a contrast here 'between the long-drawn-out conflicts of nature and the brevity of human life and happiness'.

11. Cf. the priamel in stanza 13 of FitzGerald's *Rubáiyát*, which also counsels against formulating long-range hopes:

> Some for the Glories of This World; and some
> Sigh for the Prophet's Paradise to come;
> Ah, take the Cash, and let the Credit go,
> Nor heed the rumble of a distant Drum!

12. Many of Horace's *carpe-diem* poems begin with an *ekphrasis*. A good example is *Odes* 1.9: 'See how Mt Soracte stands shining with deep snow.' Here in *Odes* 1.4 the poet depicts the coming of spring by the technique of 'the signs of', which we shall also encounter in the hymn to Venus that opens Lucretius' *De Rerum Natura* (see p. 150). The topic also opens Chaucer's *Canterbury tales* and (ironically) T.S. Eliot's 'The Waste Land'; it is also implicit in William Carlos Williams's 'Landscape with the Fall of Icarus' (see p. 77).

13. Nisbet and Hubbard, *A Commentary on Horace*, p. 65, show that springtime was traditionally associated with an increase of lightning.

14. The following temporal adverbs sketch the movement of the poem from past to present to future: 'no longer' (*neque iam*, 3), 'already' (*iam*, 5), 'while' (*dum*, 7), 'now' (*nunc*, 9), 'now' (*nunc*, 11), 'soon' (*iam*, 16), 'as soon as' (*simul*, 17), 'now' (*nunc*, 20) and 'soon' (*mox*, 20).

15. *Odes* 4.7 ('*Diffugere nives*'), one of Horace's best-known poems whose imitators include Samuel Johnson and A.E. Housman, shares a number of similarities with 1.4 (including an opening *descriptio* of the coming of spring) and incorporates most of the *carpe-diem* themes and vocabulary found in Horace.

16. See R. Woolf, *The English religious lyric in the Middle Ages* (Oxford University Press, Oxford, 1968), pp. 69–71, from whom the following example is quoted.

17. This form of empirical proof is reminiscent of Epicureanism, which based its moral principles on the observation of nature, and espoused living for pleasure (a very different sort of pleasure, to be sure) in the present, since death meant the total dissolution of the individual. The literary procedure, however, consists of an *ekphrasis* followed by a meditation. The subject need not always be nature: an epigram (*Anth. Pal.* 11.38) attributed to King Polemon (fl. c. 30 BC), which meditates on a relief sculpture depicting a jar, a loaf, a crown of fresh leaves and a skull, concludes: 'Drink,' says the relief, 'and eat, and crown yourself / with flowers; like this we suddenly become.' This example is a precursor of emblem poetry, a subgenre popular in the late sixteenth and seventeenth century. See M. Donker and G.M. Muldrow, *Dictionary of literary-rhetorical conventions of the English Renaissance* (Greenwood Press, Westport, CT, 1982), pp. 86–9.

18. Ronsard ends another famous *carpe-diem* poem 'Quand Vous Serez Bien Vieille' with the line 'Cueillez des aujourd'hui les roses de la vie'. For a survey of the '*carpe-rosam*' motif in sixteenth-century French poetry, see H. Weber, *La création poétique au XVIᵉ siècle en France* (Nizet, Paris, 1956), pp. 333–56.

19. Cf. *dum licet* at 2.11.16 and 4.12.26; *dum potes* at 3.17.13; and *dum*

. . . *patiuntur* at 2.3.15–16, all *carpe-diem* passages.

20. Cf. the seductive *carpe-diem* argument of Milton's Comus (736–54).

21. For an analysis of its logical structure, see J.V. Cunningham, 'Logic and lyric: Marvell, Dunbar, and Nashe' in *The collected essays of J.V. Cunningham* (Swallow, Chicago, 1976), pp. 162–72.

22. For the Horatian 'while we may' motif, see above, Note 19 and *iuvenes dum sumus* in the Goliardic example quoted on p. 129. Here again Marvell takes a bare motif and gives it an intense life.

23. For Marvell's characteristic use of *genera mixta*, see R.L. Colie, *My Ecchoing Song: Andrew Marvell's poetry of criticism* (Princeton University Press, Princeton, 1970), especially Chapters 4 and 5.

24. One example is 'Chant d'Automne'. 'Remords Posthume' is essentially an elaboration of lines 21–32 of the minor premiss in Marvell's poem: it has a structure similar to Ronsard's sonnet 'Quand Vous Serez Bien Vieille' — if, that is, one deleted the last two lines of exhortation from Ronsard's poem. For its relationship to the sixteenth and seventeenth century *carpe-diem* tradition, see C. Pichois (ed.), *Baudelaire, oeuvres complètes* (Gallimard, Paris, 1975), p. 895.

25. Here the mention of Eastertide gives the topic an ironic twist by recalling the Resurrection. Cf. Housman's 'The Lent Lily', where the speaker urges gathering the Lenten lily that 'dies on Easter day'.

26. Cf. the same rhymes in Thomas Carew's *carpe-diem* poem 'To A.L. Perswasions to Love': 'For that lovely face will fail, / Beauty's sweet, but beauty's frail.'

27. Cf. 'tarnished' in line 16 of Ransom's 'Blue Girls'. The last two lines recall the closing lines of A.E. Housman's *carpe-diem* poem, 'If Truth in Hearts That Perish': 'Ere to a town you journey / Where friends are ill to find'.

6

Forms of Persuasion in Hymns

In Book 10 of the *Republic* Socrates is willing to admit only two
genres of poetry into the state: 'hymns to the gods and encomia to
good men' (607A). In *Poetics* 4 Aristotle distinguishes as serious
poets those who write hymns and encomia. These two genres
constitute an important part of the poetic tradition, and we shall
devote the last two chapters to them. In this chapter we shall
analyse the formal features of hymns and prayers and examine
how they often function in longer works.

There are two major types of Greek hymns: rhapsodic and
cultic.[1] Because of their greater versatility and number, we shall
consider only the second type here. Whereas rhapsodic hymns
maintain a tone of impersonality, cultic hymns portray the
expressions of an individual worshipper: they address the god in
the second person and their tone is more private. They contain no
lengthy narratives and are composed in a variety of metres. When
cultic hymns are brief and the petition predominates, they
become indistinguishable from prayers.[2]

The prayer of Chryses at the beginning of the *Iliad* provides a
brief model for the form and style of hymns. After Agamemnon
refuses his request to return his daughter, the priest prays to
Apollo (1.37–42):

℣

'κλῦθί μευ, ἀργυρότοξ᾽, ὃς Χρύσην ἀμφιβέβηκας
Κίλλαν τε ζαθέην Τενέδοιό τε ἶ φι ἀνάσσεις,
Σμινθεῦ, εἴ ποτέ τοι χαρίεντ᾽ ἐπὶ νηὸν ἔρεψα,
40 ἢ εἰ δή ποτέ τοι κατὰ πίονα μηρί᾽ ἔκηα
ταύρων ἠδ᾽ αἰγῶν, τόδε μοι κρήηνον ἐέλδωρ·
τείσειαν Δαναοὶ ἐμὰ δάκρυα σοῖσι βέλεσσιν.'

Hear me, wielder of the silver bow, who rule over Chryse
and holy Cilla, and reign mightily over Tenedos,
Smintheus, — if ever I built a shrine that pleased you,
40 or if ever I burned fat thigh-pieces for you
of bulls and goats, fulfil this wish for me:
may the Greeks pay for my tears with your arrows.

This prayer has two major parts: an invocation and a petition.
Everything before the colon in line 41 constitutes the invocation;
line 42 is the petition. The opening imperative 'hear me' seeks the
god's attention.[3] Everything that follows is part of an argument
calculated to gain the god's goodwill so that he will grant the
request. The first word after 'hear me' is a title (epithet) of the
god, 'wielder of the silver bow', in Greek a single word,
ἀργυρότοξ'. Epithets are very important in a polytheistic system,
for individual gods have many functions, and the worshipper
must be careful to invoke the proper power of the god. Apollo, for
instance, to whom Chryses is praying, is also a god of prophecy
and medicine. By invoking Apollo as 'wielder of the silver bow',
he is singling out that attribute which he intends to exploit in the
petition, when he asks him to use his arrows of plague against the
Greeks.

Chryses continues the invocation with a relative clause, 'who
rule . . .' Because it allows the poet to add information about the
god without quitting his direct address, the relative clause is a
very common feature of hymnal style. In rhapsodic hymns it
regularly introduces the narrative of the god's deeds, while in
cultic hymns it describes the attributes and powers of the god.
Here it lists the god's abodes, three cultic centres.[4] After this
careful definition of the god's power and location, Chryses finally
gives Apollo's cultic name, Smintheus (Sminthian Apollo),[5] in
prominent position at the beginning of the line. This is a climactic
moment of the invocation, for calling on the god by name is a
serious matter.[6] Now Chryses turns to his personal relationship
with the god. When a worshipper says 'if ever' I served you in
some way, he is not calling his past into question, but indirectly
affirming his devotion to the god. Because the answer to the 'if
ever' proposition must be 'yes you did', then the response to the
request (Chryses hopes) should be positive also. 'If ever I . . .
then you' is a polite way of saying, 'Since I . . . then you'.

This recollection of past co-operation between the god and
worshipper is so common that it has a technical name: *hypomnesis*

(Greek for 'reminder'). By reminding the god of cordial past relations, the hymnist hopes that the god will continue to favour him, particularly in a time of distress. Chryses has very carefully chosen the word 'pleased' (χαρίεντ, 39). Forms of the word *charis* (χάρις), whose range of meanings includes beauty, joy, grace and favour, abound in hymns and point to the relationship the worshipper tries to establish with the god: one of pleasure and goodwill.[7] After all this careful preparation, the request comes simply and directly: 'fulfil this wish for me' (41). It achieves its desired effect: Homer tells us in the following lines that Apollo heard the prayer and came down from Olympus with his arrows rattling in his quiver. Finally, several stylistic features of Chryses' invocation belong to the formal tradition of Greek hymnody: direct addresses, relative clauses ('who rule'), anaphora ('if ever . . . if ever'), and amplification by means of lists ('Chryse . . . Cilla . . . Tenedos') and doublets ('bulls and goats').

Catullus' hymn to Diana (*Carm.* 34) provides a good Latin model.

> Dianae sumus in fide
> puellae et pueri integri:
> Dianam pueri integri
>   puellaeque canamus.
>
> 5 O Latonia, maximi
> magna progenies Iovis,
> quam mater prope Deliam
>   deposivit olivam,
>
> montium domina ut fores
> 10 silvarumque virentium
> saltuumque reconditorum
>   amniumque sonantum.
>
> tu Lucina dolentibus
> Iuno dicta puerperis,
> 15 tu potens Trivia et notho es
>   dicta lumine Luna.
>
> tu cursu, dea, menstruo
> metiens iter annuum

rustica agricolae bonis
20   tecta frugibus exples.

sis quocumque tibi placet
sancta nomine, Romulique,
antique ut solita es, bona
        sospites ope gentem.

Diana is the patroness for us
unmarried girls and boys:
of Diana, unmarried boys
    and girls, let us sing.

 5 Daughter of Latona and mighty
offspring of greatest Jove,
whom your mother bore
    by the Delian olive tree

to become mistress of the mountains
10 and green forests
and remote glens
    and resounding streams,

you are called Juno Lucina
by women in painful labour,
15 you are called powerful Trivia
    and Luna of the borrowed light.

And, goddess, as you measure the year's
journey with your monthly course,
you fill the farmer's country home
20   with good harvests.

Be hallowed by whatever name
you please, and, as you were wont
from of old, safeguard the Roman race
    with your generous aid.

Since this little hymn is particularly artful in disposing a wealth of hymnal motifs, we shall examine it in some detail. The first and last words of the opening stanza (*Dianae . . . canamus*) state the subject of the hymn and the chorus' intention to sing her praises.[8]

The hymn proper begins with an invocation: *O Latonia*, for which an imperative such as 'hear us' must be supplied. The burden of this stanza is the goddess's genealogy and birth, frequent topics of hymns. The epithets 'mighty' and 'greatest' amplify the importance of Diana and her father Jupiter, while the interlocking word order, *maximi magna progenies Iovis*, neatly magnifies the greatness of the parent and offspring. Her mother (Latona) and Delos, her birthplace and most important cult centre, are mentioned in a relative clause (*quam*, 'whom', 7), one of the most common means in hymns for adding information.

The next stanza surveys the haunts (*sedes*) over which she exercises her authority (*domina*, 10): mountains, forests, glens and streams, for she is first of all a goddess of the wilds. In the following stanza Catullus portrays her powers, and to do so he employs another standard hymnal device, anaphora. The two successive *tu*'s (13, 15) give three of her realms of influence and the cultic names associated with them: she is goddess of childbirth (Juno Lucina), goddess of crossroads (Trivia) and goddess of the moon (Luna). The fourth stanza, which continues the anaphora (*tu*, 17), elaborates her role as moon goddess by which she has control over seasonal harvests. Whereas the naming of the god was relatively straightforward in Chryses' prayer, here it is much more complicated, since Catullus is invoking several aspects of the goddess's power. Although he has been very careful not to omit any important one, as he completes the topic in the last stanza, he adds the cautious proviso: 'Be hallowed under whatever name you please.'[9] It is very important for the hymnist not to offend the god by neglecting any of his powers or names.

Before making his request, however, Catullus adds a very brief *hypomnesis*, 'as you were wont from of old', which neatly implies that Diana has been favourable for so long a time that she has become accustomed (*solita*, 23) to it. After all this preparation, the hymn ends with a simple, but powerful request: 'safeguard the Roman race with your generous aid'. Although the request applies to all of the powers mentioned in the hymn, the formal structure helps determine on which ones the emphasis falls. In portraying Diana as huntress, Catullus merely gave her haunts (9–12): clearly this is the least important power envisioned in the request. Of her powers mentioned in the three sentences begining with *tu* (13–20), the first two consist of two lines and involve proper naming. The last, her role in providing a harvest, consists

146

of an entire stanza and ends with the suggestive words, 'you fill the farmer's country home' (19–20). Since this is the last-mentioned power, since it is longer than the others, and since it mentions her bountiful gifts (*exples*, 29) and contains the word *bonis* (19) that is echoed in the request (*bona*, 23), one may assume that Catullus has it especially in mind when he asks for her aid for the Roman people.[10]

From these two examples, we can see that Graeco-Roman hymns consist of two principal parts: the invocation and the request. The purpose of the invocation is to dispose the god favourably toward the worshipper's request — in short, to secure his *charis* ('favour', 'grace'). For that reason, praise is its dominant mode, as the hymnist mentions the god's powers, *sedes*, genealogy, and amplifies them by means of superlatives, lists and inclusive doublets. In addition, the hymnist is free to expand any portion by explanations, narratives or descriptions. The style of the invocation is characterised by relative clauses, repeated addresses and additive phrasing.[11] Of course, no one hymn includes all of these elements (indeed, not even a request is necessary in hymns of praise); the following outline lists the principal topics found throughout Graeco-Roman hymns.

(1) Invocation
   (a) basic topics
      (i) name(s) (often an apostrophe)
      (ii) attributes (epithets and titles)
      (iii) genealogy (birth)
      (iv) *sedes* (abode, haunts, places of worship)
      (v) powers (over areas, actions, individuals)
      (vi) deeds

   (b) expansions
      (i) relative clauses ('you who . . .')
      (ii) repeated addresses ('you . . . you')
      (iii) explanations ('for', 'because')[12]
      (iv) *hypomneseis* ('reminders' of past interactions with the god)
      (v) *ekphraseis* (of the god, his haunts, actions, etc.)
      (vi) narratives
      (vii) attendant deities
      (viii) amplification (superlatives, impressive lists, inclusive doublets, additive phrasing, etc.)

Hymns

(2) Request (imperative)
  (a) general summons ('hear me', 'come')
  (b) specific petitions ('perform such-and-such for me')

In a given hymn any of the above elements may predominate. In the following example by Sappho, the *hypomnesis* receives particular emphasis.

ποικιλόθρον' ἀθανάτ' Ἀφρόδιτα,
παῖ Δίος δολόπλοκε, λίσσομαί σε,
μή μ' ἄσαισι μηδ' ὀνίαισι δάμνα,
πότνια, θῦμον,

5 ἀλλὰ τυίδ' ἔλθ', αἴ ποτα κἀτέρωτα
τὰς ἔμας αὔδας ἀίοισα πήλοι
ἔκλυες, πάτρος δὲ δόμον λίποισα
χρύσιον ἦλθες

ἄρμ' ὑπασδεύξαισα· κάλοι δέ σ' ἄγον
10 ὤκεες στροῦθοι περὶ γᾶς μελαίνας
πύκνα δίννεντες πτέρ' ἀπ' ὠράνωἴθε-
ρος διὰ μέσσω,

αἶψα δ' ἐξίκοντο· σὺ δ', ὦ μάκαιρα,
μειδιαίσαισ' ἀθανάτῳ προσώπῳ
15 ἤρε' ὄττι δηὖτε πέπονθα κὤττι
δηὖτε κάλημμι,

κὤττι μοι μάλιστα θέλω γένεσθαι
μαινόλᾳ θύμῳ· τίνα δηὖτε πείθω
ἄψ σ' ἄγην ἐς Fὰν φιλότατα; τίς σ', ὦ
20 Ψάπφ', ἀδικήει;

καὶ γὰρ αἰ φεύγει, ταχέως διώξει·
αἰ δὲ δῶρα μὴ δέκετ', ἀλλὰ δώσει·
αἰ δὲ μὴ φίλει, ταχέως φιλήσει
κωὔκ ἐθέλοισα.

25 ἔλθε μοι καὶ νῦν, χαλέπαν δὲ λῦσον
ἐκ μερίμναν, ὄσσα δέ μοι τέλεσσαι
θῦμος ἰμέρρει, τέλεσον· σὺ δ' αὔτα
σύμμαχος ἔσσο.

Immortal Aphrodite of the ornate throne,
wile-weaving daughter of Zeus, I beg you,
do not overwhelm my heart, mistress,
with pain or anguish,

5 but come here, if ever before
you heard my cries from afar, and,
heeding them, you left your father's
golden house and came

on your yoked chariot; beautiful swift sparrows,
10 rapidly flapping their wings, carried you
over the black earth down from heaven
through the middle of the air,

and quickly arrived. And you, blessed one,
with a smile on your immortal face,
15 asked what was wrong this time and why
this time I called,

and what my insane heart most desired
for me to have: 'Whom this time am I to
persuade to take you back as a friend? Who
20 is cheating you, Sappho?

Tell me, for if she flees, she will soon pursue;
and if she refuses gifts, she will soon be the one to give;
if she does not love, she will soon be in love,
even if she does not want to.'

25 Come to me now again, free me from my
bitter cares; bring about all that my heart
desires to happen, and you yourself
be my ally.

This poem contains most of the elements of a cultic hymn. Of the epithets that appear in the brief invocation, the last, 'wile-weaving' (2), is the most important, for it is to aid her in erotic machinations that Sappho has summoned the goddess. The request that immediately follows is cast in the negative: 'do not overwhelm my heart' (3–4), and is purposefully vague, for the *hypomnesis* will clarify more precisely the nature of Sappho's final

149

request. As in the case of Chryses' prayer, it is introduced by the formula, 'if ever . . .' (5), but here it is expanded to such an extent that it occupies five of the poem's seven stanzas. After a charming *ekphrasis* of her chariot drawn by sparrows (9–12),[13] Sappho dramatically re-enacts earlier meetings with the goddess, when she came 'with a smile' (14)[14] to aid her when she was heart-sick over a reluctant girlfriend. At this point, we can ascertain the purpose for summoning her. The final stanza, after all this preparation, contains the request: 'Come to me now again . . .' The logic is clear: 'if ever' (5) . . . 'now again' (25). By emphasising her suffering ('pain', 3; 'anguish', 3; 'bitter cares', 25–6), Sappho gives urgency to her request, while the delightful portrayal of their past relationship defines the manner in which the goddess should come 'now again' (25). The formal structure reinforces the argument. As we have seen, the hymn progresses from a rather vague, negative request: 'do not overwhelm my heart' (3–4), to a recital of previous interactions (5–24), and to a final positive request: 'be my ally' (27–8). The word ally (σύμμαχος, 28) well portrays the co-operation between man and god at which the hymnist aims.

Although a request does not necessarily come at the end of the hymn, this ability of hymnal form to lead up to a specific occasion (cf. νῦν, 25) allows hymns to function formally as parts of larger works.[15] Particularly common is the use of a hymn to introduce a poem or collection of poems. These hymns can be brief invocations (often of the Muse)[16] or long, elaborate ones:[17] for example, a hymn of 18 lines opens Aratus' *Phaenomena*, a Hellenistic treatise on astronomy of some 1,200 verses:[18] when the Roman poet Lucretius introduces his six books *On the nature of things* with a hymn, he is obliged to make it correspondingly grand, thereby producing one of the most impressive hymns in Latin literature.

> Aeneadum genetrix, hominum divumque voluptas,
> alma Venus, caeli subter labentia signa
> quae mare navigerum, quae terras frugiferentis
> concelebras, per te quoniam genus omne animantum
> 5 concipitur visitque exortum lumina solis:
> te, dea, te fugiunt venti, te nubila caeli
> adventumque tuum, tibi suavis daedala tellus
> summittit flores, tibi rident aequora ponti
> placatumque nitet diffuso lumine caelum.
> 10 nam simul ac species patefactast verna diei

et reserata viget genitabilis aura favoni,
aeriae primum volucres te, diva, tuumque
significant initum perculsae corda tua vi.
inde ferae pecudes persultant pabula laeta
15 et rapidos tranant amnis: ita capta lepore
te sequitur cupide quo quamque inducere pergis.
denique per maria ac montis fluviosque rapaces
frondiferasque domos avium camposque virentis
omnibus incutiens blandum per pectora amorem
20 efficis ut cupide generatim saecla propagent.
quae quoniam rerum naturam sola gubernas
nec sine te quicquam dias in luminis oras
exoritur neque fit laetum neque amabile quicquam,
te sociam studeo scribendis versibus esse
25 quos ego de rerum natura pangere conor
Memmiadae nostro, quem tu, dea, tempore in omni
omnibus ornatum voluisti excellere rebus.
quo magis aeternum da dictis, diva, leporem.
effice ut interea fera moenera militiai
30 per maria ac terras omnis sopita quiescant.
nam tu sola potes tranquilla pace iuvare
mortalis, quoniam belli fera moenera Mavors
armipotens regit, in gremium qui saepe tuum se
reicit aeterno devictus vulnere amoris,
35 atque ita suspiciens tereti cervice reposta
pascit amore avidos inhians in te, dea, visus,
eque tuo pendet resupini spiritus ore.
hunc tu, diva, tuo recubantem corpore sancto
circumfusa super, suavis ex ore loquelas
40 funde petens placidam Romanis, incluta, pacem.
nam neque nos agere hoc patriai tempore iniquo
possumus aequo animo nec Memmi clara propago
talibus in rebus communi desse saluti.

Mother of Aeneas' race, delight of men and gods,
nurturing Venus, who beneath the gliding stars of heaven
fill with your presence the ship-laden sea and the food-
    bearing
lands, since it is through you that every kind of creature
5 is conceived and brought forth to see the light of the sun.
When you approach, goddess, the winds flee you as do

the clouds of the sky, and at your bidding the earth in full
   variety
sprouts sweet flowers, the waters of the sea smile,
and the calmed sky shines and spreads its light.
10 For on the day that springtime shows its face
and the nourishing Zephyr blows strong and free,
the birds of the air are the first, goddess, to signal
your arrival, when your force strikes their hearts.
Then the herds leap wildly through the lush pastures
15 and swim across rushing streams: such is their eagerness,
once gripped by your charm, to follow you wherever you
   lead.
Finally, through the seas and mountains and rapid rivers,
through the woodland homes of birds and green fields,
you instill gentle love in all their hearts
20 and make each generation eagerly beget the next.
   And since you alone direct the course of nature,
and without you nothing comes forth into the bright
shores of light, nor is anything joyful or lovely,
I wish you to be my ally in composing these verses
25 which I am attempting to write about the nature of things
for my Memmius, whom you, goddess, have always
wished to excel with distinction in all things.
All the more reason, then, goddess, for you to bestow
   lasting charm
on my words. In the meantime, put to sleep the fierce
   works of war,
30 throughout the seas and all the lands, and make them rest;
since you alone can grant the joy of tranquil peace
on mortals; for strong-armed Mars, who controls
the fierce works of battle, often relaxes in your lap
when conquered by the ever-fresh wound of love:
35 in that position he throws back his smooth neck
and fills his eyes with love as he gazes open-mouthed at
   you,
goddess, and as he lies back, his breath hangs upon your
   mouth.
When he reclines, goddess, and you shed your blessed body
over him, pour upon him sweet coaxing from your lips
40 and request tranquil peace, famed goddess, for the
   Romans;
for neither can I have the peace of mind to write during a

time

of national crisis, nor can the illustrious scion of the Memmii

in such grave times withhold his aid to the common good.

As the opening epithets and appositives indicate, Venus is here invoked in her role as propagator (*genetrix*, 1), nourisher (*alma*, 2), and bringer of pleasure (*voluptas*, 1) to both men and gods. This last quality is particularly important to an Epicurean (see p. 39). The following relative clauses (*quae . . . quae*, 3) sketch her numinous presence in the sky, sea and land, while the explanatory clause (*quoniam*, 4) extends her powers over the birth of all living creatures. By means of a series of apostrophes (*te . . . te . . . te . . . tibi . . . tibi*, 6–9), he portrays the effects of her presence in the air, on land and on the sea, and yet another explanatory clause (*nam*, 10) specifies her powers over the animals in these three elements (10–20).[19]

The first 20 verses have praised the goddess in grand terms. At line 21 the poet begins the transition to the request with a combination of relative and explanatory clauses: *quae quoniam rerum naturam sola gubernas*, 'And since you alone guide the course of nature'. The words *rerum naturam* are given prominence in the sentence, since they constitute the subject of Lucretius' work. His request has two parts. The first asks for her aid in writing the poem (24–5):

te sociam studeo scribendis versibus esse
25 quos ego de rerum natura pangere conor

I wish you to be my ally in composing these verses
25 which I am attempting to write about the nature of things

The word 'ally' (*sociam*) is the Latin equivalent of 'ally' (σύμμαχος) at the end of Sappho's hymn to Aphrodite.[20] The emphatic combination of the second and first persons in the phrase *te sociam studeo*, held together with the word *sociam*, vividly portrays the synergistic effort of god and hymnist. By stating that Venus guides the course of nature (21), he disposes her well towards his subject matter (*de rerum natura*, 25 — which serves as the title of his work). In addition, having stated that she is responsible for everything that is 'joyful or lovely' (*laetum . . . amabile*, 23), he has prepared her for his additional petition to aid him in achieving an effective poetic style (28): 'bestow lasting charm (*leporem*) on my words.'

In the following verses Lucretius adds one final request, that Venus provide peace to the Romans, so that he will have the leisure to write — and Memmius to read — his work. And in order to strengthen his request for peace, the poet portrays her power over Mars, the god of war, in a lengthy *ekphrasis* (32–7) that probably derives from a Hellenistic statue or painting, for it depicts a typically Hellenistic erotic scene with figures caught in twisted positions. This description also acts as a *hypomnesis* (note *saepe*, 'often' at 33) to remind the goddess of her powers so that she will exercise them. The entire hymn is a rich, grand introduction to Lucretius' ambitious poetic treatise on nature, that announces his subject and style and expresses the hope that his poem will come into the world at a propitious moment.

Another common use of hymns is to introduce praise of mortals. Pindar, for example, often begins his victory odes with hymns.[21] These hymns regularly portray a divine background for the human action he intends to praise in the poem. A brief example is *Olympian* 12 to Ergoteles of Himera (in Sicily), who won the foot-race at Olympia in 472 BC. Civil strife in his native Cnossos had forced him to leave Crete, so he settled in Himera and subsequently won this Olympic victory for his new homeland.

Strophe

I beg you, saving Fortune, Daughter of Zeus
the Deliverer, to protect mighty Himera.
For you control the swift ships on the sea
and on land the quickly-changing wars
5 and deliberating assemblies. And meanwhile men's hopes
often rise and then tumble down, as they sail
the vain sea of lies.

Antistrophe

No mortal has yet found a trustworthy sign
from the gods about a future event,
for our minds are blind to what will come.
10 Many things happen to men unexpectedly
and bring joy's opposite, while some men,
after weathering stormy pains, in a minute exchange
their sorrows for deep good.

154

Epode

Son of Philanor, indeed, your own honour in foot-racing,
like a stay-at-home cock that fights in his own yard,
15 would have shed its leaves without fame,
    if political strife had not deprived you of your home,
    Cnossos.
But now in fact, with one crown at Olympia,
and two from Delphi and the Isthmus, Ergoteles,
you exalt the warm baths of the Nymphs where you live
    by your own fields.

In the first two lines, the familiar features of hymnal style —
address to the god, epithet, genealogy, request and the god's
name — all add important details. She is invoked as daughter of
Zeus the 'Deliverer' (1) and her epithet is 'saving' (2). Clearly the
poem will eventually be concerned with these two qualities of
fortune, while the locus of action will be the city of Himera. By
means of an explanatory clause ('For', 3), the poet describes
Fortune's powers in the rest of the strophe and the antistrophe.
The comprehensive doublets (sea–land, wars–counsels) sketch
her influence over the purposeful activities of man. The following
lines (5–12) describe how her power is experienced by mankind,
who cannot know how the future will turn out, but nevertheless
must act, and suffer unexpected reversals that bring now pain
and now joy. With the exception of the specific reference to the
city of Himera, this hymn has remained on the general level
('men's', 5; 'no mortal', 7; 'men', 10) and concerns regular
occurrences ('often', 6; 'many things', 10). As in the case of a
priamel, we await the specific instance for which this generalised
sketch serves as background, and, given the fact that it opened
with the theme of deliverance and closed with pain turning to
'deep good' (12), we might expect that the example will do the
same, and as in the case of a summary priamel provide a specific,
climactic instance.

After all this preparation, the epode opens directly with an
address to the specific man, Ergoteles, son of Philanor, whose
own career epitomises Fortune's actions, for after the pain of exile
he has been 'delivered', and experiences the great joy of an
Olympic victory. Fortune has turned out, in the end, to be
'saving' (2). By first portraying the generalised human condition
in the hymn — essentially the Greek tragic view of life — the

achievement of Ergoteles stands out as part of a greater order. This ode is a typical example of Pindar's ability to combine both of Aristotle's 'serious' forms: hymns to the gods and encomia to good men. In the next chapter we will examine another example, *Pythian* 1. Combinations of hymns and encomia continued to be written in Greek after Pindar's time. In fact Aristotle himself wrote an encomium in the Pindaric manner on the death of his friend Hermias of Atarneus, a philosopher and statesman who was treacherously captured by the king of Persia and killed when he refused to reveal Philip's plans for invading the east.

> Ἀρετὰ πολύμοχθε γένει βροτείῳ,
>   θήραμα κάλλιστον βίῳ,
>   σᾶς πέρι, παρθένε, μορφᾶς
>   καὶ θανεῖν ζηλωτὸς ἐν Ἑλλάδι πότμος
> 5 καὶ πόνους τλῆναι μαλεροὺς ἀκάμαντας·
>   τοῖον ἐπὶ φρένα βάλλεις
>   καρπὸν ἰσαθάνατον χρυσοῦ τε κρείσσω
>   καὶ γονέων μαλακαυγήτοιό θ᾽ ὕπνου.
>   σεῦ δ᾽ ἔνεκεν ⟨καὶ⟩ ὁ δῖος
> 10 Ἡρακλῆς Λήδας τε κοῦροι
>   πόλλ᾽ ἀνέτλασαν ἐν ἔργοις
>   σὰν †[. .]έποντες δύναμιν†·
>   σοῖς τε πόθοις Ἀχιλεὺς Αἴ-
>   ας τ᾽ Ἀΐδαο δόμους ἦλθον·
> 15 σᾶς δ᾽ ἔνεκεν φιλίου μορφᾶς Ἀταρνέος
>   ἔντροφος ἀελίου χήρωσεν αὐγάς.
>   τοιγὰρ ἀοίδιμος ἔργοις,
>   ἀθάνατόν τέ μιν αὐξήσουσι Μοῦσαι,
>   Μναμοσύνας θύγατρες, Δι-
> 20 ὸς ξενίου σέβας αὔξου-
>   σαι φιλίας τε γέρας βεβαίου.

Virtue, much-toiled-for by the human race,
   most noble object of life's quest,
for your beauty, virgin, even to die
   is an enviable fate in Greece
5 or to bear violent, unremitting labours,
   such is the reward you cast on the mind,
like one divine, greater than gold
   or ancestors, or soft-eyed sleep.

For your sake glorious Heracles
10 and the sons of Leda
endured much in their toils
for (?) your power.
And for desire of you Achilles
and Ajax went to Hades' abode.
15 And for the sake of your dear beauty, Atarneus'
nursling was deprived of the sun's rays.
And so, he is a subject of song because of his deeds,
and the Muses shall raise him to immortality,
those daughters of Memory, as they
20 exalt the majesty of Zeus, god of hospitality,
and his gift of steadfast friendship.

Once again, the hymn begins by sketching the power of the
goddess, here Areta ('Excellence', 'Virtue'), in broad terms
('human race', 1; 'life', 2), but instead of proceeding directly to
the addressee of the poem as Pindar did, Aristotle bridges the gap
between the divine and human realms by means of a priamel of
heroes, which includes Heracles, Castor and Pollux (sons of
Leda), Achilles, and Ajax (9–14), and culminates in the real
subject of the poem, Hermias (15), who now takes his place
among those heroes and is immortalised in song as they were.
The closing lines suggest that the qualities in Hermias which the
Muses will praise are those dear to Zeus — namely, the heroic
values of hospitality and friendship. They also offer the consolation of immortality for Hermias' virtue in the face of death. In
this brief poem Aristotle has managed to combine four of the
elements treated in this study: hymn, priamel, encomium and
consolation.

Hymns often occur in the choral portions of drama, where they
have a similar function of providing a background for the action
in the play.[22] A striking example is the 'Ode to Love' in
Sophocles' *Antigone* (781–801):

᾽Ερως ἀνίκατε μάχαν,
᾽Ερως, ὃς ἐν κτήνεσι πίπτεις,
ὃς ἐν μαλακαῖς παρειαῖς
νεάνιδος ἐννυχεύεις,
785 φοιτᾷς δ' ὑπερπόντιος ἔν τ'
ἀγρονόμοις αὐλαῖς·

καί σ' οὔτ' ἀθανάτων φύξιμος οὐδεὶς
οὔθ' ἀμερίων σέ γ' ἀνθρώ-
790 πων, ὁ δ' ἔχων μέμηνεν.

σὺ καὶ δικαίων ἀδίκους
φρένας παρασπᾷς ἐπὶ λώβᾳ·
σὺ καὶ τόδε νεῖκος ἀνδρῶν
ξύναιμον ἔχεις ταράξας·
795 νικᾷ δ' ἐναργὴς βλεφάρων
ἵμερος εὐλέκτρου
νύμφας, τῶν μεγάλων πάρεδρος ἐν ἀρχαῖς
800 θεσμῶν· ἄμαχος γὰρ ἐμπαί-
ζει θεὸς Ἀφροδίτα.

Love [Eros], invincible in a fight,
Love, you who plunder wealth,
you who keep watch on the
soft cheeks of a maiden;
785 you range over the sea
and in the abodes of the wild.
No immortal can escape you,
nor can any mortal who must
790 live day by day — and in your grip he becomes mad.

You turn even just men's thoughts
to ruinous injustice,
and you have also stirred up this
present family strife.
795 Overpowering is the desire that shines
from the eyes of an alluring
bride; that desire is enthroned in power
800 by the side of the great laws; for the unconquerable
goddess Aphrodite makes it her sport.

This hymn occurs just after Haemon, who is in love with
Antigone, has quarrelled with his father, who had condemned
Antigone to die for disobeying his edict. The chorus is disturbed
by the dissension and in this hymn meditates on the power for
good and ill of Love (Eros) and of his mother, Aphrodite. The
prominent epithet, 'invincible' (781) applied to Eros and echoed

158

at the end by 'unconquerable' (800) applied to Aphrodite, carries the leitmotif. In a series of relative clauses, the chorus portrays the extent of Love's power and influence. By mentioning that his *sedes* is on the soft cheek of a maiden (784), they may well be thinking of Antigone herself. The following lines of the strophe (785–90) sketch the extent of Love's powers by means of doublets (sea–land, wild–domestic, gods–men; cf. Lucretius' survey of Venus' territory), and conclude with his power over the individual, who is driven wild — no doubt an oblique reference to Haemon.

The strophe sketched the baneful power of love over men in general; the antistrophe uses anaphora (σὺ καί . . . σὺ καί, 791–3) to single out the power of love over justice, particularly as evidenced in the preceding scene: 'you have also stirred up this present family strife' (793–4). This is, of course, what is of most concern to the chorus, but instead of dwelling on it, the hymn concludes with a reiteration of the overpowering force of love. As in many hymnal passages in drama and encomia whose primary purpose is to praise the god (cf. Aristotle's hymn to Arete, discussed above), there is no request. This hymn, like many in drama, provides a context for the action on the stage. To Creon (and perhaps also to the Chorus), Haemon's love for Antigone and her love for her dead brother seem mad. The hymn is a meditation on a dominant theme in the play: immediately afterwards Antigone is led off to die, and Haemon will eventually commit suicide out of love for her.

Although there are many other examples of hymns that function as parts of larger works (see 'Additional Examples'), we shall turn to one that parodies hymnal language. Of all extant Latin authors, Horace excels in the number and variety of his hymns, and this witty 'Hymn to a Wine-bottle' (*Odes* 3.21) testifies to his mastery of the genre.

> O nata mecum consule Manlio,
> seu tu querellas sive geris iocos
>   seu rixam et insanos amores
>   seu facilem, pia testa, somnum,
>
> 5 quocumque lectum nomine Massicum
> servas, moveri digna bono die,
>   descende Corvino iubente
>   promere languidiora vina.

non ille, quamquam Socraticis madet
10 sermonibus, te negleget horridus:
    narratur et prisci Catonis
        saepe mero caluisse virtus.

    tu lene tormentum ingenio admoves
    plerumque duro; tu sapientium
15   curas et arcanum iocoso
        consilium retegis Lyaeo;

    tu spem reducis mentibus anxiis
    viresque et addis cornua pauperi,
        post te neque iratos trementi
20   regum apices neque militum arma.

    te Liber et si laeta aderit Venus
    segnesque nodum solvere Gratiae
        vivaeque producent lucernae,
            dum rediens fugat astra Phoebus.

O born with me when Manlius was consul,
    whether you inspire complaints or joking,
        quarrels or passionate love,
            or (o faithful wine-jar) gentle sleep,

5 by whatever name you preserve your choice
    Massic wine, that deserves to be opened on a happy day,
        come down at Corvinus' request
            to provide a mellower wine.

    Although he is steeped in Socratic
10 writings, he will not rudely pass you up;
        even old Cato is reported to have bolstered
            his courage on many occasions with wine.

    You apply gentle torment to a mind
    that is normally tough; you unlock
15   wise men's cares and their hidden thoughts
        with the jovial wine-god's help.

    You bring hope to worried minds,
    and strength and courage to the poor man,

160

who, under your spell, fears neither kings'
20   angry crowns nor soldiers' arms.

Bacchus and Venus, if she kindly attends,
and the Graces, who seldom separate from one another,
and the living lanterns will lead you on
until Phoebus returns to chase away the stars.

The ode begins with a hymnal apostrophe ('O', 1), but it is not until the fourth verse that the addressee turns out to be not a god but a wine-jar. The humour of the poem depends upon the double references of the hymnal conventions. For convenience, here is a list of the hymnal elements in the poem:[23]

apostrophe: *O* (1)
details of birth: *nata mecum* (1)
powers: *seu . . . sive . . . seu . . . seu* (2–4)[24]
epithet: *pia* (4)
name: *testa (4); quocumque . . . nomine* (5); *Massicum* (5)
request: *descende* (7)
explanatory clause: *Corvino iubente* (7)
hypomnesis: narratur et prisci Catonis . . . (11–12)
powers (in anaphora): *tu . . . tu . . . tu . . . te . . . te* (13–21)
attendant deities: *Liber, Venus, Gratiae* (21–2)

The conventional command to the god, 'come down' (*descende*, 7) [25] is cleverly applied to wine that was stored in the upper part of Roman houses, while the equally standard phrase 'by whatever name' (5) (cf. *quocumque . . . nomine* at Catullus 34.21–2) neatly turns the earnest worshipper's concern about choosing exactly the right epithet for his god to an epicure's fussiness about having the proper vintage. The container (*testa*, 4) and the contents are purposely being confused and the name of the vintage, Massic (6), is, like a cultic name, part of the deity's proper appellation. Since an explanation is often necessary to convince the god that a good reception awaits him, Horace neatly uses this motif to mention the name of his distinguished guest, M. Valerius Messalla Corvinus. This famous patron, whose literary circle included the elegiac poet Tibullus, is sure to appreciate Horace's *tour de force*. To provide further assurances, Horace adds a humorous *hypomnesis* to the effect that even Cato the Elder, that paragon of stern morals, enjoyed wine often (*saepe* occurs frequently in *hypomneseis*; cf. Lucretius' hymn to Venus, 33). After an extended doxology of the wine's powers (13–21), Horace lists its attendant deities, who, he hopes, will attend the party that will last until dawn. Both the epithet applied to Venus, 'kindly' (*laeta*, 21), and the very name of the Graces (Χάριτες in Greek) suggest the bond of *charis* that the hymnist typically seeks to establish with the god. The mood of this delightful parody perfectly fits the occasion of this party, where serious discussion (cf. 'Socratic writings', 9) will yield to relaxed enjoyment.

Before concluding this brief survey of literary hymnal form with two modern examples, we shall look at three formally similar hymns, one in Latin and two in English: Horace's 'Hymn to Fortune' (*Odes* 1.35), which in turn served as the model for hymns by Thomas Gray and William Wordsworth. Here is Horace's hymn.

O diva, gratum quae regis Antium,
praesens vel imo tollere de gradu
   mortale corpus vel superbos
     vertere funeribus triumphos,

5 te pauper ambit sollicita prece
ruris colonus, te dominam aequoris,
   quicumque Bithyna lacessit
     Carpathium pelagus carina,

te Dacus asper, te profugi Scythae
10 urbesque gentesque et Latium ferox
   regumque matres barbarorum et
     purpurei metuunt tyranni,

iniurioso ne pede proruas
stantem columnam, neu populus frequens
15   'ad arma' cessantis 'ad arma'
     concitet imperiumque frangat.

te semper anteit saeva Necessitas,
clavos trabalis et cuneos manu
   gestans aena, nec severus
20   uncus abest liquidumque plumbum.

te Spes et albo rara Fides colit

162

velata panno, nec comitem abnegat,
   utcumque mutata potentis
      veste domos inimica linquis.

25 at vulgus infidum et meretrix retro
   periura cedit, diffugiunt cadis
      cum faece siccatis amici,
         ferre iugum pariter dolosi.

   serves iturum Caesarem in ultimos
30 orbis Britannos et iuvenum recens
      examen, Eois timendum
         partibus Oceanoque rubro.

   eheu, cicatricum et sceleris pudet
   fratrumque. quid nos dura refugimus
35   aetas? quid intactum nefasti
         liquimus? unde manum iuventus

   metu deorum continuit? quibus
   pepercit aris? o utinam nova
      incude diffingas retusum in
40   Massagetas Arabasque ferrum!

O goddess, you who rule pleasant Antium,
   and come to raise up our mortal body from
      the lowest rank or to change glorious
         triumphs to funerals,

5 the impoverished peasant seeks your favour
   with anxious prayers, as does the sailor who challenges
      the Carpathian Sea in his Bithynian ship,
         since you are mistress of the sea;

   the aggressive Dacian, the retreating Scythians,
10 cities and nations and warlike Latium seek your favour,
      while mothers of foreign kings and tyrants
         dressed in purple live in fear

   that with a contemptuous kick you may topple
   the column of state and the thronging populace

15   will arouse the reluctant citizens 'to arms, to arms'
     and break their power.

Grim Necessity always precedes you,
carrying long spikes and wedges
   in her brazen hand, nor is she without
20   the stern clamp and molten lead.

Hope and uncommon Loyalty, with her hand wrapped
in white cloth, tend you and offer their companionship
   when you grow angry and leave houses
    of the powerful in mourning,

25 whereas the faithless crowd and the lying
   prostitute turn away and friends scatter
    once the wine runs out completely,
     too treacherous to share the yoke.

Safeguard Caesar when he campaigns against the Britons,
30 the furthest people on earth, and protect the fresh levy
   of young men off to daunt the eastern
    lands and the Red Sea.

Alas, how shameful are our scars and crimes
and our brothers' fates. What has our hardened
35   generation shunned? What evil have we
    left untouched? From what have our youth

drawn back their hands in fear of the gods? What altars
have they spared? O please, on a fresh anvil
   reforge our blunted steel for use
40   against the Massagetae and Arabs!

Although Fortuna is never called by name, any Roman would
have known it was she from the opening reference to Antium, on
the shore south of Rome, where her temple was. The elements of
cultic hymnal style are evident from the very beginning: the
apostrophe (*O*, 1), the honorific title (*diva*, 1), and the relative
clause (*quae*, 1) that locates her *sedes*, whose epithet 'pleasant'
(*gratum*, 1) is a synonym of the Greek *charis* and serves as a subtle
reminder to the goddess to be favourable. The word *praesens* (2)
designates her power as already immanent, obviating the need for

the conventional request to 'come'. The first power of the goddess is like that described in Pindar, *Olympian* 12: the ability to make sudden reversals in human affairs (2–4). Then a series of *te*'s surveys the scope of her influence over all conditions of men, over land and sea, wild and civilised peoples, women and men, and particularly those in power (5–16). We have noted before (see p. 147) the importance, in lists of the god's powers, of the last one mentioned, especially if it is dwelt upon. All of the fourth stanza is devoted to Fortune's power over political turmoil, and although it specifically concerns eastern tyrants (12), the words *populus* (14) and *imperium* (16) point to a larger context of politics and civil war that prepares us for the requests at the end.[26]

The next two stanzas (17–24) magnify Fortune by presenting impressive *ekphraseis* of her attendant goddesses: Necessity precedes, portrayed as a builder, whose tools symbolise the fixity of her stern work, while Hope and Fidelity ever attend her, even when she is at her harshest and the victim of her reversal has lost all his fair-weather friends. The first request comes in the eighth stanza (29–32): safeguard[27] Caesar and the armies that are setting out to fight in the north (Britain) and east (Arabia). Formally, the hymn could be considered complete at this point, but Horace adds two stanzas (33–40) that function as an explanation and *hypomnesis*, in which he reviews the horrors of the past half century of civil war that preceded the Pax Augusta. This review prepares for his final request: that Fortune will reforge the weapons the Romans have used against each other and turn them against foreign enemies. In other words, Horace reminds the goddess that the Romans have had enough tribulations and it is time for their fortune to change for the better, that the internecine violence and bloodshed that had almost destroyed the state (until Caesar Augustus took control) should now be directed against external enemies.

In the centuries during and after the breakdown of the Roman West, Christian hymns, in large part based upon psalms and meant to be sung by a congregation, effectively supplanted the literary hymn, first in medieval Latin and later in the vernacular languages.[28] In the eighteenth century, however, Thomas Gray, a classical scholar as well as a poet, returned to the Graeco-Roman tradition of the literary hymn with his 'Ode to Adversity', which, as Samuel Johnson pointed out, took its 'hint' from Horace's 'Hymn to Fortune'.

Daughter of Jove, relentless power,

Thou tamer of the human breast,
Whose iron scourge and torturing hour
The bad affright, afflict the best!
5 Bound in thy adamantine chain,
The proud are taught to taste of pain,
And purple tyrants vainly groan
With pangs unfelt before, unpitied and alone.

When first thy sire to send on earth
10 Virtue, his darling child, designed,
To thee he gave the heavenly birth,
And bade to form her infant mind.
Stern rugged nurse! thy rigid lore
With patience many a year she bore:
15 What sorrow was, thou bad'st her know,
And from her own she learned to melt at others' woe.

Scared at thy frown terrific, fly
Self-pleasing Folly's idle brood,
Wild Laughter, Noise, and thoughtless Joy,
20 And leave us leisure to be good.
Light they disperse, and with them go
The summer friend, the flattering foe;
By vain Prosperity received,
To her they vow their truth, and are again believed.

25 Wisdom, in sable garb arrayed,
Immersed in rapturous thought profound,
And Melancholy, silent maid
With leaden eye, that loves the ground,
Still on thy solemn steps attend:
30 Warm Charity, the general friend,
With Justice, to herself severe,
And Pity, dropping soft the sadly-pleasing tear.

Oh, gently on thy suppliant's head,
Dread Goddess, lay thy chastening hand!
35 Not in thy Gorgon terrors clad,
Nor circled with the vengeful band
(As by the impious thou art seen)
With thundering voice, and threatening mien,
With screaming Horror's funeral cry,

40 Despair, and fell Disease, and ghastly Poverty.

    Thy form benign, O Goddess, wear,
    Thy milder influence impart,
    Thy philosophic train be there
    To soften, not to wound, my heart,
45 The generous spark extinct revive,
    Teach me to love and to forgive,
    Exact my own defects to scan,
    What others are, to feel, and know myself a man.

This hymn[29] is perfectly regular in form. The first four lines contain the invocation, with the genealogy, epithets and relative clause that describes her powers ('whose . . .' 3–4). The next four lines give specific examples of Adversity's[30] power, and the phrase 'purple tyrants' (7) echoes Horace's *purpurei tyranni* (12). We noted how, in describing Fortune's powers, Horace ended with the one which had most bearing on the ultimate request, and Gray follows a similar procedure in the second stanza, where he tells how Adversity was the nurse for Virtue. The notion that virtue involves hardship is certainly a Classical one, beginning with Hesiod's *Works and Days* 289–91, but Gray ends the stanza with an unexpected twist, by portraying Virtue as sympathetic to others *because of* her own adversity: 'And from her own she learned to melt at others' woe' (16).[31] This attribute of Virtue is given special emphasis by its position in the hexameter at the end of the stanza, and it takes on even greater importance when the poet makes his request at the end of the poem.

The three following stanzas (17–32) magnify the goddess by listing her attendant deities (Wisdom, Melancholy, Charity, Justice and Pity) as well as those who flee her approach (Laughter, Noise and Joy) and run to Prosperity. In effect, he has amplified the few such references in Horace, and in a manner reminiscent of Milton's 'L'Allegro' and 'Il Penseroso', provides a full-scale list of personified abstractions. Once again, the emphasis falls on the deities mentioned last: we shall see that this arrangement is determined by the form and content of the request to come.

The last two stanzas contain the petitions. The prominent word 'gently' (33) insures that the goddess will appear in the proper aspect. The priamel that follows (35–41) lists the ways in which he does *not* wish her to come (as a Gorgon or Fury in the company of Horror, Despair, Disease or Poverty), in order to highlight the positive request in the last stanza: 'Thy form benign, O Goddess, wear' (41). His request for her 'philosophic train' (43) is far more specific than commentators have noticed, for the last three goddesses mentioned with Wisdom and Melancholy in stanza four (25–32) were:

> 30 Warm Charity, the general friend,
>   With Justice, to herself severe,
>   And Pity, dropping soft the sadly-pleasing tear.

The final three requests correspond exactly to the qualities of these three deities (46–8):

> Teach me to love and to forgive, [Charity]
> Exact my own defects to scan,   [Justice]
> What others are, to feel, and know myself a man.   [Pity]

Indeed, it is only with the gloss 'Exact my own defects to scan' (47) that the surprising attribute of Justice, 'to herself severe' (31), can be understood. The poet wishes, in short, to experience the right amount of adversity in order to recognise his own weakness as a man and thereby to have more generosity, love, forgiveness and sympathy for his fellow humans. Although the form is thoroughly Classical, the idea behind it, namely asking for suffering — even in a moderate amount — is a predominantly Christian–Humanist notion.[32]

Wordsworth's 'Ode to Duty' imitates Horace's and Gray's hymns: it even duplicates Gray's stanzaic form.

> Stern Daughter of the Voice of God!
> O Duty! if that name thou love
> Who art a light to guide, a rod
> To check the erring, and reprove;
> 5 Thou, who art victory and law
> When empty terrors overawe;
> From vain temptations dost set free;
> And calm'st the weary strife of frail humanity!
>
> There are who ask not if thine eye
> 10 Be on them; who, in love and truth,

Where no misgiving is, rely
Upon the genial sense of youth:
Glad Hearts! without reproach or blot;
Who do thy work, and know it not:
15 Oh! if through confidence misplaced
They fail, thy saving arms, dread Power! around them cast.

Serene will be our days and bright,
And happy will our nature be,
When love is an unerring light,
20 And joy its own security.
And they a blissful course may hold
Even now, who, not unwisely bold,
Live in the spirit of this creed;
Yet seek thy firm support, according to their need.

25 I, loving freedom, and untried;
No sport of every random gust,
Yet being to myself a guide,
Too blindly have reposed my trust:
And oft, when in my heart was heard
30 Thy timely mandate, I deferred
The task, in smoother walks to stray;
But thee I now would serve more strictly, if I may.

Through no disturbance of my soul,
Or strong compunction in me wrought,
35 I supplicate for thy control;
But in the quietness of thought:
Me this unchartered freedom tires;
I feel the weight of chance-desires:
My hopes no more must change their name,
40 I long for a repose that ever is the same.

Stern Lawgiver! yet thou dost wear
The Godhead's most benignant grace;
Nor know we anything so fair
As is the smile upon thy face:
45 Flowers laugh before thee on their beds
And fragrance in thy footing treads;
Thou dost preserve the stars from wrong;
And the most ancient heavens, through Thee are fresh and
strong.

To humbler functions, awful Power!
50 I call thee: I myself commend
Unto thy guidance from this hour;
Oh, let my weakness have an end!
Give unto me, made lowly wise,
The spirit of self-sacrifice;
55 The confidence of reason give;
And in the light of truth thy Bondman let me live!

There is a progression in these three hymns that exemplifies the
transition from Classical to Romantic. Horace's ode has an
entirely public function: the purpose behind his hymn to Fortune
is to request her favour on the Roman state, specifically on
Caesar Augustus and the armies. Gray, on the other hand, is
concerned entirely with himself. His request is for a greater
personal sympathy for others; of importance is the emphasis on
feeling: 'Thou tamer of the human breast' (2); 'my heart' (44); 'to
feel, and know myself a man' (48). There is no sense of a nation or
of any relationship more general than that between man and
man. Wordsworth's poem, however, has a tone that is even more
personal because he includes autobiographical details.

The opening shows a deft handling of traditional hymnal
elements. The initial epithet 'stern' (repeated at line 41) presents
a side of the goddess which the poet is careful to mollify before
making his request. The genealogy ('Daughter . . . of God') mixes
pagan with Christian elements that Gray avoided in his
'Daughter of Jove', but Wordsworth returns to a Graeco-Roman
context with the conventional proviso: 'if that name thou love'
(2). The two relative clauses ('who . . . who', 3–5) relate her
powers in guiding men. In the second stanza Wordsworth
switches from the powers of the goddess to the kinds of
worshippers who need her support. Ideally, with 'love' (10, 19) as
the sole guide, mankind would have no need of Duty, but since
man cannot perfectly live up to the 'spirit of this creed' (23), Duty
must be on hand to offer support. In the manner of a priamel,
these generalised examples lead up to the case of the poet himself,
introduced by the emphatic 'I' of the fourth stanza (25).[33] These
two stanzas, in which the poet demonstrates his need for her help
now that his 'freedom' (25, 37) has become too burdensome, are
remarkable for the confessional tone that makes this poem so
much more subjective than Gray's.

The following stanza (41–8) returns to the goddess for the final requests. Like Gray, Wordsworth defines the way in which he wishes Duty to come to him before offering his petitions. Her dread aspect quickly yields to a kindly one:

> Stern Lawgiver! yet thou dost wear
> The Godhead's most benignant grace;
> Nor know we anything so fair
> As is the smile upon thy face.

The words 'grace' and 'smile' are, as we have seen, standard terms in the worshipper's strategy to dispose the deity favourably. By portraying her powers over the greatest of natural phenomena ('Thou dost preserve the stars from wrong', 47), he can then appeal (*a fortiori*) for her aid in much less demanding tasks: 'To humbler functions, awful Power! /I call thee' (49–50). The requests of the final stanza, though less mechanically than those in Gray's poem, ask for gifts that have been defined as belonging to Duty's power in the body of the poem. In particular, 'guidance' (51) recalls 'guide' (3) and 'light' (56) echoes 'light' (3). The poem is remarkable in Wordsworth's collection both for its traditional formality and its gesture away from radical Romanticism toward Graeco-Roman, specifically Stoic, values.[34]

Although hymnal elements can be found in many twentieth-century poems,[35] the formal hymn has not been a popular poetic form in this century. There are, however, a number of poems entitled prayers that draw upon the Graeco-Roman tradition. We shall conclude with two examples bearing identical titles, 'A Prayer for my Son', by W.B. Yeats and Yvor Winters. Yeats's poem contains an unusual structural feature.

A Prayer for my Son

> Bid a strong ghost stand at the head
> That my Michael may sleep sound,
> Nor cry, nor turn in the bed
> Till his morning meal come round;
> 5 And may departing twilight keep
> All dread afar till morning's back,
> That his mother may not lack
> Her fill of sleep.

Bid the ghost have sword in fist:
10 Some there are, for I avow
Such devilish things exist,
Who have planned his murder, for they know
Of some most haughty deed or thought
That waits upon his future days,
15 And would through hatred of the bays
Bring that to nought.

Though You can fashion everything
From nothing every day, and teach
The morning stars to sing,
20 You have lacked articulate speech
To tell Your simplest want, and known,
Wailing upon a woman's knee,
All of that worst ignominy
Of flesh and bone;

25 And when through all the town there ran
The servants of Your enemy,
A woman and a man,
Unless the Holy Writings lie,
Hurried through the smooth and rough
30 And through the fertile and waste,
Protecting, till the danger past,
With human love.

The most obvious formal innovation in this poem is the reversed order of the request and the invocatory justification. Indeed, the reader does not know until the third stanza who is being addressed. The poem divides into halves: two stanzas devoted to requests and two to the *hypomnesis*. The first two stanzas, which open with the imperative 'bid' (1, 9), seek protection for the baby, but with different emphases. The first stanza concerns the infant's basic needs and sustenance; the second concerns vague threats to the child's future development of his potential greatness.

The third stanza begins with a brief aretalogy of Christ (who is never named in the poem). Like Wordsworth, who mentioned Duty's power over the stars and heavens before summoning her to 'humbler functions' (49), so Yeats surveys the vast power of the god ('Though You can fashion everything / From nothing every day, and teach / The stars to sing', 17–19) before concentrating on the details most relevant to his situation. The rest of the poem is a *hypomnesis* consisting of two parts that correspond to the two requests made earlier in the poem. The first part in the third stanza (20–4) refers to the Nativity and reminds Christ that he too was once an infant entirely dependent upon his mother. The second part, which occupies the final stanza, refers to the Flight into Egypt, when the child was protected from Herod, who wished to prevent him from fulfilling his destiny.[36] By thus reminding Christ of his own past, the poet wishes to gain his sympathy for his own requests. Particularly forceful is the final line, 'With human love' (32), which attempts to bind the god in common effort with the child's parents. This inversion of the usual order places greater emphasis on the *hypomnesis* and justification than on the actual requests, with the result that the last half of the poem is more memorable than the first: indeed, the requests at the beginning seemed dwarfed by the ending.

In contrast, the form of Winters's poem is regular.

A Prayer for my Son

> *'Tangled with earth all ways we move.'*
> — Janet Lewis

      Eternal Spirit, you
      Whose will maintains the world,
      Who thought and made it true;
      The honey-suckle curled
    5 Through the arbutus limb,
      The leaves that move in air,
      Are half akin to him
      Whose conscious moving stare
      Is drawn, yet stirs by will;
   10 Whose little fingers bend,
      Unbend, and then are still,
      While the mind seeks an end.
      At moments, like a vine,
      He clambers through small boughs;
   15 Then poised and half divine,
      He waits with lifted brows.
      To steep the mind in sense,

173

Yet never lose the aim,
Will make the world grow dense,
20 Yet by this way we came.
Earth and mind are not one,
But they are so entwined,
That this, my little son,
May yet one day go blind.
25 Eternal Spirit, you
Who guided Socrates,
Pity this small and new
Bright soul on hands and knees.

Winters's prayer opens with an invocation of an 'Eternal Spirit' and in two relative clauses supplies the deity's powers. It then closes with a second address to the god, a brief *hypomnesis*, which reminds him of another human he assisted ('you / who guided Socrates', 25–6), followed by the final request (27–8). The most striking feature is the long central portion of lines 4–24. Formally, it is also a *hypomnesis*, for it reminds the god of the child's need for his guidance and 'pity' (27). It also includes elements of *descriptio*, for the poet vividly describes the movements of the child crawling around outdoors, exploring his environment. The two relative clauses that give the god's powers are densely packed with terms and ideas that are repeated and exemplified in the long *hypomnesis*. The word 'will'(2), for example, is repeated at line 9, 'world' (2) at line 19, and 'thought' (3) is echoed by 'mind' at 12, 17 and 21. Like many of Winters's poems, this one concerns the relationship between the sensuous world or 'earth' (as mentioned in the epigraph and in line 21 and portrayed through the concrete details of the description) and the mind's ability to perceive (cf. 'conscious stare', 8) and understand it.[37] The *hypomnesis* ends by stating that if the proper balance between them is not maintained a metaphysical blindness can result (21–4): 'Earth and mind are not one, / But they are so entwined, / That this, my little son, / May yet one day go blind.' After this careful preparation and the reminder of previous help to Socrates (26), the request, although simple, has considerable intellectual and emotional force: 'Pity this small and new / Bright soul on hands and knees.' The position of the child even suggests that of a suppliant. Whereas Yeats's poem draws on Christian belief, Winters's poem belongs to a tradition of philosophical hymns that stretches back to Cleanthes' 'Hymn to Zeus'.

Notes

1. Rhapsodic hymns take their name from the 'rhapsodes', bards who recited Homeric epic poetry at festivals or gatherings. They are characterised by being in epic metre (dactylic hexameter), by addressing the god in the third person, and by using extensive narrative. Some of these hymns, called Homeric hymns, appear to have served as preludes to a recital of epic poetry: indeed, two (31 and 32) end with an announcement that the singer will proceed to sing the deeds of men and one (6) asks for help in winning the actual contest. Surviving examples are few: 33 Homeric hymns and a few later imitations by Callimachus and Theocritus. For a brief treatment of some formal features of Greek hymns and a bibliography, see W.H. Race, 'Aspects of rhetoric and form in Greek hymns', *Greek, Roman, and Byzantine Studies*, vol. 23 (1982), pp. 5–14. For an ancient discussion of cultic hymns with many sub-classifications, see the first treatise of Menander Rhetor in D.A. Russell and N. Wilson (eds), *Menander Rhetor* (Oxford University Press, Oxford, 1981), pp. 2–29.

2. In general, the intention of hymns is to praise, while that of prayers is to supplicate, but in practice the two intentions are frequently combined to such an extent that the distinction becomes academic. Thus, for example, Menander Rhetor, whose treatise contains the most important ancient discussion of hymns, makes no distinction between hymns and prayers. Indeed, he calls the prayer of Chryses (quoted below) a κλητικὸς ὕμνος, an 'invocatory hymn' (335.13).

3. The two words κλῦθί μευ, forcefully juxtapose the second person implicit in the imperative '(you) hear' and the first person 'me', thereby establishing a close I–Thou relationship with the god. The same conjunction occurs at the end of the invocation 'fulfil for me' (μοι κρήηνον, 41), and is present in the petition: '*your* arrows' and '*my* tears'. As a general rule in hymns, the speaker attempts to harmonise the god's power ('your arrows') with his own needs ('my tears'), a procedure known as 'binding' the god in Near Eastern hymnology.

4. The place which the god rules or frequents is often called his *sedes*, from the Latin for 'seat', 'abode'. Greek gods were worshipped in a variety of places and ways, and Chryses undoubtedly has connections with these three centres, all near his home in the eastern Aegean.

5. Greek gods were worshipped under various names, and it was very important for the worshipper to call the god by the proper name. Obviously Chryses worships him as the Sminthian. Often a hymnist will mention more than one name or will simply say 'by whatever name you wish to be called'. The *locus classicus* is the hymn to Zeus at Aeschylus, *Agamemnon* 160–2: 'Zeus, whoever he is, if he is pleased to be called by this name, then this is what I call him.' At Exodus 3.13 Moses asks specifically for God's name.

6. This is true as well in Judeo-Christian religion: cf. 'You shall not take the name of the Lord your God in vain' (Exodus 20.7) and the expression 'in the name of' throughout the New Testament.

7. For a brief treatment of *charis* in Greek hymns, see W.H. Race, 'Aspects of rhetoric and form in Greek hymns', pp. 8–10.

8. This opening statement of intention is similar to that of many Homeric Hymns (e.g. hymn 6: 'I shall sing of venerable Aphrodite . . .'). Since Diana is a virgin goddess and cares particularly for the young, she will be pleased by the fact that the choir is composed of unmarried girls and boys. From the very beginning Catullus is intent on establishing a relationship of *charis* with the goddess.

9. The word *placet* corresponds to the word *charis* in Greek hymns: see above, Note 7.

10. As a general rule, the last item in a list (especially if it is longer or given more impressive treatment) is the most important, even if it is not clearly marked as the climactic term in a priamel.

11. Many Graeco-Roman hymns have elaborate preparations before the request, giving rise to the stricture at Matthew 6.7: 'And in praying do not heap up empty phrases as the Gentiles do; for they think that they will be heard for their many words.' In contrast, the invocation of the 'Lord's Prayer' is very brief and only includes a title, a relative clause giving the *sedes*, and a reference to God's name: *Pater noster, qui es in caelis, sanctificetur nomen tuum.* The rest of the prayer consists of petitions. The opening title 'father' is especially important for establishing an intimate bond between the god and the worshipper.

12. Explanations are very frequent in hymns, usually introduced by γάρ in Greek and *nam, enim* or *quoniam* in Latin. They are part of the overall strategy of persuading the god to be well disposed.

13. For the association of sparrows with eroticism, see p. 113, Note 3. Sappho is particularly adept at *descriptiones*. Cf. *fr.* 2, also a hymn (or prayer) to Aphrodite, where the lovely description of the grove to which she summons the goddess provides an early example in lyric poetry of the topic of the *locus amoenus*: see p. 85, Note 49.

14. Aphrodite's smile may express indulgent mockery, but is an important reminder of the goddess's favour on past occasions.

15. In this respect, they are similar to priamels: the foil consists of the many possibilities inherent in the *hypomnesis* ('if ever') and the climactic term is *this* (cf. τόδε in line 41 of Chryses' prayer) *present* (cf. νῦν in line 25 of Sappho's prayer) occasion.

16. Cf. the three brief hymns that open Theognis' collection of poems or the hymn that opens Hesiod's *Works and days*.

17. The hymn to the Muses that opens Hesiod's *Theogony* is 115 lines long, more than a tenth of the entire work.

18. Aratus' hymn with translation can be found in the Loeb edition of A.W. and G.R. Mair, *Callimachus, hymns and epigrams, Lycophron, Aratus* (Heinemann, London, 1955), p. 206. Aratus' hymn combines a number of hymnal elements with a priamel in order to introduce the subject of the work and request the god's help in writing it: it was undoubtedly one of the models for Lucretius' hymn.

19. For the technique of suggesting something's power by portraying its effects on others, see p. 54, Note 15. This passage is also a fine example of the *topos* 'signs of spring' (see p. 140, Note 12) and of amplification by means of triplets (sky, land and sea) that sketch the whole universe, which we saw on Achilles' shield.

20. Aphrodite is the Greek counterpart of Venus. Although the two

poets address the same deity and use the same formal elements, the contrast between their poems' styles, intentions and content points up the flexibility of the hymnal genre to accommodate very different poetic intentions.

21. Odes that open with hymns include *Ol.* 4, 5, 8, 14; *Pyth.* 1, 8, 11; *Nem.* 7, 8, 11; and *Isth.* 7.

22. One of the most famous, the hymn to Zeus near the beginning of Aeschylus' *Agamemnon* (160–83), introduces a major theme of the trilogy, gaining knowledge through suffering. For a detailed treatment of this hymn, see P.M. Smith, *On the hymn to Zeus in Aeschylus' Agamemnon* (Scholars Press, Chico, California, 1980).

23. E. Norden, *Agnostos Theos* (1913; repr. Teubner, Stuttgart, 1974), pp. 143–63 was the first to analyse in detail the hymnal elements in this poem. For further religious overtones in the words *moveri* (6), *bono die* (6), *laeta* (21) and *producent* (23), see S. Commager, *The odes of Horace* (Indiana University Press, Bloomington, 1962), pp. 126–7 and G. Williams, *The Third Book of Horace's odes* (Oxford University Press, Oxford, 1969), pp. 116–17.

24. Divine powers and names are often sketched in disjunctive form.

25. Horace begins his hymn to Calliope (*Odes* 3.4) with *Descende caelo* ('Descend from the sky'). Cf. Milton's hymn to Urania at P.L. VII, 1: 'Descend from Heav'n . . .'

26. This stanza elaborates Fortuna's role as protector of the State. Fortune was requested to keep watch over Himera in Pindar's *Olympian* 12: in the Hellenistic period she was regularly associated with guardianship of States.

27. The word 'safeguard' (*serves*, 29) recalls Fortune's epithet 'saving' in Pindar's *Olympian* 12: the same word appears in the hymn to the wine-jar, where the jar 'preserves' (*servas*, 6) the Massic wine.

28. The transition from Classical hymns to doctrinal Christian hymns can be seen in the twelve hymns attributed to Ambrose: for example, his 'Deus Creator Omnium' is in regular Classical form, while 'Iam Surgit Hora Tertia' dispenses with the formal features of literary hymns and simply sets forth elements of Christian faith. The Nicene Creed is a good example of Christian adaptation of hymnal elements to articles of faith.

29. From the time of its publication, there was considerable confusion whether to entitle the poem a 'hymn' or an 'ode', indicating that the distinction between the two was becoming blurred. Gray ultimately preferred 'ode' and was followed by Wordsworth, who called his 'hymn' to Duty an 'ode'.

30. Like Horace, he never states her name in the hymn: but whereas in Horace the mention of her *sedes* at Antium clearly indicated to a Roman audience who Fortuna was, without Gray's title, we could only guess the identity of Adversity who has no Graeco-Roman counterpart — certainly not Ate, as some have suggested.

31. The idea that hardship can make a person more sympathetic to others can be found in Graeco-Roman authors, the most famous example being at *Aeneid* 1.630, where Dido says, 'Not ignorant of ill do I learn to befriend the unhappy' (*non ignara mali miseris succurrere disco*). As R. Lonsdale (ed.), *Gray, Collins and Goldsmith* (Longman, New York, 1969),

p. 71, notes, Vergil's passage was undoubtedly in Gray's mind, but nowhere in antiquity is such a notion applied to Virtue. For the Greek view of virtue, compare the hymn of Aristotle (discussed on p. 157). By making melting at others' woe an attribute of Virtue, he is, in effect, elevating that disposition itself to a virtue.

32. This Christian suffering stems from the *imitatio Christi*. Cf. 'A Hymn to God the Father', by Ben Jonson, which begins 'Hear me, O God! / A broken heart, / Is my best part'; and the sonnet of John Donne, 'Batter My Heart, Three-personed God'.

33. The expressions 'There are who' (9) and 'they . . . who' (21–2) are reminiscent of the foil in Horace, *Odes* 1.1–28 — see p. 38.

34. For an example of a Graeco-Roman hymn with predominantly Romantic ideas, cf. Shelley's 'Ode to the West Wind'.

35. Examples from the two authors quoted below include Y. Winters's sonnet 'To a Portrait of Melville in my Library', and the third stanza of Yeats's 'Sailing to Byzantium'. Yeats's well-known poem 'A Prayer for my Daughter', contains few formal features of Graeco-Roman hymns because it is addressed to no specific deity: rather, it consists of a series of wishes introduced by 'may'.

36. In the context of a *hypomnesis*, the clause, 'Unless the Holy Writings lie', should not imply any uncertainty, for it is part of the strategy of making the god recall past actions by posing an hypothesis, as in Chryses' prayer to Apollo. Given Yeats's scepticism toward Christianity, however, there may be some room for irony. Cf. A.E. Housman's 'Easter Hymn'.

37. For an account of the philosophical themes in Winters's poetry, see G. Powell , *Language as being in the poetry of Yvor Winters* (Louisiana State University Press, Baton Rouge, 1980). See also D. Davis, *Wisdom and wilderness: the achievement of Yvor Winters* (University of Georgia Press, Athens, 1983), whose title reflects the Wintersian dichotomy between 'Earth and mind' at line 21.

7

Praise and Counsel: Eulogy

Eulogy pervades our poetic tradition. We have already seen it
combined with many other forms: with hymns (Lucretius' 'Hymn
to Venus'), with lament (Milton's 'Lycidas'), consolation (W.H.
Auden's 'In Memory of W.B.Yeats'), with priamels (Martial's
epigram on the Colosseum) and with *ekphrasis* (Vergil's description of Aeneas' shield). It bears an especially close relationship to
the hymn, for an important function of all hymns is to praise the
god's powers and benefactions — 'Praise the Lord!' is the
opening of many psalms — whether or not the praise ultimately
issues in a specific request. Many of the strategies of hymnal
praise can easily be adapted to praise men: indeed, eulogy is
essentially a secularisation of hymnal praise.[1]

Eulogy, including praise, encomium and panegyric, consti-
tuted such an important part of ancient rhetoric that it
dominated an entire division called the *epideictic* ('display')
branch. Numerous ancient rhetorical treatises discuss its proper
subject, form and inherent topics, as well as offering instructions
on how to compose it.[2] In general terms, eulogy is a communal
celebration of ἀρετή, 'excellence', and τὸ καλόν, 'the good', as
embodied in the person or thing praised.[3] Thus, it supposes a
public occasion,[4] and, as we shall see, it is intimately connected
with ethical philosophy (which also concerns 'excellence' and 'the
good' as manifested in human action). In their practical
instructions, rhetoricians divided praise of human beings (in
prose or poetry) under specific headings. Here is a brief synopsis
of the major topics:[5]

    (I) Parentage
       (a) native land
       (b) progenitors

(II) Natural endowments

(III) Upbringing

(IV) Education

(V) Accomplishments

(VI) Gifts of fortune or the gods (such as power, wealth, beauty and health)

(VII) Deeds (according to the virtues: courage, wisdom, temperance, justice, etc.)
    (a) in war
    (b) in peace

(VIII) Comparisons with famous examples

In practice, each eulogy selects different topics for emphasis, and few poets or prose writers would attempt to include all of them.[6] There is, however, a poem that manages to incorporate all of the topics listed above — one whose other claim to merit is brevity — by Nicholas Grimald on Mistress Awdley (no. 141 in *Tottel's miscellany*).[7]

> Deserts of Nymphs, that ancient poets show,
> Are not so couth, as hers, whose present face,
> More than my Muse, may cause the world to know
> A nature nobly given, of worthy race,
> 5 So trained up as honour did bestow.
> Cyllene, in sugared speech, gave her a grace.
> Excel in song Apollo made his dear,
> No fingerfeat Minerve hid from her sight.
> Expressed in look, she hath so sovereign cheer,
> 10 As Cyprian once breathed on the Spartan bright.
> Wit, wisdom, will, word, work, and all, I ween,
> Dare no man's pen presume to paint outright.
> Lo luster and light, which if old time had seen
> Enthroned, shine she should with goddess Fame.
> 15 Yield, Envy, these due praises to this dame.

It opens with a comparison (VIII): she surpasses the 'deserts' of

Nymphs in the Graeco-Roman tradition. She is 'of worthy race' (I), she has a 'nature nobly given' (II), and was well 'trained up' (III, IV). Her accomplishments (V) include prose, poetry and handicraft. She also has the gifts of fortune (VI): beauty (comparable [VIII] to Helen's), wit and wisdom. Since she is a woman, she necessarily has few deeds to mention (VII), but they are alluded to in the 'word' and 'work', which the poet tactfully declines to depict. The conclusion echoes the beginning with an implicit comparison (VIII) to famous ladies of 'old time', and the poem ends with a request that Envy will not begrudge his 'praises' of the lady.[8]

Since most eulogies are long, it is impossible to treat many here. In addition, eulogy is often combined with other generic forms, as for example, with consolation in Yeats's 'In Memory of Major Robert Gregory'. I have therefore concentrated on one species of eulogy, which might be called political eulogy, and selected only four poems for comment: one Classical Greek, one Hellenistic Greek, one Roman and one English. All four are to powerful men and all four illustrate the strategies and difficulties of praising great leaders.

We shall begin with Pindar, the greatest of the Greek lyric poets, who was a master of eulogy. Four of his 17 books of poems were written to celebrate athletic success. We have already looked briefly at one of his short odes, *Olympian* 12 to Ergoteles of Himera (see p. 154), which treats four of the topics listed above: the athlete's native land (Ergoteles was exiled), his natural endowments (he was a gifted runner), his fortune (the subject of the opening hymn) and, most importantly, his deeds (the victories in the great games). In other odes, Pindar will emphasise the victor's parentage (especially when relatives are successful athletes), upbringing and education (especially when a parent or famous trainer has contributed to the success) and physical endowments, but here in *Olympian* 12 he concentrates on the fact that Ergoteles has (with Fortune's help) turned hardship into joy.

Olympian 12 is a brief poem to a private citizen. The poem I wish to examine in detail, *Pythian* 1, is to one of the most powerful men of the time, Hieron, tyrant of Syracuse, on the occasion of his team's victory in the chariot race at the Pythian games at Delphi in 470 BC. The event itself may seem quite minor, and indeed the poet only mentions the actual race in passing; but Hieron's victory in the national games becomes the focal point for a celebration of Greek life in general, of which athletic victory is but one part. Because it is one of Pindar's grandest odes, and since it incorporates many of the forms we have previously examined (hymn, *ekphrasis* and priamel), we shall treat it in detail, although it is too long to quote in Greek. It opens with a hymn to the personified Lyre.[9]

Strophe 1

Golden Lyre, possession of Apollo and the violet-haired Muses
who acts as their spokesman, to you the footstep listens
    as it begins the splendid celebration,
while the singers heed your signals,
whenever your vibrations strike up the choir-leading preludes.
5 You quench even the thunderbolt's spear
of eternal fire. And the eagle sleeps on the sceptre of Zeus,
    relaxing his swift wings at his sides,

Antistrophe 1

that king of birds, when you have shed over his curved head
a black-hooded cloud, sweet seal for his eyelids. And as he slumbers,
he ripples his smooth back, held in check
10 by your volley of notes. Yes, even violent Ares puts aside
his sharp-pointed spears and delights his heart
in sleep. And your shafts also soothe the minds of the gods,
    through the skill of Leto's son and the deep-breasted Muses.

The initial epithet of the Lyre, 'golden', is frequently applied in Classical poetry to divine objects to indicate their superlative quality. The *sedes* of the Lyre is in the company of the gods when its possessors, Apollo and the Muses, entertain the divine hosts. The burden of the hymn is the Lyre's power, initially over the footsteps of the dancers and the voices of the singers, but then extending to all who hear its sound. Even Zeus' awesome thunderbolt is temporarily extinguished, and in a brief *ekphrasis* (6–10) the poet vividly portrays the Lyre's relaxing effect on the other symbol of Zeus' power, the eagle.[10] Even Ares, the god of

182

war, rests from his normal delight in battle. Throughout this section, the poet conveys the power of the Lyre by describing its effects on others, a topic we have noted before in hymns and *ekphraseis* (see pp. 127 and 153).

The strophe and antistrophe form a unit by means of a device of early Greek poetry known as 'ring-composition', in which the end is signalled by a near repetition of the beginning. The phrase 'of Apollo and the violet-haired Muses' (1) is echoed by 'of Leto's son (i.e. Apollo) and the deep-breasted Muses' (12), and provides a sense of closure for this scene in heaven, which has vividly portrayed the Lyre's power to calm the hearts of the gods and to control martial power. This opening hymn could have stopped here and Pindar could have gone directly to the occasion of the ode (the actual celebration of Hieron's victory), but he continues in the epode to hymn the powers of the Lyre, and by concentrating on the martial function of music, he reminds us that for the Greeks music was not just a pastime, but also played a vital role in warfare, for Greek armies marched to music and often sang hymns as they went into battle.[11] The effect of the Lyre's music on those who are enemies of Zeus is thus very different.

Epode 1

But those creatures without Zeus' love are terrified
   when they hear the shout of the Pierian Muses, those on
      land and in the overpowering sea —
15 especially the one lying in dreadful Tartarus, enemy of the
      gods,
Typhon the hundred-headed, who was once reared
   in that famous Cilician cave, but now
   the sea-fencing cliffs above Cymae
   and Sicily weigh upon his shaggy chest, and a skyward
      column constrains him,
20 snowy Mt Aetna, year-round nurse of biting snow.

Strophe 2

From its depths belch forth holiest springs
   of unapproachable fire. By day its rivers pour forth a
      blazing stream of smoke,
   but at night the tumbling red flame

183

carries boulders into the deep expanse of the sea with a
crash.
25 That monster sends up those terrible springs
of Hephaestus' fire — an awesome portent to behold, a
wonder even to hear about from witnesses,

Antistrophe 2 (beginning)

such is that creature confined between Aetna's dark-leaved
peaks
and the plain, as his jagged bed goads the entire length of
his outstretched back.

This *ekphrasis* of the eruption of Mt Aetna was one of the most
famous in antiquity. In contrast to the Olympian gods, who relax
as they listen to the Lyre, Typhon, the last enemy to challenge
Zeus' reign (cf. Hesiod, *Theogony* 820–80), cringes in fear and
writhes in pain when he hears the 'shout' (14) of the Pierian
Muses. Apollo's music has a two-fold function: it cheers those
who are good and disheartens those who are evil.[12] The
description of Typhon, who is portrayed as stretched between the
cliffs at Cymae (Mt Vesuvius on the Bay of Naples) and Mt
Aetna (the volcanic mountain in eastern Sicily north of Syracuse), ends with the motif of wonder (26–8), standard in
ekphraseis. The emphasis that falls on Cymae and Aetna in this
description seems disproportionate at this point, but Cymae will
prove to be the site of Hieron's naval victory, while it was as a
citizen of Aetna and not of Syracuse that Hieron had accepted his
Pythian victory. Although he was well known as the ruler of
Syracuse, he had just founded Aetna with settlers from Sicily and
the mainland. Pindar tactfully follows his patron's lead in asking
for prosperity for the new city rather than for the older one.

Antistrophe 2 (conclusion)

Grant us, O Zeus, favour in your sight,
30 you who rule this mountain, the forehead of a fruitful land,
whose neighbouring city that bears its name
was honoured by its glorious founder,
when at Pytho's racecourse the herald proclaimed it as he
announced Hieron's victory

Epode 2

with the chariot. First blessing for sailors when setting out
on a voyage is the coming of a favouring wind, since it
augurs well
35 for a more prosperous return at the end. And this saying,
given this present success, inspires the expectation that the
city
will hereafter be famous for its crowns and its horses,
and be celebrated in tuneful feasts.
Lycian Apollo, ruler of Delos, you who love the Castalian
spring on Mt Parnassus,
40 graciously take this to heart and make this a land of good
men.

This section begins with a prayer to Zeus and ends with a prayer
to Apollo (another example of 'ring-composition' marking off a
part of a Pindaric ode). The new city of Aetna has had a
successful beginning — with the gods' favour it may also have a
bright future. To a reader acquainted with the conventions of
eulogy, and especially with epinician poetry, this praise of the city
should be a signal that more direct praise of the 'glorious founder'
(31) will be forthcoming.

Strophe 3

For the gods provide all the means for human
achievements,
be it inborn wisdom, or strength of hand and eloquence. In
my eagerness to praise
that man, I hope
not to throw, like an athlete, the bronze-cheeked javelin
whirling from my hand outside the boundary,
45 but to cast it far beyond my competitors'.
May all time to come continue to grant him
such happiness and prosperity,
and make him forget his hardships.

Antistrophe 3

Surely it would recall those wars and battles,
in which he stood his ground with steady soul,

and with divine help he and his family won
such honour as no other Greek has reaped
> 50 to crown his wealth with esteem. But now,
like another Philoctetes,
he has taken to the field, when even the proud man
was compelled to seek his friendship. They say
that the god-like heroes came to fetch him
from Lemnos, wasting from his wound,

Epode 3 (beginning)

Poeas' archer son,
who destroyed Priam's city and ended
the Greeks' toils.
55 He walked on weak flesh, but he fulfilled his destiny.
In like fashion may the god sustain Hieron
in time to come, and give him due measure
of his desires.

To our surprise, the praise of Hieron is quite general. We gather
that he has been a very successful commander, but Pindar
provides no specific details. In fact, we do not know what
campaign it was that calls forth the comparison with
Philoctetes.[13] We must wait until later in the poem for Hieron's
'deeds of war' to be specified: in the meantime, the poem takes
another unforeseen direction, when the poet suddenly turns to
Hieron's young son, who was (we discover) nominally in charge
of the new city.

Epode 3 (conclusion)

Muse, I beg you to include Deinomenes too in the
celebration
of this chariot victory, for the joy of his father's success
is as his own.
60 Join me, then, in composing a loving hymn for Aetna's
king.

Strophe 4

His city was founded in divinely based freedom
by Hieron under the laws of Hyllus' rule. For the

descendants of Pamphylus
and of Heracles' sons, who dwell
under the slopes of Mt Taügetus, are determined to retain
    the institutions of Aegimius and remain
65 Doric. Their prosperous ancestors came down
from Mt Pindus and took Amyclae, to become
    glorious neighbours of the white-horsed Tyndarids;
    and the fame of their spears flourished.

Antistrophe 4 (beginning)

Zeus, you who determine the end of all, may men's true
    report
always ascribe such good fortune as this to the citizens
    and their king by the waters of the Amenas.
For with your help, a ruler may,
70 with his son as viceroy, honour his people and turn them
    to harmonious peace.

The abundant information in this passage would be out of place
— a mere digression — if its only purpose were to tell more about
the new city of Aetna (only briefly introduced earlier). However,
Pindar also indirectly praises its founding father by placing
Hieron and his governance in the venerable political tradition of
the Doric branch of Greek culture, which was thought to have
made its way during the so-called Dark Age (c. 1000 BC) from Mt
Pindus in the north of Greece to Amyclae in the south. The
colonists of the new city are under Doric laws whose traditions go
back to the time of Hyllus and the sons of Heracles. Pindar had
ended his initial praise of the city in Epode 2 with a prayer for its
prosperity: here he does the same, but the emphasis is appropriately political — the hope is that Hieron and his son may turn the
people to 'harmonious peace' (σύμφωνον . . . ἡσυχίαν, 70). These
two words bring together two of the important themes of the
poem: music and repose, which we saw in the opening tableau of
the Lyre's power over the gods. However, Pindar uses the
mention of 'harmonious peace' to recall its antithesis, war, and in
the prayer that follows he returns to the battles of Hieron that
were only hinted at earlier.

Antistrophe 4 (conclusion)

I beseech you, son of Cronus, make the

Phoenicians and Etruscans keep their war cry
>   quietly at home, now that they have seen their
>   aggression
>   bring woe to their fleet before Cymae,

Epode 4

>   such defeat did they suffer at the hands of the Syracusans'
>   chief,
>   when he cast their youth from their swift ships into the sea
> 75 and delivered Greece from grievous slavery. I shall earn
>   the Athenians' favour as my reward by telling of Salamis
>   and the Spartans' by telling of the battles before Mt
>   Cithaeron,
>   where the curve-bowed Persians were beaten;
>   but beside the well-watered banks of the Himeras
>   Deinomenes' sons are the subject of my hymn,
> 80 which they earned with their valour by defeating their
>   enemies.

The battle mentioned in lines 72–5 is that of Cymae, when in 474 BC Hieron defeated an Etruscan fleet that was threatening the Greek settlements in southern Italy, thereby effectively ending Etruscan sea power. The battle mentioned in lines 79–80 is the earlier Battle of Himera (480 BC), in which a coalition of Sicilian cities under the leadership of Gelon[14] (Hieron's older brother whom he succeeded as tyrant of Syracuse) and Theron of Acragas devastated a 100,000–man army of Carthaginians. At the same time the Greeks on the mainland were defending themselves against a massive invasion of Persians under Xerxes. In the priamel that follows (75–80), Pindar mentions the Battle of Salamis (when the Athenians engineered a sea victory over the Persians in 480 BC, supposedly on the same day as the Battle of Himera), and the Battle of Plataea (when the Spartans defeated the Persian army in 479 BC), but reserves the climactic position for the Battle of Himera. The description of each battle is one line longer than the preceding one, and there is no doubt about where the emphasis falls. Although Pindar does not say that the Battle of Himera is greater than the other battles (a claim that would be an exaggeration), he definitely implies that it was on a par with them. What unites them is the fact that each helped to deliver Greece 'from grievous slavery' (75) to an outsider.

We noted in the outline of topics on p. 180 that deeds naturally divide into those of war and those of peace. When Pindar rounds off the section in which he praises Hieron's deeds of war, the generically conscious audience will expect to hear about his peacetime accomplishments as a political leader. Pindar suspends this expectation, however, interrupting himself to meditate on the possible effects on his audience of the forthcoming praise. In the lines that pass from deeds of war to those of peace (81–4), the poet himself suddenly appears,[15] and exhorts himself to be concise in his praise by citing two reasons: the audience will become restive if he goes on at great length, and some may even resent hearing a fellow citizen being highly praised. In other words, Pindar implies that he has a great deal to say, but will hold back for fear of offending any members of his audience.

Strophe 5 (beginning)

81 If you tell the gist by combining the strands of many things
    in brief, men are less apt to criticise, for nagging
    tedium dulls keen expectation;
    then too, citizens can be grieved in their secret hearts,
        especially when they hear of another's success.

This is, of course, highly sophisticated rhetoric. Pindar does indeed intend to praise Hieron, but he will manage to do so without offence to anyone by couching his praise in exhortation. As we noted at the beginning, eulogy is closely related to ethical philosophy, since both concern *arete* and the good. A passage in Aristotle's *Rhetoric* 1.9, which illustrates just how close they are in practice, provides a good account of Pindar's procedure here (67b37):

Praise and counsel are a common type, for what you recommend in counselling becomes encomium by a change of phrase. So, when a certain action or character is required, we should change the phrasing by inversion and state it as a recommendation. For example, 'One should not be proud of success due to fortune but of that due to oneself,' becomes praise when changed to: 'He is not proud of what he acquires through fortune but what he gains himself.' Consequently, if you wish to praise, consider what you would counsel, and if you wish to counsel, consider what you would praise.

Pindar had mentioned before that he was eager to praise Hieron (42), and the praise of his martial accomplishments was indeed full. Now that he turns to his domestic policy, he intends to exercise caution, lest any fellow citizens be offended.[16] In the following lines, however, he turns suddenly to Hieron (and Deinomenes too), and says, in effect: just because fear of envy may make me temper my praise, that same fear should not stop you from continuing to succeed. To substantiate his point, he refers to the proverbial saying that it is better to be envied for success than pitied for failure.

Strophe 5 (conclusion)

85 But nevertheless, since it is better to be envied than pitied,
      do not forego any noble things. Guide your people
          with a rudder of justice; forge your words
          on an anvil of truth.

Antistrophe 5

Even a slight thing, you know, becomes an important
      matter
if it chances from you. Many things are in your control, but
      many are the sure witnesses for good or ill.
Abide in flourishing high spirits,
90 and if you love always to be well spoken of,
      do not trouble too much about the costs,
      but let out the sail, like a ship captain,
      to the wind. Do not be deceived,
          my friend, by shameful gains,
          for the posthumous acclaim of fame

Epode 5

alone reveals the life of men who have died
to writers and poets. The loving-minded excellence of
      Croesus does not perish,
95 but that man of pitiless mind, Phalaris, who burned others

in his bronze bull, is overwhelmed by universal execration,
and no lyres in banquet halls welcome him
into gentle fellowship with boys' voices.
Success takes first prize, and high esteem
      comes second; but the man who can try for both
100 and wins them earns the highest crown.

These lines, which incorporate a small treatise on good government based on principles of justice, truth, honesty and generosity, simultaneously praise Hieron for his high ideals and advise
him to live up to them. The final piece of advice (92) is negative
— 'Do not be deceived by shameful gains' — and is accompanied
by the warm interjection of the poet, 'my friend'. The reward for
following these precepts is fame, and in the final epode, Pindar
offers two examples. The one, Croesus, was a wealthy king of
Lydia about 550 BC, who was legendary for his generous offerings
to Delphi and for being a friend of the Greeks. The other,
Croesus' contemporary Phalaris, the tyrant of Acragas in Sicily,
used to roast his victims in a great bronze bull, so constructed
that their screams sounded like bellowing. These examples, one
positive, the other negative, give point to Pindar's closing
reflection that success accompanied by good repute is the highest
goal.

Having thus sketched the movement of the poem as a whole,
we can now attempt to tie it together thematically. In the broadest terms, the poem is a hymn to Zeus' order in the universe as
embodied in the music of Apollo's lyre. Those who join in the
celebration of that order enjoy a pleasurable relaxation, but those
who do not are, like Typhon, tormented by its sound. On the
national level, those Greeks who obey the music of the lyre in
their celebrations also participate in right order, and have proven
its effectiveness in four great battles within six years — in the east
(Salamis and Plataea against the Persians) and west (Himera
against the Carthaginians and Cymae against the Etruscans) —
when their culture was threatened with destruction.

On the level of the *polis*, Apollo's lyre embodies the principles
of good government necessary for turning the citizenry 'to
harmonious peace' (70). Not only does the poem celebrate the
defeat of national enemies, but also the founding of a new city,
Aetna, and the extension of the Doric laws and traditions that
have helped to make Hellas great. (The poem itself is composed
in Doric metre and dialect). Finally, on the level of the individual,

Hieron and his young son Deinomenes — counterparts on earth of Zeus' order in the universe — must model their rule on the precepts and examples that Pindar provides in the poem.

From beginning to end the ode celebrates the power of music to make life pleasant and meaningful for those who join in its fellowship. Those who defy its harmony suffer defeat and execration. Typhon lies imprisoned in painful frustration, the aggressive national enemies are defeated in battle after battle, and Phalaris is excluded from the fellowship of his own nation. However, Hieron, who has twice performed Panhellenic service by rescuing Greek civilisation from slavery, and who even now is extending its boundaries with a new city that has gained a victory at Apollo's Panhellenic festival at Delphi, participates in the music of Pindar's ode, which will be his incentive to follow the example of Croesus, whose 'loving-minded excellence' (φιλόφρων ἀρετά) does not perish (94). This remarkable poem maintains a balance between the divine and human, history and poetry, universal and particular, precept and example, and praise and counsel.

Werner Jaeger has rightly called attention to the poem as an early example of a *Fürstenspiegel*, 'Mirror for Princes', in which the author advises the ruler by holding up an ideal of conduct.[17] The poem praises, but it also advises: when the praise might threaten to become tedious flattery, Pindar converts it to admonition. As Erasmus points out in his *Institutio Principis Christiani*, when a young monarch hears himself called 'Father of his Country', he should be instructed to 'act in such a way as to appear worthy of that title. If he thinks of it in that way, it will be a warning; but if he takes it otherwise, it will be fawning adulation'.[18] In this manner epideictic poetry can retain its seriousness. The Latin phrase *laudando praecipere* sums up the procedure: 'to counsel by praising'.

In order to gauge the restraint of Pindar's praise, we shall briefly compare his poem with another eulogy of a king, written in the Hellenistic period about 272 BC by Theocritus. His *Idyll* 17 presents a full-scale encomium of Ptolemy II of Egypt. Since it is too long to quote in its entirety, we shall only single out some salient points of comparison. The most obvious difference is the form. Pindar's ode was in complex choral lyrics meant to be sung and danced by a choir, perhaps of boys (cf. verse 98). Theocritus' encomium is written in dactylic hexameter and meant to be recited. Its model is the Homeric hymn (see p. 175, Note 1).

Eulogy

Whereas Pindar's introductory hymn to the Lyre tactfully suggested analogies between Hieron and Zeus, Theocritus begins by making a bold parallel between Ptolemy and Zeus and goes so far as to declare Ptolemy the most excellent of men.

Ἐκ Διὸς ἀρχώμεσθα καὶ ἐς Δία λήγετε Μοῖσαι,
ἀθανάτων τὸν ἄριστον, ἐπὴν †ἀείδωμεν ἀοιδαῖς·
ἀνδρῶν δ' αὖ Πτολεμαῖος ἐνὶ πρώτοισι λεγέσθω
καὶ πύματος καὶ μέσσος· ὃ γὰρ προφερέστατος ἀνδρῶν.

Let us begin with Zeus, and you Muses end with him,
since he is the greatest of the immortals for us to sing;
but of men let Ptolemy be mentioned first,
last and in the middle, for he is most excellent of men.

After an indication of the helplessness (*aporia*) before his vast subject (9–12), he treats Ptolemy's lineage on his father's side (13–33) and then on his mother's side (34–52). The priamel that introduces his birth puts him at the end of a series including Diomedes and Achilles, thereby suggesting that he can stand comparison with Homer's greatest heroes (53–7):

'Αργεία κυάνοφρυ, σὺ λαοφόνον Διομήδεα
μισγομένα Τυδῆι τέκες, Καλυδωνίῳ ἀνδρί,
55 ἀλλὰ Θέτις βαθύκολπος ἀκοντιστὰν 'Αχιλῆα
Αἰακίδᾳ Πηλῆι· σὲ δ', αἰχμητὰ Πτολεμαῖε,
αἰχμητᾷ Πτολεμαίῳ ἀρίζηλος Βερενίκα.

You, Deipyle, a dark-browed Argive, bore people-slaying
Diomedes
to your husband Tydeus, a man from Calydonia;
55 and deep-breasted Thetis bore javelin-throwing Achilles
to Peleus, son of Aeacus; but you, spear-wielding Ptolemy,
were born to the warrior Ptolemy from illustrious Berenice.

Whereas Pindar had concentrated on the mature Hieron and did not mention his ancestors, upbringing, education or youthful accomplishments,[19] Theocritus' poem runs through a catalogue of topics in an effort to be complete. In fact, it seems to have served as a model for later rhetorical handbooks containing instructions on how to compose encomia for Roman emperors.[20] After setting forth in considerable detail the favourable conditions of Ptolemy's birth (58–76), a typical topic in hymns, Theocritus describes the vast extent of the monarch's political power (77–94) and praises him for the generous use of his great wealth, which wins him fame (107–20).[21] Finally, he is praised for his piety toward his parents and his devotion to his wife (121–34) — the two are even compared with Zeus and Hera. The end of the poem continues the hyperbolic praise with a remarkable hymnal tribute:

135   Χαῖρε, ἄναξ Πτολεμαῖε· σέθεν δ' ἐγὼ ἶσα καὶ ἄλλων
       μνάσομαι ἡμιθέων, δοκέω δ' ἔπος οὐκ ἀπόβλητον
       φθέγξομαι ἐσσομένοις· ἀρετήν γε μὲν ἐκ Διὸς αἰτεῦ.

135   Hail, King Ptolemy; I shall sing of you no less than of the other
       demigods, and I believe that I shall speak poetry which future
       generations will not reject. As for success, ask that of Zeus.

Instead of the usual hymnal farewell to the god, Theocritus bids farewell to Ptolemy himself and goes so far as to call him a demigod. Pindar used hymnal elements to frame his praise of Hieron: Theocritus' poem is virtually a hymn to Ptolemy.

The very different attitudes these poems display toward their subjects point up the changes that occurred during the two centuries that separate them and their respective Classical and Hellenistic periods. Pindar offers advice to Hieron, and even addresses him as 'my friend' (92): Theocritus views Ptolemy as nearly divine,[22] and nowhere does he offer advice as a counsellor or equal. By the Hellenistic period, poetry has lost much of its serious political force:[23] advice yields to adulation. This is not to say that all encomium has become mere flattery, but that the position of the poet has changed: he admires from a distance as a political subject rather than advising as an intellectual equal.[24] In short, there is little of the tension that had required Pindar's tact and poetic skill when he had to mediate between the ideal he was recommending and the reality of the subject's achievement.

Among Horace's odes, some (e.g. 1.12, 4.4 and 4.14) are straightforward encomia in the Hellenistic tradition. In others, however, we have seen one way in which he solved the problem of praising great men such as Augustus and Agrippa while still maintaining his own integrity: by pretending to refuse to write proper encomia of them (see pp. 8–18). In *Odes* 1.37, however, he uses a different means to celebrate Octavian's victory at Actium. This battle, which we saw as the central event depicted on Aeneas' shield at *Aeneid* 8.675–713, was regarded by the Augustan poets as a turning-point in history. Yet in celebrating it, he appears to show such respect for the defeated Cleopatra that the poem is commonly known as the 'Cleopatra Ode', even though she is nowhere named.

> Nunc est bibendum, nunc pede libero
> pulsanda tellus, nunc Saliaribus
>   ornare pulvinar deorum
>   tempus erat dapibus, sodales.
>
> 5 antehac nefas depromere Caecubum
> cellis avitis, dum Capitolio
>   regina dementes ruinas,
>   funus et imperio parabat
>
> contaminato cum grege turpium
> 10 morbo virorum, quidlibet impotens
>   sperare fortunaque dulci
>   ebria. sed minuit furorem
>
> vix una sospes navis ab ignibus,
> mentemque lymphatam Mareotico
> 15   redegit in veros timores
>   Caesar ab Italia volantem
>
> remis adurgens, accipiter velut
> molles columbas aut leporem citus
>   venator in campis nivalis
> 20   Haemoniae, daret ut catenis
>
> fatale monstrum. quae generosius
> perire quaerens nec muliebriter
>   expavit ensem nec latentes
>   classe cita reparavit oras.
>
> 25 ausa et iacentem visere regiam
> vultu sereno, fortis et asperas

    tractare serpentes, ut atrum
      corpore combiberet venenum,

    deliberata morte ferocior;
30 saevis Liburnis scilicet invidens
    privata deduci superbo
      non humilis mulier triumpho.

Now is the time to get drunk, now with free feet
to stomp the ground, now it is high time, comrades,
    to spread the couches of the gods
      with Salian feasts.

5 Until now it was forbidden to break out Caecuban wine
from our grandfathers' storerooms, so long as a queen
    was threatening insane ruin of the Capitol
      and destruction to the empire

with her polluted herd of men disgraced by
10 vice, for she was wild enough to hope for anything,
    drunk with sweet fortune.
      But her fury lessened

when scarcely one ship escaped the flames
and Caesar brought her mind maddened
15   with Egyptian wine to face true
      terrors, chasing her with his ships

as she fled from Italy, like a hawk
after soft doves or a swift hunter
    after a rabbit over the fields of snowy
20   Thessaly, to put in chains

the deadly monster. But she sought
a more noble death, for she had no effeminate
    fear of arms, nor did she sail in haste
      to some secret shores;

25 she even dared to look calmly upon her
defeated realm and was brave enough
    to handle fierce snakes, so as to
      inject their deadly poison into her body,

hardened by her resolve to die;
30 for that proud woman refused to be taken
on enemy ships, and, stripped of her
title, be led in glorious triumph.

The poem begins with joyous celebration at the great relief
following Actium. Cleopatra is at first portrayed in strongly
negative terms: she has insane delusions of power and her
associates (Antony is tactfully not named) are called a 'polluted
herd' (*contaminato . . . grege*, 9). In lines 12–21, Caesar is praised
for bringing her back to reality and is duly compared with a hawk
or hunter,[25] in his determination to capture the 'deadly monster'
(*fatale monstrum*, 21). Until this point the ode has no real tension
between the ideal and the real, for the two protagonists are
simply drawn in black and white. At 21, however, the relative
pronoun *quae* ('But she') takes the poem in an unforeseen
direction that rescues it from simplistic praise of Caesar, for the
rest of it rehabilitates Cleopatra, who ultimately emerges as a
queen too proud to submit to the humility of being led as a
private citizen (*privata*, 31) in a Roman triumph. The *litotes* of the
compliment to her in the last stanza of the poem makes all the
greater impression: *non humilis mulier* (32), 'no lowly woman'.

What might have been a conventional eulogy of a victorious
commander has been turned into a miniature tragedy of
Cleopatra. Since Horace plays down Octavian's role and devotes
the last third of the poem to the defeated queen, many readers
have sensed an ironic criticism in the poem, but there is no reason
(within the poem or from other sources) to think that Horace felt
any ambivalence about the outcome of Actium. What has been
tempered, however, is the outburst of enthusiasm of the opening
lines: *nunc est bibendum*. In the end, Cleopatra proves to have been
a more worthy opponent than she appeared at first to be, and as a
result Octavian has won no hollow victory. Just as Achilles finds
a noble opponent in Hector or Aeneas in Turnus, so Cleopatra's
final heroism adds seriousness to Octavian's victory. The poem
has much the same effect as the ending of the *Aeneid* when Aeneas
plunges his sword into Turnus: it forces us to reconsider the event
being celebrated and adjust our reaction more carefully because
the event turns out to be more complex than we had anticipated.
We must also recall that the Battle of Actium was the termination
of a *civil* war, so that although celebration was definitely in order,

gloating certainly was not. Horace is no flatterer of the *princeps*; his poem should provoke a sober reflection on the costs of victory.

We shall conclude with the English poem that in many ways comes closest to Horace's manner, Andrew Marvell's 'An Horatian Ode Upon Cromwell's Return from Ireland', which, although longer and grander, clearly looked to *Odes* 1.37 as a model, as many scholars have pointed out. It has been called 'the greatest of political poems in English',[26] and it deserves quotation in full.

> The forward youth that would appear
> Must now forsake his Muses dear,
>   Nor in the shadows sing
>   His numbers languishing:
>
> 5 'Tis time to leave the books in dust,
> And oil the unusèd armour's rust,
>   Removing from the wall
>   The corslet of the hall.
>
> So restless Cromwell could not cease
> 10 In the inglorious arts of peace,
>   But through adventurous war
>   Urgèd his active star;
>
> And like the three-forked lightning, first
> Breaking the clouds where it was nursed,
> 15   Did thorough his own side
>   His fiery way divide.
>
> For 'tis all one to courage high,
> The emulous or enemy;
>   And with such to inclose
> 20   Is more than to oppose.
>
> Then burning through the air he went,
> And palaces and temples rent;
>   And Caesar's head at last
>   Did through his laurels blast.
>
> 25 'Tis madness to resist or blame
> The force of angry heaven's flame;

And if we would speak true,
Much to the man is due,

Who, from his private gardens, where
30 He lived reservèd and austere
    (As if his highest plot
    To plant the bergamot),

Could by industrious valour climb
To ruin the great work of time,
35 And cast the kingdom old
    Into another mould;

Though Justice against Fate complain,
And plead the ancient rights in vain;
    But those do hold or break,
40 As men are strong or weak.

Nature, that hateth emptiness,
Allows of penetration less,
    And therefore must make room
    Where greater spirits come.

45 What field of all the civil wars,
Where his were not the deepest scars?
    And Hampton shows what part
    He had of wiser art;

Where, twining subtle fears with hope,
50 He wove a net of such a scope
    That Charles himself might chase
    To Carisbrooke's narrow case,

That thence the royal actor borne
The tragic scaffold might adorn;
55 While round the armèd bands
    Did clap their bloody hands.

He nothing common did or mean
Upon that memorable scene,
    But with his keener eye
60 The axe's edge did try;

Nor called the gods with vulgar spite
To vindicate his helpless right;
    But bowed his comely head
    Down, as upon a bed.

65 This was that memorable hour
Which first assured the forcèd power:
    So, when they did design
    The Capitol's first line,

A bleeding head, where they begun,
70 Did fright the architects to run;
    And yet in that the state
    Foresaw its happy fate.

And now the Irish are ashamed
To see themselves in one year tamed;
75   So much one man can do
    That does both act and know.

They can affirm his praises best,
And have, though overcome, confessed
    How good he is, how just,
80   And fit for highest trust.

Nor yet grown stiffer with command,
But still in the republic's hand —
    How fit he is to sway
    That can so well obey!

85 He to the Commons' feet presents
A kingdom for his first year's rents;
    And, what he may, forbears
    His fame to make it theirs;

And has his sword and spoils ungirt,
90 To lay them at the public's skirt:
    So when the falcon high
    Falls heavy from the sky,

She, having killed, no more does search
But on the next green bough to perch;

95   Where, when he first does lure,
      The falconer has her sure.

    What may not, then, our isle presume,
    While victory his crest does plume?
      What may not others fear,
100   If thus he crown each year?

    A Caesar he, ere long, to Gaul,
    To Italy an Hannibal,
      And to all states not free
      Shall climactéric be.

105 The Pict no shelter now shall find
   Within his parti-coloured mind,
      But from his valour sad
      Shrink underneath the plaid;

    Happy if in the tufted brake
110 The English hunter him mistake,
      Nor lay his hounds in near
      The Caledonian deer.

    But thou, the war's and fortune's son,
    March indefatigably on!
115   And for the last effect,
      Still keep thy sword erect;

    Besides the force it has to fright
    The spirits of the shady night,
      The same arts that did gain
120   A power must it maintain.

Like the events surrounding Actium, the English civil wars, the rise of Cromwell, and the beheading of Charles were complicated affairs, and no single response (whether of joy or despondency) was sufficient to the occasion. Although both Actium and Charles's death marked major turning-points in the histories of the two nations and pointed the State in directions of which both Horace and Marvell approved, the cost in citizens' lives was so great that any gloating was out of place. Horace admired Augustus, and Marvell admired Cromwell, but both poets avoid writing mere flattery by carefully restraining their enthusiasm. Indeed, Marvell is so careful to avoid adulation that, like Horace, he has been accused of actually disapproving of the man he praises. However, such misunderstandings result when critics isolate the poem from its generic tradition, and by concentrating on subtle nuances of language detect a web of irony and ambivalent loyalties in it.[27] We must never lose sight of the fact that Marvell named this poem 'An Horatian Ode'.[28]

The parallels between the Roman and English situations are obvious: Octavian and Cromwell were both young, both came to sudden power during civil war, and both made momentous changes in the government. Furthermore, in their securing of power, both Octavian and Cromwell had to defeat a regal foe. We have already seen the sympathetic treatment Horace metes out to Cleopatra, who partly redeems her previous misconduct by her heroic death. So too, Marvell gives Charles tragic stature at his death (53–64), at that 'memorable hour' (65), when a new age began. Marvell took great care to portray that 'memorable scene' (58) in a striking *ekphrasis*, for it is meant to remind both Cromwell and us of the price that was paid for his rise to power — and of his obligation to the State now that he has secured it.

The lasting interest in Marvell's treatment of Cromwell's spectacular career, when he 'cast the kingdom old / Into another mould' (35–6), stems in part from his powerful portrayal of the opposing forces that met in this tragic and historic event (37–40):

> Though Justice against Fate complain,
> And plead the ancient rights in vain;
>> But those do hold or break,
> 40   As men are strong or weak.

However, it also stems from his refusal to gloss over the ugly aspects of Charles's execution, or to deny the king his personal triumph, even though it may seem to detract from Cromwell's glory, just as Cleopatra's heroism in part detracted from Octavian's triumph. By such details as 'While round the armèd bands / Did clap their bloody hands' (55–6), he intensifies the horror of the drama and by contrast increases the stature of Charles, who 'nothing common did or mean' (57). He even includes a reference to the 'bleeding head' (69). There is no doubt that this portrayal is very sympathetic to Charles, but it would be rash to see this as a criticism of Cromwell, for the two stanzas that complete this section clearly give Marvell's assessment of the event (65–72):

> 65 This was that memorable hour
> Which first assured the forcèd power:
> So, when they did design
> The Capitol's first line,
>
> A bleeding head, where they begun,
> 70 Did fright the architects to run;
> And yet in that the state
> Foresaw its happy fate.

The words 'bleeding' and 'fright' are Marvell's addition to the story in Pliny (*Nat. Hist.* 28.4.15): they point to the horror of the beheading, 'and yet' (71) the dreadful event portends a 'happy fate' (72) for the State. This positive conclusion is immediately followed by an example of what that 'happy fate' is (73–6):

> And now the Irish are ashamed
> To see themselves in one year tamed;
> 75 So much one man can do
> That does both act and know.

This stanza effects the transition from Cromwell's rise to power to his use of that power. Although the second part of the poem (73–120) concentrates on Cromwell's military prowess, the fact that he is acting on behalf of Parliament against foreign enemies makes it correspond with the 'deeds of peace' topic of eulogy, and its spirit is very similar to that of an Horatian passage we have already examined (see p. 163), when, at the end of his 'Hymn to Fortune', Horace prays for Rome's success in foreign wars as compensation for all the horrors of the past civil wars:

> Safeguard Caesar when he campaigns against the Britons,
> 30 the furthest people on earth, and protect the fresh levy
> of young men off to daunt the eastern
> lands and the Red Sea.
>
> Alas, how shameful are our scars and crimes
> and our brothers' fates. What has our hardened

35   generation shunned? What evil have we
          left untouched? From what have our youth

          drawn back their hands in fear of the gods? What altars
          have they spared? O please, on a fresh anvil
              reforge our blunted steel for use
40   against the Massagetae and Arabs!

Like Horace, Marvell hopes that English swords can now be pointed out against foreign enemies rather than against each other, and lines 97–112 joyfully prophesy tremendous success abroad: 'A Caesar he, ere long, to Gaul / To Italy an Hannibal' (101–2). The last two stanzas of the poem (113–20) are a stirring exhortation to Cromwell to use his power in foreign campaigns.

However, this second section (73–120) does not consist merely of jubilation: it too is tempered by sober reflections that not only praise Cromwell but, just as importantly, counsel him on the proper use of his military power. Like the closing part of *Pythian* 1, these lines offer counsel on the correct conduct of a leader. The ringing lines 'How good he is, how just, / And fit for highest trust' (79–80) and 'How fit he is to sway / That can so well obey!' (83–4) are equally praise and advice. Cromwell must use his abilities in the service of his country.[29] The simile of the falcon, that waits for the bidding of his master before going out to make another kill (91–6), vividly portrays the proper relationship that should obtain between Cromwell and the government. The hope conveyed in the ode that Cromwell's military prowess abroad will be accompanied by civil order at home is pointedly expressed in an epigram attributed to Marvell, 'On a Portrait of Oliver Cromwell' ('In Effigiem Oliveri Cromwell'):

Haec est quae toties inimicos umbra fugavit,
    At sub qua cives otia lenta terunt.

This shadow [image] often put enemies to flight,
    But under its shade the citizens enjoy calm leisure.

The poem is a sobering tribute to a remarkable man, and when seen in the tradition of political eulogy we have sketched, it stands out as one of the finest examples.

As in the case of Pindar and Horace, what makes this poem more than a mere recital of achievements is the poet's recognition of the complexity of the situation and his refusal to smooth over the real moral and political problems involved in the proper exercise of power: he maintains an objective distance and never capitulates to mere congratulation. By presenting themselves as spokesmen for their cultures, these three poets can address the powerful men of their times — Hieron, Octavian, Cromwell — freely, as intellectual equals.

Notes

1. Often the distinction between them is blurred. Pindar calls his poems in praise of athletes ὕμνοι ('hymns'), ἀοιδαί ('songs'), ἐγκώμια ('encomia') and ἐπινίκια ('epinicians'), with apparently no generic difference. The more the poet wishes to 'divinise' his subject, the more hymnal his style tends to become, as we shall see with the example of Theocritus.

2. Among the most important are Aristotle, *Rhetoric* 1.9, the *Rhetorica ad Alexandrum* 35, [Cicero], *Rhetorica ad Herennium* 3.10–15, Cicero, *De Oratore* 2.340–8, Quintilian, *Institutio Oratoria* 3.7 and the treatises on epideictic speeches by Menander Rhetor and pseudo-Dionysius of Halicarnassus (the latter conveniently translated in D.A. Russell and N.G. Wilson, *Menander Rhetor*, pp. 362–81). Encomia were also exercises in the *progymnasmata* (see p. 80, Note 2). The best survey still remains that of T.C. Burgess, *Epideictic literature* (University of Chicago Press, Chicago, 1902). Other important studies are V. Buchheit, *Untersuchungen zur Theorie des Genos Epideiktikon von Gorgias bis Aristoteles* (Max Hueber, Munich, 1960); T. Viljamaa, *Studies in Greek encomiastic poetry of the early Byzantine period* (Helsingfors, Helsinki, 1968); and O.B. Hardison, Jr., *The enduring monument: a study of the idea of praise in Renaissance literary theory and practice* (University of North Carolina Press, Chapel Hill, 1962), D.L. Peterson, *The English lyric from Wyatt to Donne: a history of the plain and eloquent styles* (Princeton University Press, Princeton, 1967) and R.S. Peterson, *Imitation and praise in the poems of Ben Jonson* (Yale University Press, New Haven, 1981). For an excellent treatment of panegyric in the seventeenth century, see J.D. Garrison, *Dryden and the tradition of panegyric* (University of California Press, Berkeley, 1975).

3. Cf. the definition of ἐγκώμιον in the *Progymnasmata* of Theon: 'a speech that emphasises the greatness of deeds done according to virtue (ἀρετή) and of the other good things (ἀγαθά) that concern a person' (2.109.20 Sp.).

4. Eulogy is essentially 'occasional'. Menander Rhetor gives numerous occasions for which speeches of praise could be delivered: speeches to emperors and governors, arrival and farewell speeches, epithalamia, birthday speeches, funeral speeches, ambassadorial speeches and festival speeches.

5. For a detailed survey of the topics of encomia, see T.C. Burgess, *Epideictic literature*, pp. 119–26. See also Curtius, *European literature*, pp.

162–82. The topics find common acceptance in sixteenth-century English poetry through the rhetorical treatises of Rainolde, Cox, Puttenham and Wilson. See D.L. Peterson, *The English lyric*, and A. Leigh Deneef, 'Epideictic rhetoric and the Renaissance lyric', *Journal of Medieval and Renaissance Studies*, vol. 3 (1973), pp. 203–31.

6. In this dry list of topics lurk some of the most influential genres of literature: epic, history, biography and hagiography, as well as important issues of ethics, political science and education. Inasmuch as eulogy seeks to measure the particular against set standards and models of conduct, implicit in its praise are tensions between the ideal and real, nature and nurture, aspiration and fulfilment, past and present, universal and particular, and will and fortune. To follow these tensions from Homer to the present is to chart much of the literary tradition's history.

7. I take this example from D.L. Peterson, *The English lyric*, p. 59, who shows its indebtedness to rhetorical treatises, particularly in its oratorical structure.

8. It an an axiom of eulogy that praise, especially high praise, may arouse envy in those who resent being surpassed; therefore eulogists often explicitly exorcise it. Cf. the expulsion of Envy at the end of Callimachus' 'Hymn to Apollo' (p. 4) and Pindar's careful avoidance of it in praising Hieron, (p. 190).

9. The ode is divided into five metrical units called triads. Each triad contains two matching stanzas, called strophe and antistrophe, and ends with a metrically different stanza called an epode. Many elements contribute to the total effect of Pindar's grand style in this poem, including the stately rhythm (Doric or, technically, dactylo-epitritic), the wealth of proper names and epithets, the hymnal language, the circumlocutions, the bold metaphors and sudden transitions — all of which can be seen in the opening strophe and antistrophe.

10. The *ekphrasis* gains point from the fact that coins from Aetna portray a seated Zeus with a thunderbolt in his right hand and an eagle perched beside him.

11. The paean, usually a hymn to Apollo, was often sung before and after battle. Like Apollo himself, music has both peaceful and martial attributes.

12. These two functions of music correspond to the positive and negative sides of epideictic rhetoric: praise and blame. For a theoretical discussion of praise and blame in archaic lyric and epic poetry, see G. Nagy, *The best of the Achaeans* (The Johns Hopkins University Press, Baltimore, 1979), pp. 222–64.

13. Philoctetes, the son of Poeas, was bitten in the foot by a snake at the outset of the Trojan War and was abandoned on the island of Lemnos by the Greeks because they could not endure his suffering. However, since Troy was destined to fall only to him and his bow, after years of futile warfare the Greek commanders eventually recanted and fetched him. Comparisons are an integral part of encomia (see V. Buchheit, *Untersuchungen zur Theorie des Genos Epideiktikon*, pp. 15–26): this one suggests that Hieron is a saviour to the Greeks, a man of the hour upon whose friendship all depend.

14. Deinomenes' sons are Gelon, Hieron and two younger brothers. Hieron's own son Deinomenes (mentioned in 58) is named for his grandfather.

15. Twice before the authorial voice appeared: in lines 42–5, when the poet hoped that his enthusiasm would not carry him away, and in line 58, when he asked the muse to help him to compose a 'loving hymn' for Deinomenes.

16. For an instructive parallel of a speaker who is afraid of arousing the envy of townsmen, cf. the opening of Pericles' 'Funeral Oration' (Thucydides 2.35).

17. W. Jaeger, *Paideia*, trans. G. Highet (Oxford University Press, Oxford, 1945), vol. 1, pp. 205–22. For a detailed survey of the form, see P. Hadot, 'Fürstenspiegel', *Reallexikon für Antike und Christentum* (A. Hiersemann, Stuttgart, 1972), vol. 8, cols 555–632.

18. Translated by L.K. Born, *The education of a Christian prince by Desiderius Erasmus* (Columbia University Press, New York, 1964), p. 198. In pp. 44–124, Born surveys the tradition (mostly in prose) from Isocrates to the Middle Ages. Erasmus goes on to say:

> When the prince hears his various titles from the provinces, let him not immediately swell with conceit as if he were the absolute master of so many affairs, but let him think to how many he is morally obliged to be a good prince (198–9).

This is very close to Pindar's: 'Many things are in your control, but many are the sure witnesses for good or ill' (88). What is given in praise is withheld by warning.

19. Pindar is a master of selecting the 'gist' (cf. *Pythian* 1.81) for elaboration, as we saw in *Olympian* 12, which concentrated on the role of Fortune in Ergoteles' success. By selecting what is essential to each person he praises, Pindar avoids mechanical praise and makes each ode interesting in its own right.

20. For a detailed analysis of the poem in conjunction with Menander Rhetor's instructions for composing a *basilikos logos*, see F. Cairns, *Generic composition in Greek and Latin poetry* (Edinburgh University Press, Edinburgh, 1972), pp. 100–12.

21. Just as Pindar urged Hieron to be generous and to keep in mind 'the posthumous acclaim of fame' (92) and ended his poem with 'Success takes first prize, and high esteem comes second; but the man who can try for both and wins them earns the highest crown' (99–100), so Theocritus says, 'And what could be more noble for a prosperous man than to win good fame among men?' (116–17). The virtuous man needs poets to keep alive his fame and the poets need virtuous men to give them occasions for writing serious verse.

22. There are many brief hymns to gods and demigods throughout Pindar's odes, and he frequently adapts hymnal elements to praise his subject, but Theocritus has gone a step further by writing a formal hymn to a man, thereby consciously blurring the distinction between god and man, a confusion stemming from Alexander's assumption of divine honours and continued by his Seleucid and Ptolemaic successors, in the latter case also encouraged by Egyptian belief in the pharaoh's divinity.

23. In the Classical period, poets such as Hesiod, Solon and Alcaeus (and the Athenian dramatists) freely mixed poetry and politics by admonishing princes and citizens. By the end of the fifth century, however, serious political thought became a specialised province of prose treatises, particularly in the writings of Isocrates, Plato, Aristotle and members of the other philosophical schools. At the same time, eulogistic poetry tended to become praise *tout court*, and aimed at completeness and exaggeration. For a survey of one branch of this tradition that issued into 'panegyrical biography', see M.P. Rewa, *Reborn as meaning: Panegyrical biography from Isocrates to Walton* (University Press of America, Washington, D.C., 1983).

24. The position of the poet of praise in the Hellenistic period is strikingly dramatised by Theocritus in *Idyll* 16, where the Graces of his poetry must go begging to find someone to praise. Although he finds a worthy subject in Hieron II of Syracuse (a descendant of Pindar's Hieron), the rather abject state of the stay-at-home poet characterises the difficult role of the encomiastic poet since the days of the free *polis*.

25. Praising military exploits by means of similes drawn from nature derives from Homeric practice and is common throughout eulogy. For examples in Horace cf. *Odes* 4.4.1–16 and 4.14.20–34. Of particular note here is the comparison of Cleopatra to a dove or hare, suggesting her feminine weakness that is belied at the end of the poem.

26. See J. Hollander and F. Kermode (eds), *The Oxford anthology of English literature*, (Oxford University Press, Oxford, 1973), p. 1162. For a balanced treatment of the poem and its Latin sources, see A.J.N. Wilson, 'On "An Horatian Ode Upon Cromwell's Return from Ireland."' *Critical Quarterly*, vol. 2 (1969), pp. 325–41 (repr. in A. Pollard (ed.), *Andrew Marvell, poems: a casebook* (Macmillan, London, 1980), pp. 176–98). For a survey of English panegyric verse through Dryden and brief analyses of Marvell's 'An Horatian Ode' and 'The First Anniversary', see Garrison, *Dryden and the tradition of panegyric*.

27. For example, some have detected ambivalence in lines 77–80, which refer to Cromwell's brutal Irish campaigns: 'They [the Irish] can affirm his praises best, / And have, though overcome, confessed / How good he is, how just, / And fit for highest trust.' However, it is a commonplace in antiquity (as well as today) that the most convincing witness is one that has every right to be hostile. And in one of his encomia, *Odes* 4.4, Horace himself uses the topic when he says that defeated Hasdrubal (*Hasdrubal devictus*, 38–9) is a witness (38) to the deeds of the Nerones and later has Hannibal himself testify to their ability (50–76).

28. For a good, brief discussion of the importance of the title, see L. Lerner, 'Titles and timelessness' in L. Lerner (ed.), *Reconstructing literature* (Barnes and Noble, Totowa, NJ, 1983), pp. 184–8.

29. It should be noted that while the poem concentrates on the military and political abilities of Cromwell, Marvell also praises his personal qualities such as his love of leisure (1–5), his courage (17), his austere life (30), his bravery in battle (45–6), his shrewdness (48), his goodness and justice (79) and his trustworthiness (80).

Conclusion

Classics students will, I hope, gain new insights from the preceding chapters into the workings of ancient generic forms, as well as profiting from seeing how English poets subsequently reused and adapted them, since the later examples, by realising latent potentialities, often serve as valuable commentaries on the earlier ones. Students of English poetry will also, I hope, discover new features in familiar poems by viewing them in the light of generic traditions.

Throughout this study I have tried to maintain a balance between generic analysis and literary history, for the two approaches usefully complement each other. In each chapter I have therefore presented a kind of generic cross section of literary history, for the purpose of revealing the interplay between the universal form and the particular example, between synchronic and diachronic perspectives, and between tradition and individual poets. To take an example not treated in the study, a reader who compares the priamel in Wordsworth's 'Scorn Not the Sonnet' with one by, say, Horace or Spenser, will gain insight not only into the subtle effects of Wordsworth's poem, but also into the individual character of each poet's programme and into the general concerns of his literary period.

In this way, generic cross sections can effectively highlight major developments in literary history. In the chapters on the *recusatio*, *ekphrasis* and eulogy, for example, I have tried to demonstrate a fact — too often overlooked by students of English poetry — that the Graeco-Roman tradition really contains two very different strains, Classical and Hellenistic; and that both of these (often in tension with each other) continue to inform all subsequent poetry influenced by Graeco-Roman models. The

209

Hellenistic strain, which has only in recent years begun to be studied with the seriousness it deserves, is much more important in shaping the modern poetic tradition than many realise. Indeed, it may arguably be more influential than the Classical strain — Callimachus probably counts more followers than Pindar. Of the modern poets treated in this study, for instance, William Carlos Williams probably comes closest to the Hellenistic spirit in his depiction of diminutive scenes and everyday events. And when Yeats, in 'Politics' (the final poem of *Last poems*), refuses to write political poetry and concludes a brief priamel with 'But O that I were young again / And held her in my arms', he is writing squarely in the Hellenistic vein.

The very word 'genre' and its offspring 'rhetoric', 'commonplace' and 'convention' have, since the end of the eighteenth century, become bywords for derivative (and hence insincere, unimaginative) poetry. It is true that when generic formulations are regarded as mere recipes, poor writing results: poetry composed strictly according to Menander Rhetor's formulae will surely be dreary. However, as long as poets write about recurring human experiences (*quidquid agunt homines*, as Juvenal puts it), they will necessarily (whether consciously or not) employ topics, arguments, generic forms and rhetorical strategies that were developed by Graeco-Roman writers. Far from being static entities, generic forms have proved flexible enough to permit their own change, mixture, parody and renewal, and continue to serve as valuable aids for ordering the particulars of experience. As C. Guillén points out (*Literature as system*):

> A genre is an invitation to form. Now, the concept of genre
> looks forward and backward at the same time. Backward,
> toward the literary works that already exist. Forward, in the
> direction of the apprentice, the future writer, the informed
> critic.

A knowledge of generic forms provides the poet as well as the critic with a point of departure. Whether he intends it or not, a poet will ultimately be judged according to existing models.

As stated in the Introduction, the present work is a beginning. Not only are there more examples in English poetry of the seven types sketched in this study, but also many more in other literatures, samples of which appear in 'Additional Examples'. There are also many more generic issues to be explored, such as the topics and rhetoric of invective and satire, the forms of Christian hymns, ancient and modern concepts and uses of irony, the motif of the voyage as an analogue of experience, the relationship of genre and style, the topographical *ekphrasis*, the rhetoric of complaints, the forms and functions of epigrams and the structure and purpose of catalogues, to mention a few. If, however, the present study has succeeded in demonstrating the importance of genre for understanding individual poems, it can serve as a guide for further investigations.

Additional Examples

Additional *recusationes*

Horace (65–8 BC), *Odes* 1.7.1–14: rejects praise of other cities for praise of Tibur; 1.38: rejects elaborate accoutrements at a drinking party for simplicity, thereby reflecting stylistic preferences as well; 2.12: rejects writing a history of Augustus' campaigns for love themes; 4.15: rejects martial themes for themes of peace; *Satires* 2.1.1–29: rejects writing panegyrics for writing satire; *Epistles* 2.1.245–70: rejects writing of Augustus' achievements in favour of satire.

Propertius (c. 50–c. 15 BC), *Elegies* 1.7: rejects martial epic poetry for love poetry; 2.1: an extensive *recusatio*, addressed to Maecenas, it refuses to celebrate Augustus' triumphs (it contains priamels as well); 3.1: rejects martial poetry for love elegy; 3.9: also addressed to Maecenas, it reaffirms the poet's allegiance to Callimachean poetics.

Ovid (43 BC–17 AD), *Amores* 1.1: Ovid wishes to write about battles in epic metre, but Cupid steals one foot from every other line, turning his heroic lines into love elegy; 2.1: Ovid tried to write grand poetry, but his mistress slammed the door and he had to take up love elegy to get her back; 3.1: a dramatised *recusatio* in which Ovid must choose between Dame Tragedy and Dame Elegy.

Manilius (fl. c. 14 AD), *Astronomica*: *recusationes* in the form of priamels open Books 2 and 3.

Martial (c. 40–c. 104 AD), *Epigrams* 4.49: rejects tragic bombast and mythological themes for epigrams; 8.3: relegates writing tragedy and epic to 'serious' (*graves*, *severi*) poets, and instead will treat life (*vita*).

Juvenal (c. 60–c. 140 AD), *Satires* 1.1–30: like Persius and Martial, the poet is weary of epic, drama, love poetry and declamation; when he looks at all the folly around him, he declares: 'It is difficult *not* to write satire' (*difficile est saturam non scribere*).

Joannes Secundus (1511–36), *Elegy* 1.1: rejects martial poetry for love poetry in the tradition of Ovid.

Guillaume de Salluste Du Bartas (1544–90), 'Uranie' (translated by Joshua Sylvester as 'Urania, Or the Heavenly Muse'): a long poem in which Urania suddenly appears to direct him to writing religious poetry.

Sir Philip Sidney (1554–86), *Astrophil and Stella*, Sonnet 3 ('Let dainty wits call on the sisters nine'): rejects grand-style writing for simply copying what nature has written in Stella's face; Sonnet 6 ('Some lovers speak when they their Muses entertain'): a priamel contrasts other love poets' subjects and styles with his own; Sonnet 15 ('You that do search for every purling spring'): contrasts far-fetched aids to writing with those provided by Stella; Sonnet 28 ('You that with allegory's curious frame'): eschews learned eloquence for the simple inspiration of love.

212

Samuel Daniel (1563–1619), *Delia*, Sonnet 46 ('Let others sing of knights and paladins'): rejects Spenserian romance for amatory sonnets.

George Herbert (1593–1633), 'Jordan I': rejects 'fictions' and elaborate language for simple statement.

John Milton (1608–74), *Paradise Lost* IX.13–47: the poet refuses to write in the manner of a traditional Classical or medieval epic.

Anne Bradstreet (c. 1612–72), 'The Prologue' to *The Tenth Muse*: an elaborate poetic apology for attempting ambitious verse, full of variations on the 'modesty *topos*'.

Thomas Traherne (1637–74), 'The Author to the Critical Peruser': eschews 'curling metaphors' for 'the naked truth'.

Robert Burns (1759–96), 'Epistle to J. Lapraik, an Old Scottish Bard': rejects learned Classical poetry for a 'homely' Muse, but one that 'may touch the heart'.

A.E. Housman (1859–1936), 'Terence, This is Stupid Stuff': defends his stoical verse against those who prefer optimistic poetry.

W.B. Yeats (1865–1939), 'On Being Asked for a War Poem': rejects political subjects for those appropriate to a young girl or an old man (cf. 'Politics'); 'Sailing to Byzantium': rejects poetry about ephemeral subjects (e.g., youth, sexual love) in favour of that which concerns 'monuments of unageing intellect' as represented by the art and culture of 'Byzantium'; 'The Circus Animals' Desertion': after reviewing the old themes that have deserted him, the speaker returns to the source of his inspiration: 'the foul rag-and-bone shop of the heart'.

Dylan Thomas (1914–53), 'In My Craft Or Sullen Art': defines its subject (love poetry) in priamels that reject various motives for writing and various kinds of readers.

Wallace Stevens (1879–1955), 'The Man on the Dump' and 'Sailing after Lunch': for a discussion of these poems, see G. Davis, 'The disavowal of the grand (*recusatio*) in two poems by Wallace Stevens', *Pacific Coast Philology*, vol. 17 (1982), pp. 92–102.

Czeslaw Milosz (1911–   ), 'No More': renounces Romantic, Bohemian views of poetry in favour of verses that are 'arranged'. See D. Davie, *Czeslaw Milosz and the insufficiency of lyric* (University of Tennessee Press, Knoxville, 1986), pp. 22–6.

Additional priamels

Homer (c. 750 BC), *Iliad* 9.378–91: Achilles uses two priamels to reject Agamemnon's offer of reconciliation; 9.406–9: Achilles emphasises the preciousness of human life; 14.315–28: Zeus portrays the extent of his passion for Hera; 23.315–18. Nestor counsels his son to use 'skill' in chariot-racing (compare the witty adaptation of Ovid, *Ars Amatoria* 1.3–4).

——, *Odyssey* 5.118–29: Calypso accuses the gods of jealousy in her case; 24.87–92: a summary priamel praising the splendour of Achilles' funeral.

——, *The Homeric Hymn to Apollo* 30–49: the travels of the pregnant Leto culminate in Delos; 140–8: Apollo's delight in his Delian festival culminates in the wondrous singing of the Delian Maidens.

Tyrtaeus (c. 650 BC), *fr.* 9 (12 W): lines 1–9 praise valour in war above all else.

Pindar (518–438 BC), *Olympian* 1.1–7: a priamel highlights the supremacy of the Olympian games.

Horace (65–8 BC), *Odes* 1.7.1–12: a priamel selects Tibur for praise; 1.12: a priamel singles out Augustus for hymnal praise; 1.31: a priamel highlights the poet's request in his prayer to Apollo; 2.18.1–11: a priamel highlights the plain delights of the poet's Sabine farm; 4.3.1–12: a priamel singles out the gift of Melpomene to the poet.

Tibullus (c. 55–19 BC), *Elegies* 1.1.1–6: a priamel rejects wealth and war for love.

Propertius (c. 50–c. 15 BC), *Elegies* 2.34.85–94: a list of poets and their lovers culminates in Propertius and Cynthia; cf. Ben Jonson's 'An Ode' ('Helen, did Homer never see').

Ovid (43 BC–17 AD), *Amores* 1.10.25–9: the poet censures his mistress's venality; 2.1.29–34: Ovid rejects Homeric themes for love poetry; *Ars Amatoria* 2.373–7: the fury of a wife who discovers her husband in bed with another woman; 3.121–7: Ovid's delight in living in a sophisticated age.

Persius (34–62 AD), *Satires* 5.52–62: various pursuits culminate in Cornutus' choice of Stoic philosophy.

Martial (c. 40–c. 104 AD), *Epigrams* 1.61: a catalogue of authors' birthplaces culminates in that of the poet.

Boethius (480–524 AD), *The Consolation of Philosophy*, Book 5, metron 5: a priamel singles out the uniqueness of man.

Chaucer (c. 1340–1400), 'Wife of Bath's Tale', 931–40: the thing women love best.

François Villon (c. 1431–62), 'Ballade des Femmes de Paris': Parisian women take the prize for talking; 'Je Congnois Bien . . .': the poet knows everything — but himself.

Sir Thomas Wyatt (c. 1503–42), Sonnet 9 ('Caesar, when that the traitor of Egypt'): the examples of Caesar and Hannibal lead (after a summarisation) to the case of the poet.

Joachim Du Bellay (1522–60), *Regrets* 68: a catalogue of traits the poet hates culminates in 'un sçavoir pedentesque' (pedantry).

Pierre de Ronsard (1524–85), 'Le Houx': a priamel singles out the holly tree for praise.

Edmund Spenser (1552–99), *Ruines of Rome*, Sonnet 2 ('Great Babylon her haughtie walls will praise'): Rome surpasses all wonders. This is an imitation of Du Bellay, *Les Antiquités de Rome*, Sonnet 2, which is itself an adaptation of Martial's *De Spectaculis Liber* 1.

Sir Philip Sidney (1554–86), *Astrophil and Stella*, Sonnet 75: an ironic sonnet in which an initial summary priamel selects Henry IV for praise while a second singles out his abdication as his greatest achievement.

William Shakespeare (1564–1616), Sonnet 18: a list of vicissitudes which can occur during a real summer (summed up by 'every', 7) is foil for 'thy eternal summer' which exists in the poet's verse.

Ben Jonson (c. 1573–1637), 'An Ode' ('Helen, did Homer never see'): a catalogue of poets and the women they celebrated culminates in the poet and his mistress.

Robert Burton (1577–1640), 'The Author's Abstract of Melancholy', a prefatory poem to his *Anatomy of melancholy* containing a series of priamels that culminate in melancholy.

George Herbert (1593–1632), 'Virtue': a priamel singles out Virtue's capacity for lasting sweetness.

Milton (1608–74), *Comus* 19–29: the attendant Spirit uses a priamel to introduce 'this Isle'.

John Dryden (1631–1700), 'To my Honour'd Friend, Dr Charleton': a priamel of English scientists culminates in Charleton.

Christopher Smart (1722–71), 'A Song to David': stanzas 72–86 are a series of priamels, which Smart in his note to the poem calls 'an amplification in five degrees'.

William Blake (1757–1827), 'London': a priamel singles out 'the youthful Harlot's curse' as the most blatant woe of man.

William Wordsworth (1770–1850), 'Scorn Not the Sonnet, Critic': a list of poets who wrote sonnets culminates in Milton; 'Nuns Fret Not at Their Convent's Narrow Room': a series of examples leads to the poet's choice of writing sonnets.

Samuel Taylor Coleridge (1772–1834), 'Work Without Hope': a brief priamel contrasts the activity in nature with the inactivity of the poet.

John Keats (1795–1821), 'Ode to Apollo': the climax of this priamel fails to equal the expectation aroused by the foil.

Robert Browning (1812–89), 'Summum Bonum': a priamel sums up everything in the 'kiss of one girl'.

Charles Baudelaire (1821–67), 'Le Poison': a priamel singles out the most powerful poison; 'Le Vin du Solitaire': a priamel highlights the power of a bottle of wine.

Ezra Pound (1885–1972), 'Amities': a priamel humorously characterises three friends.

T.S. Eliot, (1888–1965), 'Little Gidding' 35–9: a brief priamel singles out the present moment in England; the priamel in verses 43–5 leads up to the real purpose for coming to Little Gidding.

W.H. Auden (1907–73), 'Spain': a priamel in lines 1–16 culminates in 'But to-day the struggle'.

Additional *ekphraseis*

pseudo-Hesiod (c. 600 BC), *Shield of Heracles* 139–320: a description of Heracles' shield, modelled on that of Achilles.

Sophocles (c. 496–406 BC), *Oedipus at Colonus* 668–93: a lovely description of Colonus, an example of the *locus amoenus*.

Apollonius of Rhodes (c. 295–c. 215 BC), *Argonautica* 1.730–67: a description of Jason's robe. For a discussion of the scenes and their relationship to Hellenistic poetry and painting, see H.A. Shapiro,

'Jason's cloak', *Transactions of the American Philological Association*, vol. 110 (1980), pp. 263–86.

Moschus (c. 150 BC), *Europa* 43–62: a description of Europa's basket in the tradition of Hellenistic *ekphrasis*.

Vergil (70–19BC), *Aeneid* 1.466–93: a description of the scenes on Dido's temple to Juno; 6.20–33: a description of the scene on the doors of Apollo's temple; 7.170–91: a description of King Latinus' palace.

Ovid (43 BC–17AD), *Metamorphoses* 2.1–18: description of the Palace of the Sun; 12.39–63: a description of Rumour's temple; *Amores* 3.1.1–14: a humorous description of Dames Tragedy and Elegy, an early example of allegorical description that became so popular in late antiquity and the Middle Ages.

Statius (c. 45–96 AD), *Silvae* 1.3: a description of Vopiscus' villa that prefigures the later country-house poems; 2.2: a companion description of Pollius' villa.

Ausonius (d. c. 395 AD), 'The Moselle': a 483–line descriptive poem on the Moselle River in the style of Statius.

Corippus, *In Laudem Iustini* (c. 567 AD): a detailed account in four books of Justinian's accession with extended *descriptiones*.

Paul the Silentiary (d. c. 575 AD) wrote a long ekphrastic poem on Santa Sophia; for the text and commentary, see P. Friedländer, *Johannes von Gaza und Paulus Silentiarius* (Teubner, Leipzig, 1912), and for a sample, see I. Fletcher and D.S. Carne-Ross, 'Ekphrasis: lights in Santa Sophia, from Paul the Silentiary', *Arion*, vol. 4 (1965), pp. 563–81.

Chaucer (c. 1340–1400), 'Knight's Tale' 1881–2088: a description of the lists in heroic style.

Ben Jonson (c. 1573–1637), 'To Penshurst': a famous description of the Sidney estate in praise of its owners and first of many country-house poems.

Milton, 'L'Allegro' and 'Il Penseroso': much of these poems consists of *ekphraseis*; *Paradise Lost* I, 710–32: the description of Pandaemonium.

Andrew Marvell (1621–78), 'Upon Appleton House': a lengthy and diffuse treatment in the tradition of country-house poems that began with Jonson's 'To Penshurst'.

W.C. Williams (1883–1963), 'The Dance': an *ekphrasis* of Brueghel's *Wedding Dance in the Open Air*, also the subject of one of his later *Pictures from Brueghel*.

Yvor Winters (1900–68), 'To a Portrait of Melville in my Library': combines ekphrastic and hymnal elements; 'On the Portrait of a Scholar of the Italian Renaissance': a description of the painting leads to a meditation on universals and particulars.

W.H. Auden (1907–73), 'The Shield of Achilles': a satiric description of an Achilles' shield for modern warfare; 'In Praise of Limestone': in part a description of landscape and sculpture; 'Woods': a brief *ekphrasis* of Piero di Cosimo's paintings and a meditation on the modern attitude towards nature.

Randall Jarrell (1914–65), 'The Knight, Death, and the Devil': an *ekphrasis* of Dürer's famous engraving.

Additional *lamentationes* and *consolationes*

Homer, *Iliad*, 22.477–514: Andromache's lament for Hector.

Pindar (c. 518–c. 438 BC), *Pythian* 3: an ode of consolation to Hieron of Syracuse. For an analysis, see W.H. Race, *Pindar* (G.K. Hall, Boston, 1986), pp. 50–62.

Sophocles (c. 496–406 BC), *Electra* 121–250: the chorus tries in vain to console Electra.

Euripides (c. 485–c. 406 BC), *Alcestis*: the first two-thirds of the play contains most of the standard topics of lament and consolation.

Catullus (c. 84–54 BC), *Carm.* 8: Catullus employs the topics of manly consolation in a vain attempt to give up his girlfriend; *Carm.*101: a lament at the tomb of his brother.

Vergil (70–19 BC), *Eclogue* 10: a lament for the love-sick poet, Gallus.

Horace (65–8 BC), *Odes* 1.28: a lament for Archytas.

Propertius (c. 50–c. 15 BC), *Elegies* 3.7: a lament for the drowned Paetus; 3.18: a lament for Marcellus (d. 23 BC), ending with his apotheosis.

Ovid (43 BC – 17 AD), *Amores* 3.9: an elegy for the poet Tibullus which contains many of the topics of lament and consolation; for a comparison with *Amores* 2.6 see E. Thomas, 'A comparative analysis of Ovid, 'Amores' II, 6 and III, 9', *Latomus*, vol. 24 (1965), pp. 599–609. '*Consolatio ad Liviam*': a long consolatory poem to Livia on the death of her son, Drusus, doubtfully attributed to Ovid.

Statius (c. 45–96 AD), *Silvae* 2.1: a poem of consolation to Melior on the death of his foster-son; see O.B. Hardison, *The enduring monument* (University of North Carolina Press, Chapel Hill, 1962), pp. 119–20 for an analysis; 2.4: a mock lament for a parrot in the style of Ovid; 5.3: a lament for his father.

Nemesianus (c. 275 AD), *Eclogue* 1.35–80: a pastoral lament for Meliboeus.

Paulinus of Nola (c. 353–431 AD), *Carm.* 31, 'Lament for Celsus': the first fully Christian *consolatio*.

Fortunatus (c. 540–c. 600 AD), '*De Gelesuintha*': a long lament on the untimely death of a Spanish princess; see G. Davis, '*Ad Sidera Notus*: strategies of lament and consolation in Fortunatus' *De Gelesuintha*', *Agon*, vol. 1 (1967), pp. 118–34.

Geoffrey of Vinsauf, *Poetria Nova* (c. 1210), 368–430: a full lament on the death of Richard the Lionhearted.

Geoffrey Chaucer (c. 1340–1400), *Canterbury Tales*, 'The Knight's Tale' 2987–3074: Theseus' speech of consolation over the dead Arcite.

Robert Garnier (c. 1544–90), 'Elégie Sur le Trespas de Pierre de Ronsard': bewails the state of France and ends with a vision of Ronsard in the Isles of the Blessed.

Edmund Spenser (1552–99), 'Astrophel': a lament on the death of Sidney.

Ben Jonson (c. 1573–1637), 'To the Immortal Memory and Friendship of That Noble Pair, Sir Lucius Cary and Sir H. Morison': a consolatory poem in Pindaric form, drawing mainly on the Senecan consolatory tradition; 'On My first Son': a brief example of manly consolation.

Thomas Carew (1595–1645), 'An Elegy upon the Death of the Dean of Paul's, Dr John Donne': his famous lament for Donne and eulogy of his poetry.

Izaak Walton (1593–1683), 'An Elegy upon Dr Donne': this elegy emphasises the lament over the praise.

Andrew Marvell (1621–78), 'Upon the Death of the Lord Protector': a long elegy on Cromwell.

John Dryden (1631–1700), 'Ode to Mrs Anne Killigrew': a grand-style ode of consolation and praise that opens with a hymn to the lady and includes such topics as complaints, an *ekphrasis* (Killigrew was a painter), and the contrast between past and present ('Now all those charms').

Percy Bysshe Shelley (1792–1822), 'Adonais': a long pastoral elegy on the death of Keats.

Alfred, Lord Tennyson (1809–92), 'In Memoriam A.A.H.': this long series of poems exhibits the topics and form of lament and consolation.

Matthew Arnold (1822–88), 'Thyrsis': a pastoral lament for a fellow poet, Arthur Hugh Clough.

A.E. Housman (1859–1936), 'To an Athlete Dying Young': this sardonic poem elaborates the consolatory topic of 'escaping the world's ills'.

Hart Crane (1899–1933), 'Praise for an Urn, In Memoriam: Ernest Nelson': a brief lament with little (if any) consolation.

Federico García-Lorca (1898–1936), 'Llanto por Ignacio Sánchez Mejías': despite some surrealistic passages, a traditional lament with the consolation of immortality in verse promised at the end.

W.B. Yeats (1865–1939), 'In Memory of Alfred Pollexfen': by means of a priamel, Yeats singles out this third Pollexfen for lament; 'In Memory of Major Robert Gregory': a priamel singles out Major Robert Gregory for lament and praise.

W.H. Auden (1907–73), 'In Memory of Sigmund Freud': a summary priamel opens this tribute to Freud.

Additional *carpe-diem* poems

Theognis (fl. c. 540 BC), *Elegies* 973–8: a brief statement of the inevitability of death with a *carpe-diem* resolution.

Aeschylus (525–456 BC), *Persians* 840–2: the ghost of Darius gives a brief *carpe-diem* message as he departs.

Palatine anthology 5.74, 5.79 and 5.118: in all three epigrams, the poet gives his beloved an apple or garland to remind him or her of the brevity of life.

Anacreontea: poems 7, 8, 32, 36, 38 and 40 (in J.M. Edmonds, *Greek elegy and Iambus II, with Anacreontea* (Loeb Classical Library, Cambridge, Mass., 1931)) contain many variations of *carpe-diem* themes.

Horace (65–8 BC), *Odes* 1.9: begins with a brief description of Mt Soracte to set up the *carpe-diem* message; 2.3: contains most of the motifs covered; 2.11: advises not to be so preoccupied with distant concerns

218

Statius (c. 45–96 AD), *Silvae* 5.4: a charming prayer to Sleep; cf. Wordsworth's sonnet 'To Sleep' and see J.V. Cunningham, 'Classical and Medieval: Statius on sleep' in *The collected essays* (Swallow, Chicago, 1976), pp. 147–61.

St Ambrose (c. 340–97 AD), 'Deus Creator Omnium': a Christian hymn in Classical form.

Boethius (c. 480–524 AD), *Consolation of Philosophy*, Book 3, metron 9: a 'philosophical' hymn to God (cf. Cleanthes' 'Hymn to Zeus'.)

Spenser (1552–99), Four Hymns: long, complex poetic hymns. For the generic background of these hymns, see P.B. Rollinson, 'A generic view of Spenser's *Four Hymns*', *Studies in Philology*, vol. 68 (1971), pp. 292–304.

John Milton (1608–74), 'L'Allegro' and 'Il Penseroso': companion hymns to Euphrosyne and Melancholy; *Paradise Lost*: elaborate invocatory hymns open Books I, III and VII.

James Thompson (1700–48), 'An Ode on Aeolus' Harp': a hymn to the Aeolian harp that describes its powers and requests inspiration.

Percy Bysshe Shelley (1792–1822), 'Hymn to Intellectual Beauty': a long philosophical hymn; 'Ode to the West Wind': a good example of hymnal form with Romantic content.

John Keats (1795–1821), 'Ode to Psyche': a good example of Romantic adaptation of hymnal form; 'Hymn to Pan' (in *Endymion* I.247–306): a choral hymn.

Winters, Yvor (1900–68), 'To a Portrait of Melville in My Library': combines *ekphrasis* and hymnal elements.

W.H. Auden (1907–73), 'At the Grave of Henry James': like Winters's 'To a Portrait of Melville', only much longer, it prays to the dead author to aid the poet in his programme; 'Winds': the last section is a hymn to the 'Goddess of winds and wisdom' to inspire the poet, a good example of Auden's reuse of a traditional form.

Additional eulogies

Pindar (c. 518–c. 438 BC), *Pythian* 5: an encomium of King Arcesilas IV of Cyrene.

Bacchylides (c. 505–c.450 BC), *Epinicians* 3 and 5: encomia of Hieron of Syracuse.

Theocritus (c. 300–c. 260 BC), *Idyll* 16: an encomium of Hieron II of Syracuse, which portrays the difficulty of finding a worthy subject to praise.

Horace (65–8 BC), *Odes* 1.12: an extended priamel that praises Augustus and asks for Jupiter's protection; 4.4: a eulogy of young Drusus and his famous family on the event of a military victory; 4.5: praise of Augustus as if to a god; 4.14: praise of Drusus and Tiberius for military victories; 4.15: praise of the Pax Augusta.

Tibullus (c. 55–c. 19 BC), *Elegies* 1.7: a birthday ode that praises the military exploits of his patron Messalla.

Statius (c. 45–96 AD), *Silvae* 4.1: a poem celebrating Domitian's seventeenth consulship, full of adulation.

Ben Jonson (c. 1573–1637), 'To the Memory of My Beloved, the Author Mr William Shakespeare and What he Hath Left Us': Jonson's famous eulogy of Shakespeare; 'To the Immortal Memory and Friendship of That Noble Pair, Sir Lucius Cary and Sir H. Morison': Jonson's Pindaric ode that combines consolation and praise.

John Milton (1608–74), 'On Shakespeare, 1630': a sonnet in praise of Shakespeare.

Edmund Waller (1606–87), 'A Panegyric to My Lord Protector': a eulogy of Cromwell that artfully combines praise and counsel; see W.L. Chernaik, 'Waller's *Panegyric to My Lord Protector* and the poetry of praise', *Studies in English Literature*, vol. 4 (1964), pp. 109–24.

John Dryden (1631–1700), 'Heroic Stanzas': another eulogy of Cromwell that praises his character, deeds of war and deeds of peace.

Alfred, Lord Tennyson (1809–92), 'Ode on the Death of the Duke of Wellington': after the *lamentatio*, the last two sections contain a stirring eulogy.

W.B. Yeats (1865–1939), 'In Memory of Major Robert Gregory': contains extended praise of Gregory.

Allen Tate (1899–1978), 'Ode to the Confederate Dead': Although the title implies praise, the poem is more concerned with the unheroic modern temper (particularly its solipsism); cf. Robert Lowell (1917–77), 'For the Union Dead', another poem that despairs of praise.

Select Bibliography

The following bibliography is not exhaustive: it includes general works of importance as background and does not include all works cited in the Notes and 'Additional Examples'

Abrams, M.H. (1953) *The mirror and the lamp*, Oxford University Press, Oxford

Alexiou, M. (1974) *The ritual lament in Greek tradition*, Cambridge University Press, Cambridge

Bate, W.J. (1946) *From Classic to Romantic*, Harper and Row, New York

Braden, G. (1978) *The Classics and English Renaissance poetry: three case studies*, Yale University Press, New Haven

Bramble, J.C. (1974) *Persius and the programmatic satire: a study in form and imagery*, Cambridge University Press, Cambridge

Burgess, T.C. (1902) *Epideictic literature*, University of Chicago Press, Chicago

Cairns, F. (1972) *Generic composition in Greek and Latin poetry*, Edinburgh University Press, Edinburgh

Clark, D.L. (1948) *John Milton at St Paul's School: a study of ancient rhetoric in English Renaissance education*, Columbia University Press, New York

Cody, J.V. (1976) *Horace and Callimachean aesthetics*, Latomus, Brussels

Colie, R.L. (1970) *My Ecchoing Song: Andrew Marvell's poetry of criticism*, Princeton University Press, Princeton

—— (1973) *The resources of kind: genre-theory in the Renaissance*, B.K. Lewalski (ed.), University of California Press, Berkeley

Commager, S. (1967) *The odes of Horace*, Indiana University Press, Bloomington

Curtius, E.R. (1973) *European literature and the Latin Middle Ages*, trans. W.R. Trask, Princeton University Press, Princeton

Deneef, A.L. (1973) 'Epideictic rhetoric and the Renaissance lyric', *Journal of Medieval and Renaissance Studies*, vol. 3 (1973), pp. 203–31.

Donker, M. and G.M. Muldrow (1982) *Dictionary of literary-rhetorical conventions of the English Renaissance*, Greenwood Press, Westport CT.

Fowler, A. (1982) *Kinds of literature: an introduction to the theory of genres and modes*, Harvard University Press, Cambridge, Mass.

Garrison, J.D. (1975) *Dryden and the tradition of panegyric*, University of California Press, Berkeley

Guillén, C. (1971) *Literature as system: essays toward the theory of literary history*, Princeton University Press, Princeton

Hardie, A. (1983) *Statius and the Silvae: poets, patrons and epideixis in the Graeco-Roman world* (ARCA Classical and Medieval Texts, Papers and Monographs, vol. 9), Redwood Burn, Trowbridge, Wiltshire

Hardison Jr, O.B. (1962) *The enduring monument: a study of the idea of praise in Renaissance literary theory and practice*, University of North Carolina Press, Chapel Hill

Harrison, T.P. (1939) *The pastoral elegy*, University of Texas Press, Austin

Hendrickson, G.L. (1905) 'The origin and meaning of the ancient characters of style', *American Journal of Philology*, vol. 26, pp. 249–90

Hirsch Jr, E.D. (1967) *Validity in interpretation*, Yale University Press, New Haven

—— (1976) *The aims of interpretation*, University of Chicago Press, Chicago

Jenkyns, R. (1982) *Three Classical poets: Sappho, Catullus, and Juvenal*, Harvard University Press, Cambridge, Mass.

Lattimore, R. (1962) *Themes in Greek and Latin epitaphs*, University of Illinois Press, Urbana

Lewalski, B.K. (1973) *Donne's anniversaries and the poetry of praise*, Princeton University Press, Princeton

—— (1979) *Protestant poetics and the seventeenth-century religious lyric*, Princeton University Press, Princeton

Lindley, D. (1985) *Lyric*, Methuen, London

Mack, M. and G. deF. Lord (eds) (1982) *Poetic traditions of the English Renaissance*, Yale University Press, New Haven

Martz, L.L. (1954) *The poetry of meditation: a study in English Religious literature of the seventeenth century*, Yale University Press, New Haven

Menander Rhetor (1981) *Menander Rhetor*, D.A. Russell and N. Wilson (eds), Oxford University Press, Oxford

Nisbet, R.G.M. and M. Hubbard (1970) *A commentary on Horace: Odes Book I*, Oxford University Press, Oxford

—— (1978) *A commentary on Horace: Odes Book II*, Oxford University Press, Oxford

Norden, E. (1973) *Agnostos Theos*, Teubner, Stuttgart

Onians, J. (1979) *Art and thought in the Hellenistic age: the Greek world view*, Thames and Hudson, London

Peterson, D.L. (1967) *The English lyric from Wyatt to Donne: a history of the plain and eloquent styles*, Princeton University Press, Princeton

Pollitt, J.J. (1986) *Art in the Hellenistic age*, Cambridge University Press, Cambridge

Raby, F.J.E. (1953) *A history of Christian-Latin poetry from the beginnings to the close of the Middle Ages*, 2nd edn, Oxford University Press, Oxford

Race, W.H. (1982) 'Aspects of rhetoric and form in Greek hymns', *Greek, Roman, and Byzantine Studies*, vol. 23, pp. 5–14.

—— (1982) *The Classical priamel from Homer to Boethius*, E.J. Brill, Leiden

—— (1986) *Pindar*, G.K. Hall, Boston

Rosenmeyer, T.G. (1969) *The green cabinet: Theocritus and the European pastoral lyric*, University of California Press, Berkeley

Rosmarin, A. (1985) *The power of genre*, University of Minnesota Press, Minneapolis

Russell, D.A. (1981) *Criticism in antiquity*, University of California Press, Berkeley

Sacks, P.M. (1985) *The English elegy: studies in the genre from Spenser to Yeats*, Johns Hopkins University Press, Baltimore

Spengel, L. (1853–6) *Rhetores Graeci*, 3 vols, Teubner, Leipzig

Strelka, J.P. (1978) *Theories of literary genre*, Pennsylvania State University Press, University Park

Trimpi, W. (1962) *Ben Jonson's poems: a study of the plain style*, Stanford University Press, Stanford, Calif.

Viljamaa, T. (1968) *Studies in Greek encomiastic poetry of the early Byzantine period.* (*Commentationes Humanarum Litterarum Societas Scientiarum Finnica*, vol. 42.4), Helsingfors, Helsinki

Williams, G. (1968) *Tradition and originality in Roman poetry*, Oxford University Press, Oxford

—— (1969) *The Third Book of Horace's Odes*, Oxford University Press, Oxford

Wimmel, W. (1960) *Kallimachos in Rom. Die Nachfolge seines apologetischen Dichtens in der Augusteerzeit.* (*Hermes Einzelschriften*, vol. 16), F. Steiner, Wiesbaden

Woolf, R. (1968) *The English religious lyric in the Middle Ages*, Oxford University Press, Oxford

Zanker, G. (1987) *Realism in Alexandrian poetry: a literature and its audience*, Croom Helm, London

Index of Authors and Works

Index of Subjects

233